The Wartime Broadcasts
of Francis Stuart
1942–1944

Edited by Brendan Barrington

THE LILLIPUT PRESS
DUBLIN

First published 2000 by
THE LILLIPUT PRESS LTD
62–63 Sitric Road, Arbour Hill,
Dublin 7, Ireland
www.lilliputpress.ie

A CIP record for this title is available from
The British Library.

1 3 5 7 9 10 8 6 4 2

ISBN 1 901866 54 8

*The Lilliput Press receives financial assistance
from An Chomhairle Ealaíon / The Arts Council of Ireland.*

Set in Adobe Garamond
Printed in Ireland by Betaprint, Clonshaugh, Dublin

Contents

Introduction / 1

Acknowledgments / 61

Note on the Text / 63

THE BROADCASTS / 67

Appendix / 201

Sources / 205

Index / 214

Introduction

In March 1924, Sinn Féin published a sixteen-page pamphlet entitled *Lecture on Nationality and Culture*.[1] Its author was a young
man named Francis Stuart. Although not quite twenty-two years
old, Stuart was a man of experience. He had been married for
nearly four years to Iseult Gonne, daughter of Maud Gonne; he
had fought on the anti-Treaty side in the Irish civil war and been
interned by the Free State; and his poems had been awarded the
Young Poet's Prize of the distinguished American magazine *Poetry*.[2]

In the *Lecture*, Stuart wrote bitterly of the physical reconstruc-
tion of Dublin then taking place:

Under this Free State we are watching contractors raise from the ruins a
Dublin that will be an exact replica of an average English city. Personal and
national needs and tastes are not consulted. The plans are designed in English or Anglo-Irish offices without the slightest knowledge or thought of
what they are building in France, in Germany, in Russia: it's a case of 'England is good enough for us!'

1. The title of the pamphlet, published by the Sinn Féin Ard-Chomhairle and dated
March 1924, suggests that Stuart's 'lecture' might have been delivered orally to a Sinn Féin
audience; but there is no reference to the date, location or circumstances of its delivery. In
1972 the literary historian W.J. Mc Cormack wrote that 'Mr Stuart has no recollection of
the circumstances in which the lecture was given.' See Mc Cormack, ed., *A Festschrift for
Francis Stuart on His 70th Birthday*, p. 55.
2. Later in 1924, W.B. Yeats was the instigator of a ceremony at the Royal Irish Academy
in which awards were given to writers whose works had conferred 'honour and dignity
upon Ireland'. Stuart was one of four recipients, for his book of poems *We Have Kept the
Faith*. See Joseph Hone, *W.B. Yeats, 1865–1939*, 2nd ed., p. 363. Also in that year, with Yeats's
support, Stuart was a joint founder and editor of *To-morrow*, a literary magazine which produced two provocative numbers before folding.

England may be good enough for the English, and English cities may be suitable to a money-mad, sterile civilization; but will it do for us? We want to know about the cities of France, of Germany, of Europe in fact.[3]

Stuart also wrote of the influence of the mass media on national consciousness, expressing concern at the dominance of British radio – its music and its 'censored news' – in Ireland. He added: 'I don't for a moment want to condemn the wireless; I think, on the contrary, that it is one of the few achievements of this century of which mankind can be proud'.[4]

He went on to declare that if Ireland were to fall 'short of a Republic by one slight word or one inch of ground, our struggle would be useless'[5] – an orthodox anti-Treaty stance that would have been consistent with the views of his Sinn Féin audience. Then he turned again to the Continent, comparing Ireland's situation with that of Austria – a country 'of which I myself had personal experience':

Austria, in 1921, had been ruined by the war, and was far, far poorer than Ireland is to-day, for besides having no money she was overburdened with innumerable debts. At that time Vienna was full of Jews, who controlled the banks and factories and even a large part of the government; the Austrians themselves seemed about to be driven out of their own city.

Stuart stated that the Austrians, 'determined ... not to lose Austria', had used their strength in local government ('the only administrative organisations that were, at least to a large extent, composed of Austrians') to create a building society and other such communitarian bodies.[6] Just as Austria had overcome the Jewish influence, Stuart suggested, Ireland must overcome a lingering British influence.

3. Stuart, *Lecture on Nationality and Culture*, p. 4.
4. Ibid., p. 7.
5. Ibid., p. 11.
6. Ibid., p. 12. Stuart travelled in central Europe in 1921/2, and spent some three or four months in Vienna; his remarks here echo mainstream Austrian anti-Semitism of the time. See George E. Berkley, *Vienna and Its Jews*; and Bruce F. Pauley, 'Political Antisemitism in Interwar Vienna', in Oxaal, et al., eds, *Jews, Antisemitism and Culture in Vienna*.

It was a strikingly premonitory piece of writing. Stuart couldn't have known, as he wrote of buildings rising from the 'ruins' of Dublin and of the need to emulate continental architecture, that one of the dominant images of his later novels would be the toppled masonry of wartime and post-war Germany. He couldn't have known, as he praised the wireless but deplored the effects of British radio in Ireland, that he would earn notoriety for making broadcasts from the Third Reich to neutral Ireland during the Second World War – seeking, among other aims, to counteract the 'censored news' of British wartime radio. And he couldn't have known, as he attributed the former ills of Austria to the influence of the Jews, that three quarters of a century later, long after the near-total destruction of European Jewry, he would be in the dock of public opinion in Ireland, accused of making an anti-Semitic remark on a television documentary.

The *Lecture on Nationality and Culture* is the earliest published evidence of the range and intensity of Stuart's political beliefs. It is not a part of the established narrative of Stuart's career, which defines his artistic achievement in terms of a handful of post-war novels and views his pre-war and wartime writings and activities strictly within the terms established by the post-war books. If the ideas expressed within the *Lecture* had never resurfaced in Stuart's writing, we might sensibly write it off as a youthful anomaly. In fact, the *Lecture* adumbrates a number of themes that would recur consistently in his work. Along with various writings of the 1930s, it helps to make explicable what might have seemed inexplicable: Stuart's decision to move in 1940 from neutral Ireland to Nazi Germany, where he had been offered a position at Berlin University; his decision to work in German radio propaganda translating news bulletins and writing scripts for William Joyce ('Lord Haw-Haw'); and his decision to broadcast his own talks to Ireland.

I

The present volume brings to light Francis Stuart's most significant unpublished work: some forty-five thousand words spoken
into the microphones of the Irland-Redaktion, the Third Reich's
radio propaganda service for Ireland, between March 1942 and
February 1944, and transcribed by Irish military intelligence and
BBC monitors.[7] The surviving transcripts represent between two
thirds and three quarters of Stuart's talks.[8] Anyone who has read
Stuart's fiction will recognize the voice: its tone, diction and
rhythm are unmistakable. It is, moreover, unmistakably the same
voice as that of the young pamphleteer of 1924, with some of the
same preoccupations: the importance of true and total Irish independence from Britain and closer engagement with the culture of
continental Europe; the perils of the 'money-mad, sterile civilization' he saw ascending. One element of the 1924 argument that
does not figure in the surviving Irish and British transcripts is the
characterization of Jews as a malign force: these transcripts contain
not a single explicit reference to Jews.[9] The significance of this
silence will be discussed in some detail below; for the moment, it
is enough to observe that whereas what we might politely call the
'debate' over Francis Stuart has tended to fixate on the question of
his attitude to Jews, the broadcasts published herein shed little
light on the question, but suggest that anti-Semitism was not at
the core of Stuart's enthusiasm for Hitler and the National Socialist project.

7. There is also a German transcript of a talk by Stuart, dated 9 February 1942 – five
weeks before Stuart's first appearance in the Irish and British monitoring files: see the
Appendix for this transcript and for a discussion of its status.
8. For the circumstances under which Stuart's broadcasts were transcribed and the nature
of the surviving transcripts, see the Note on the Text. The transcripts have been quoted
piecemeal in a handful of previous books, notably Robert Fisk's *In Time of War*, Geoffrey
Elborn's *Francis Stuart: A Life*, and David O'Donoghue's *Hitler's Irish Voices*.
9. But see the German transcript of 9 February 1942, in the Appendix.

The most notable aspect of the 1924 *Lecture* is its essentially political character. This is notable because Stuart's allegiances to the anti-Treaty side in the Irish civil war and to the Third Reich in the Second World War have usually been explained as arising from non-political forces in his psyche: a sense of adventure, a compulsion to betray, a mystical desire to suffer.[10] These forces were undoubtedly present, but they existed alongside a political consciousness that was far more highly developed, and also rather more discriminating and conventional, than has generally been recognized. The wartime broadcasts – which, contrary to a strangely durable myth, touch hardly at all on literary matters – are concerned primarily with politics, and could not have been written by someone as politically naïve, or gormless, or blindly revolutionary as Stuart has usually been depicted as being.

Stuart's participation in the Irish civil war – as a gun-runner and then as an armed fighter – has frequently been described as an apolitical adventure, or as one in which an initial enthusiasm for the republican cause quickly gave way to intense disillusionment with it.[11] This view of Stuart's attitude, so difficult to square with the uncompromising opinions expressed in the Sinn Féin pam-

10. Eileen Battersby, for example, has argued that 'It is pointless placing him in a polit-ical context, his preoccupations were almost exclusively interior.' See *Irish Times*, 3 February 2000. The most articulate and perhaps the most uncompromising statement of this view was made by Colm Tóibín during the controversy over Stuart in 1997. Tóibín wrote: 'Coming from a unionist background, Stuart (and indeed [his fictional alter ego] H) would become a republican, even though the politics meant nothing to him; and later, in the 1930s when liberal opinion (and indeed most other opinion) considered Hitler's Germany to be a place of evil, he would go there, he would live there during the war, he would broadcast to Ireland, and he would know what the consequences were going to be. And all this, his novel *Black List, Section H* makes clear, had nothing to do with politics, with anti-Semi-tism, or fascism, or Nazism, but arose from something darkly and deeply rooted in his psy-che – the need to betray and be seen to betray. It arose from something else too – a passionate belief that every organised structure, and that includes liberal democracy, is rot-ten.' See *Sunday Independent*, 7 December 1997.
11. J.H. Natterstad, for example, declares that 'His involvement in the Civil War was his first overt act of rebellion against the established order, though by the time of his impris-onment he had become wholly disillusioned with the Republican leaders and their cause'. See Natterstad, 'Francis Stuart: A Voice from the Ghetto', p. 8.

phlet which appeared mere months after the defeat of the Irregulars, takes its cue (as do most of the prevailing views of Stuart's attitudes) from his autobiographical novel *Black List, Section H*:

The civil war created doubt and confusion, and thus a climate in which the poet could breathe more easily. Instead of uniting in a conformity of outlook that had to appeal to dull-witted idealists as well as those with intelligence, it divided people. And once the process of division had started, H foresaw it continuing, and subdivisions taking place, especially on the Republican side, perhaps creating small enclaves of what he looked on as true revolutionaries whose aim had less to do with Irish independence than in casting doubt on traditional values and judgments.

He was spending a lot of time at the bedside of a Republican officer who'd been wounded in an attempt, with some of his men, to join up with the Four Courts garrison at the start of the fighting. This was because H sensed in him a mode of consciousness closer to his own than that of the few members of that I.R.A. he'd met at his mother-in-law's. Theirs, as hers, he'd had the feeling, was a one-track, political approach to something that for him had other more complex aspects. He realized how little politics could ever concern him with their large-scale, impersonal values.[12]

Can the character being described here be the young man who, within two years, would declare that if Ireland fell 'short of a Republic by one slight word or one inch of ground, our struggle would be useless'? Who would call for 'a constructive and national distribution of products based upon a universal plan of organisation of production' as the only way to 'save the country'?[13] Who would compare Ireland's struggle with England to Austria's struggle, carried out by means of 'administrative organisations', against the perceived dominance of the Jews? Clearly not; and what is striking is not the disparity between what Stuart said in 1924 and what he wrote several decades later in *Black List*, but the degree to which a work of fiction has been taken as a reliable guide to the young Stuart's state of mind and political beliefs.

12. *Black List, Section H*, p. 72. All references to *Black List* are to the identical Lilliput and Penguin editions currently in print; obvious typographical faults in these editions, some of which perpetuate errors from the 1975 Martin Brian & O'Keeffe edition, are silently corrected here.
13. *Lecture on Nationality and Culture*, p. 12.

The question of Stuart's politics is not merely a detail of literary biography, as it would be for many writers. The widespread view of Stuart as a poet–adventurer of no fixed political abode, a view deriving largely from *Black List*, has obscured the fact that many of his writings are filled with politics, and that the political vision they communicate is highly consistent. One need only read these works to see that this is so; but in case there are any doubts about the intentions and implications of texts that frequently defy straightforward interpretation, we have Stuart's own words to guide us. In his broadcast of 13 November 1943, to take the starkest instance, Stuart said that some of his pre-war books 'were primarily political, and I only mention them now because I want those of you who listen to me to be sure that what I say now is, in different words, what I said then'.

To which of the pre-war books might he have been referring? Stuart's second novel, *Pigeon Irish*, published in 1932, imagines a future world war in which Ireland is the last outpost of Western civilization and its spiritual values. This chimes with comments in his wartime broadcasts depicting Ireland as such an outpost, though he also decried the perceived assault on continental civilization by the Anglo-American forces. In his talk of 13 January 1943, Stuart said:

Over ten years ago I wrote a book called *Pigeon Irish* in which I foresaw the coming war and the part we [*i.e. Ireland*] would have to play in it, and although a few of the outward facts are different I still see our part very much as I saw it then. It is to keep to true and lasting values in the face of the war hysteria and diversion of truth and hypocrisy all around us.

The comment that 'a few of the outward facts are different' is an understatement: although Stuart does not go into much detail about the nature of the war taking place on the Continent in *Pigeon Irish*, it is clear that Ireland is not neutral in the war, but allied to a number of liberal states including Britain and the US, against an enemy that seems to be a version of the USSR. Otherwise, though, the reference is apt: in the novel, as in his comments about the actual war a decade later, Stuart envisaged Ireland as a refuge of spirituality and truth.

The Coloured Dome, also published in 1932, depicts an Ireland not radically different from the actual Ireland Stuart inhabited in the early thirties, in which a bookmaker's clerk achieves a spiritual apotheosis by volunteering to martyr himself to the republican cause. As in *Pigeon Irish*, in which Ireland has achieved the status of a republic but is led by men who betray the nation's revolutionary vision, the country's political leaders in *The Coloured Dome* (here obviously 'Free Staters') are depicted as spiritually lacking. In these novels, politics and war are means to spiritual or mystical ends; but the political scenery is not merely incidental. Stuart's characters feel themselves alienated in the face of modernity as represented by the enemy power in *Pigeon Irish*, and by the compromised mediocrity of the Irish state in both novels. Their struggles are inseparable from these political contexts.

Stuart's two novels of 1933 evoke the political crisis that was brewing in Europe at the time. In *Try the Sky*, Stuart's characters, travelling across the Continent, find themselves in the midst of a riot by brownshirts in Munich. Stuart referred to this scene in his broadcast of 13 November 1943, saying that in the novel he had 'described a clash between brownshirts and government forces in Munich, in which I did not hide my sympathies for the revolutionaries, as they then were'.[14] In the aftermath of the fighting, the four main characters befriend one Dr Graf, a Nazi who has built a mysterious aircraft. Dr Graf promises that the maiden flight of this craft will have revolutionary implications. The plane, flying west, makes a rather mundane refuelling stop in Ireland, where the

14. Stuart was obviously stating that his sympathies were with the brownshirts of the SA as against the Weimar state; but it is possible that a subtle criticism of the Third Reich was intended as well: in 1931 Hitler had ordered the SA to cease street fighting, and in 1934 he liquidated the leadership of the SA, which was viewed as nurturing dangerously revolutionary tendencies even after the Nazis took power.

Stuart-like character and his girlfriend gratefully disembark. The allegorical implications of the book are not easily discerned, and certainly *Try the Sky* is not Nazi agitprop.[15] But Stuart's comment to his listeners in 1943 that the book expressed his pro-brownshirt 'sympathies' – in the same broadcast Stuart said he 'admired Hitler from the first days of power in Germany' – indicates that the book's political dimension is not simply a matter of local colour.

Stuart's next novel, *Glory*, is an astonishingly bizarre book with a plot even more curious and complicated than that of *Try the Sky*. A company called Trans-Continental Aero-Routes builds an aerodrome on land purchased from a County Galway farmer, Mike O'Byrne. O'Byrne's teenage daughter, Mairead, befriends one of the company's top men, a General Porteous, and soon learns that his intentions for the company are more than purely commercial. Porteous tells Mairead of his vision of the future:

'It [the world] is going to become more and more self-complacent, more and more standardised, more and more benevolent on a large material scale. But cold and ruthless to those who outrage its conventions. To those who threaten its order and organisation. And it will be ruled by a Company. And a student of history might have foreseen it,' he added. 'That is the logical conclusion of all the observable tendencies in the last few centuries.'
'By what sort of Company?' Mairead asked.
'By this Company. By Trans-Continental Aero-Routes,' he said.[16]

Porteous goes on to tell Mairead: 'I want to shatter the smugness of the world. All the cold smugness that believes in humanity, that believes in itself. All the pride and self-complacency that

15. A mostly negative review of *Try the Sky* by Seán O'Faoláin in *The New Statesman and Nation* does not mention the brownshirt riot or the fact that Dr Graf is a Nazi, sympathetically drawn. One possible interpretation of this is that sympathy for National Socialism was not a particularly notable sentiment in Britain and Ireland in 1933. In any case, there can be no warrant for Hayden Murphy's claim that 'As he had shown in *Try the Sky* he was not blind to the evil of Nazism.' The book has nothing to do with any view that Nazism was evil, as Stuart's own comments demonstrate. See Murphy, 'Case for the Cause of Francis Stuart', p. 9.
16. *Glory*, pp. 140–1.

it has sunk into. And I will use their own tools to do it. Their own machines.'

Mairead is bewitched by Porteous's vision, viewing him as 'one of those lonely figures feared and despised by the world he hated so much'.[17] It is agreed that she will accompany him on his mission, to places and towards ends still unknown to her. Mairead knows only that 'I want to be on the winning side'.[18] Porteous is similarly sanguine:

'I've the brain,' he said, 'and you've the desire, the passion. That's the combination that wins great victories.'

Yes, yes, that is what she wanted. To ride in triumph by his side. That desire might be mad, preposterous in the eyes of a civilised world. But did not all desire cut across civilisation and society? There were two madnesses, the conqueror's and the saint's. They should have died with the past, with all the discarded outworn glamour of the past. But they had not died. [...] And the drab world would look up from its money-making, shocked and startled, and hear of them again.[19]

En route to eastern China, base of operations for the Company's 'campaign in the East', Porteous and Mairead stop in London. Stuart describes Mairead in her hotel room:

While she sat on the bed, half undressed, waiting for the dresses to arrive, she felt that desire, vague and yet poignant, kindle in her again. A thirst for triumph [...]

Mairead got up and walked across the room, paused a moment at the window and then stepped out upon the little balcony. She leant with her hands on the balustrade. She smiled with that frank spontaneous joy of a child when he first sees, say, the tree on Christmas morning. Then she straightened herself and raised a bare arm in a little arrogant gesture to a world whose crowds already, in her imagination, were shouting to her from below.[20]

Shortly after they reach China, Mairead realizes that Porteous is armed with poison gas. He leaves her behind for his first campaign, telling her: 'I want you to have the fruit but not to see the

17. Ibid., p. 150.
18. Ibid., p. 152.
19. Ibid., p. 177.
20. Ibid., p. 189.

gathering.'[21] Left to the pleasure of a local warlord who is allied to Porteous, she begins to be disillusioned:

She began to see that the true arrogance lay in being quite alone. Unknown to the world and to glory. That was the height after which the noble soul must strive—a deep aloneness. To leave all the fussiness, the pettiness, the gregariousness of the world and be alone. Not to try to conquer it or triumph over it. To desire nothing from it. To be alone.[22]

Porteous, rampaging murderously across Asia, becomes an international hate-figure, known as the Butcher of Benares; as the Chinese warlord's consort, Mairead is the subject of lurid press coverage as well. When Porteous finally returns, he declares that the whole experience has made a woman of Mairead, and suggests that this was the point of the exercise. She is sceptical:

'But do you think a god would upset a world and kill thousands for the sake of making one vain, silly little girl into a woman with a little wisdom and a little humility?'

'It has been done like that before,' he said. 'The gods have their own ways. They will change history by the fall of an acorn or the cackle of a bird and uproot a whole civilisation to mould one little life. But perhaps I am the first person who had ever been allowed to see them at work. Usually no one knows anything about it until afterwards, or not at all.'

'But why should I be chosen for such a lesson, to be so moulded?'

'I will tell you what I think,' he said. 'You have had the world shocked at you and jeer at you and be afraid of you, and you've learnt not to care. Not merely to exult in its hostility, but just not to care. You've learnt to be an outcast, as your generation must learn, and when I say "generation," it may only be a handful, because it is a handful in every generation who mould thought, as they say. They will be outcast from the smug, the self-complacent, from the vast societies of organised benevolence, from the capitalists and the communists. And you shall be the first of these outcasts, the first of the tragic generation.'[23]

Porteous has his hands cut off by the Chinese warlord and dies of his wounds; Mairead retaliates by killing the warlord, then travels home to Galway. There she finds that an anti-Porteous faction

21. Ibid., p. 218.
22. Ibid., p. 230.
23. Ibid., pp. 240–1.

in the Company is sitting in judgment on the others, with whom
Mairead allies herself. They receive her as a saviour:

'But I have nothing,' she said, 'and I am an outcast.'

'A girl shall lead them,' he said, repeating the words he had spoken the
last night she had seen him.

'Where?' she asked. 'To death and torture and disaster. That's all I'm
good for.'

'They have no one else,' he said. 'This generation is full of outcasts
searching for they don't know what. No hero, or conqueror or saint could
lead them because they have lost belief in heroism and in sanctity. There has
been too much wasted heroism and too much mock sanctity.' [...]

'Take us where you will,' Maklakov said. 'Out of this hell, this futility.' He
spoke as though, not only for himself, but for others as well. For many others.[24]

The saviour, predictably enough, is found guilty and executed,
following a bombastic summation by the prosecutor accusing her
of various crimes against civilization.

As is often the case in his novels of the 1930s, Stuart manages
in *Glory* to be at once didactic and puzzling. Like *Try the Sky*,
Glory is allegorical but rather incoherently so. It is possible to read
the novel as a study in the value of aloneness and suffering, and in
the folly of lusting for power, fame and victory. But Stuart's vision
is defined by the fact that, although these two sides of life are in
tension throughout the book – initially in the narrator's consciousness, and eventually in Mairead's – he does not present it as
a matter of either-or. Glory and suffering are sides of the same
coin, linked by common enemies: respectability, sham 'benevolence', 'self-complacency'. While General Porteous represents one
side of this coin, and the O'Byrnes' mystic hermit neighbour
Frank de Lacy the other, Mairead fuses both within herself. As he
made clear in his next book, *Things to Live For*, Stuart believed
that to be fully human one must attempt to achieve such a fusion
of extremes, and that all else was mediocrity and deadness.[25]

24. Ibid., pp. 268–9.

25. It is tempting, and not as absurd as it may seem, to read *Glory* as a parable of Hitler's

In *Things to Live For* (1934), a volume of autobiography and philosophical musing, Stuart paints himself as a fighter and adventurer who is all at sea in polite society:

I crouch in my dugout under the barrage, cutting a sorry figure, I dare say, but all the same a less sorry one I hope in the eyes of God than the staff colonels strutting at the base who have never been under fire. Living in bombarded dugouts does not fit one for shining in society. [...]

How often have I felt that anger in drawing rooms, at cocktail parties, at luncheon parties. Oh God, their chatter, their gossip, their nonsense, and I with an aching heart because of the damned awfulness of things, and if it was my own fault what the hell consolation is that? Take the soldier from the line that was broken after a day-long attack. Dizzy and defeated and tired to death, put him down amongst the intellectuals or the social Moguls. He'll cut a pretty poor figure all right.[26]

Much later, Stuart returns to the image of himself as soldier:

I have learnt to glory in the knowledge that there is nothing between me and the enemy, nothing but my own will that will not allow me to surrender. That is the greatest pride of all, the pride of the soldier, gripping a useless rifle, covered with mud, deafened and dizzy, a sorry figure, and yet deep down with that little spark still glowing white that can never be put out and is the most precious thing in the world. Blind faith it has been called. It is at those moments that one gives that yea to life in all its fullness.[27]

---

rise, and to view Mairead as a pre-vision of Stuart himself going to Nazi Germany in the face of all respectable opinion. In this schema, the mystic Frank de Lacy, who stays in Galway and who resembles his creator in a number of obvious respects, represents another side of Stuart, the Stuart who had lived an isolated life in County Wicklow with his wife and children (though this existence was punctuated by extended trips to London) for close to a decade and who would continue to do so until he went to Germany. J.H. Natterstad, a sympathetic commentator on Stuart since the early 1970s, adhered for many years to the view of Stuart as essentially apolitical, but revised this assessment fundamentally in a 1991 essay in which he identified a fascistic strain in Stuart's work and wrote that 'There is no mistaking the kinship of General Porteous and Hitler.' See Natterstad, 'Locke's Swoon: Francis Stuart and the Politics of Despair,' pp. 66–7. Interestingly, in *Things to Live For* Stuart appears to suggest that he identifies himself with Porteous: 'I have always put myself into my books. This is part of the fun of it. Putting oneself against this background and against that, with these people and with those. I have made myself a general, a bookie's clerk, a racehorse trainer, an aeroplane pilot. I live in my books the things I have not time to live in life. And of course I always cut a much better figure on the printed page.' See *Things to Live For*, p. 52.

26. *Things to Live For*, pp. 92, 93.
27. Ibid., p. 182.

Stuart's 1921/2 visit to Austria, which gave rise to his remarks on that country in the 1924 *Lecture*, is remembered in *Things to Live For*, as, in rather different form, is the political climate of Vienna at that time. Interestingly, from one who had spoken of 'Austrians' being in danger of being driven out of Vienna by Jews, Stuart here writes of befriending a Jewish fur-dealer:

The Jew was also interested in diamonds. I used to go round the shops with him looking at stones. In those days one got thousands of kronen to the pound. If I had been shrewder I would have bought a diamond, but I bought a motor car instead. The fact is I have never been very shrewd in money matters. All the same, we had fun driving outside Vienna in the snow, Iseult, a German girl called Paula, and myself. Once I had the car I did not see so much of the Jew, who was quietly making a fortune smuggling the diamonds out to England. He gave up his fur-dealing because of his fear of anthrax. He was a timid individual. One night when there was an anti-Jewish demonstration in the streets I found him locked in his room in the hotel.

'Have they passed? Have they gone?' he asked trembling.

'They aren't touching anyone. Only breaking windows.'

'Ach, how terrible.'

'My God,' I said, 'it's a pity they don't break your head.'

I was suddenly angry with him, because there he was making money and I was only wasting it. The car I had bought had broken into pieces. Part of it blew off one wild morning into the Donau Canal.[28]

It is important to remember that *Things To Live For* is a pre-*Kristallnacht* and pre-Holocaust book: we cannot tax Stuart with our knowledge of what the broken windows were leading to. Even so, Stuart's cavalier attitude to organized racism is startling. He admits the petty origin of his anger, but this cannot obscure the contrast, from one chapter to the next, between his attitude to himself – 'in the dugout', gripping his 'useless rifle', heroically weathering the slings and arrows of 'the intellectuals or the social Moguls' – and his attitude to the Jew in Vienna, cowering from what Stuart decorously calls a 'demonstration'. (The 'demonstration' itself receives no further comment.) The gulf between the drama Stuart can wring from his own social awkwardness and the

28. Ibid., p. 108.

matter-of-factness with which he evokes an anti-Semitic riot might seem inexplicable if we didn't know, from his own words of 1943, about his 'sympathies'.[29]

In *Things to Live For* Stuart also makes an extended attack on democracy:

Once Dublin was a city of adventure and romance. [...] Those days are over and Dublin has become drab, respectable and dead. [...] I walk through those streets that I once fought to defend, feeling a little like a stranger. And it was this spirit of smugness and deadness that we fought against and were defeated by. The spirit of liberal democracy. We fought to stop Ireland falling into the hands of publicans and shop-keepers, and she has fallen into their hands. [...]

[...] Democracy is the ideal of those whose lives as individuals are failures and who, feeling their own futility, take refuge in the mass and become arrogant in the herd. The productive worker, who takes pride in his work and exults in it, is never democratic because he feels no need for this refuge. He stands alone. He does not believe in the rule of the majority because he does not feel himself to be one of the majority.[30]

A glimpse at another dimension of Stuart's political thought is provided by an essay on Eamon de Valera, published in 1935 as part of a book called *Great Contemporaries*. This is an admiring portrait of a man Stuart terms a 'democratic genius' – although Stuart's endorsement of de Valera's method of looking into his heart to know what the Irish people wanted suggests that it is this rather undemocratic tendency, and the Chief's obeisance to the dead generations, that Stuart particularly admired.[31]

According to Stuart, de Valera 'has attempted as a political leader to live for his people as a father and a shepherd, taking his

---

29. In *Black List, Section H* – in many important respects a post-Holocaust book – the Jewish fur-trader and diamond-smuggler appears as Mr Isaacs; he is streetwise rather than timid, and there is no 'demonstration'.

30. *Things to Live For*, pp. 253–5.

31. W.B. Yeats reportedly defended de Valera's comment about looking into his heart, asking: 'Where the devil else would he look?' In July 1933 Yeats wrote: 'De Valera has described himself ... as an autocrat expressing the feeling of the masses. If we must have an autocrat let him express what Swift called the "bent & current" of a people not a momentary majority.' See Elizabeth Cullingford, *Yeats, Ireland and Fascism*, p. 199.

inspiration from saints rather than from statesmen'. Stuart specu-
lates that the success of such an attempt 'might be the one effective answer that has yet been given to such impersonal systems as
Communism and Fascism'. He endorses de Valera's opposition to
the Treaty, and writes that during the civil war 'He was no longer
the leader and protector and father of his people, but an outcast,
a fanatic, an embittered extremist in the eyes of the majority of
them.'[32] For Stuart, 'outcast' and 'fanatic' are terms of praise, and
the beliefs of the 'majority' are to be viewed with extreme mistrust.

Had de Valera accepted the treaty he would doubtless be where Cosgrave and
the others of the pro-treaty party are today, completely and, I think, finally
discredited. As it is, he is still the strongest force in Ireland because he has
shown himself in 1916 and in 1922 capable of going his own way towards the
goal that he sees, whether the people whom he loves follow him or not.[33]

Stuart concluded his essay with a dark suggestion that de
Valera was becoming too much the democrat:

Already there are signs that he has finally bowed to the wishes of the people
whose servant he considers himself, has finally renounced those flashes of

32. 'President de Valera', pp. 64–5.
33. Ibid., p. 65. The protagonist of *Black List, Section H* has a pointedly different attitude
to de Valera's performance during the civil war, indicating once again that it is a mistake to
view H as a direct cipher for Stuart:

'He opened the door of a compartment where there were only two girls and an elderly
man and stepped in. Both girls were looking up at him, wide-eyed and pale, not avoiding
his glance.
Was this the moment that they, like him, had been waiting for, when familiar habits and
conventions were swept away and nobody was safe who didn't want to be, nothing was dis-
allowed to the daring, and whatever could be imagined could be made come true?
He looked boldly into the face of the younger girl and she smiled at him as her sister
exclaimed, "Up the Republic! Up de Valera!"
H was sobered and brought back to earth from the start of one of his fantasies. He certainly didn't share their enthusiasm for de Valera. De Valera was one of the most reactionary
of the leaders on either side. He had an integrity and vision that the Free State lot lacked,
but this merely ensured that he wouldn't compromise on the national issue; as a revolutionary leader, in the sense that interested H, he had nothing to offer.' (p. 83)

While the events in the novel are taking place a dozen years before Stuart wrote his essay,
it is difficult to imagine that the author of the latter could have been as disillusioned with
de Valera during the civil was as H is.

undemocratic fire that led him into the 1916 rebellion and into the civil war of 1922. If that is so there can be only one end. The people for whom he has sacrificed himself will finally throw him over. Because, in their hearts, although it may take a long time for those hearts to realize it, they will only follow, year in, year out, a leader who dares to lead them to the heights; to those heights of national aspiration which it is so hard for anyone outside Ireland to understand.[34]

Stuart's hostility to democracy, his sympathy for the brown-shirts and nonchalance towards anti-Semitism in Vienna, and the implicit politics of several of his novels of the 1930s collectively raise the spectre of fascism. Was Stuart a fascist at this time? It is an obvious question, but perhaps not a terribly useful one. During the 1920s and 1930s, fascism was many things to many people; and it exercised a particularly plastic fascination on writers and intellectuals. There is little evidence that Stuart was interested in fascism *per se*. Italian fascism, upon which W.B. Yeats cast an intermittently indulgent eye over the years between Mussolini's rise and his own death, figures not at all in Stuart's pre-war writings, and Italy is invoked only fleetingly in the wartime broadcasts. There does not appear to be a single reference to the Spanish civil war in Stuart's writings of the 1930s; this silence may have had something to do with the political orientation of Franco's Irish supporters.[35] Irish civil-war politics would also have ensured that Ireland's only indigenous fascist movement, the Blueshirts, held no appeal for Stuart.

In the 1935 essay Stuart suggested that de Valera's political persona as 'a father and a shepherd' 'might be the one effective answer that has yet been given to such impersonal systems as Communism and Fascism'; and in *Things to Live For* he went so far as to claim that 'I know little of politics and, for an Irishman, I have little interest in them'. But a declared lack of interest in fascism as a 'system', and in politics generally, does not end the discussion. One of

34. 'President de Valera', p. 66.
35. See Fearghal McGarry, *Irish Politics and the Spanish Civil War*.

the attractions of fascism, particularly to artists, was its claim to be above politics: it drew upon aesthetics and appealed to spiritual rather than strictly political sensibilities. As Walter Benjamin famously had it, 'The logical result of Fascism is the introduction of aesthetics into political life.'[36] It follows from this that those of an aesthetic disposition – particularly in faraway lands – might be peculiarly inclined to embace the aesthetics of fascism without fully realizing that they were adopting a politics as well.

What Stuart had in common with the famous writers of this era whom we associate with fascism – Yeats, Pound, Céline, Wyndham Lewis, and many others – was a hostility to democracy, rational-ism, materialism and modernity (not to be confused with Mod-ernism). Beyond these things, it is difficult to generalize about a literary tendency that has proved far easier to identify than to define; and it is correspondingly difficult to locate meaningful parallels or divergences between Stuart and the famous 'literary fascists'. It might be useful to observe that whereas these writers were broadly linked by what they were against, they took very dif-ferent paths in terms of what they were for, and these paths tended to be defined by personal circumstances. Just as friendship with Pound coloured Yeats's attitude to Italian fascism, so Stuart's trav-els in Germany and Austria in 1921/2, and his sympathy for an uncompromising Irish republican element that was willing to col-laborate with the Nazis, helped to provide the spiritual and prac-tical foundations for the non-literary activities to which his own fascist leanings eventually led him.

The question of literary anti-Semitism is cognate to that of fas-cism, but not identical with it. Yeats was sympathetic to fascism, and late in his life wrote a pamphlet called *On the Boiler* in which he advanced a hair-raising defence of eugenics and looked forward to the coming of war with something approaching glee; but he was

36. Walter Benjamin, 'The Work of Art in the Age of Mechanical Reproduction', in *Illu-minations*, p. 234. See also Alastair Hamilton, *The Appeal of Fascism*.

not, so far as we know, an anti-Semite. T.S. Eliot *was* an anti-Semite, and he felt some of the 'cultural despair' (Fritz Stern's term) that characterized the literary fascists, but his politics were not fascist in any meaningful sense.[37] The same could be said of said of several other anti-Semitic writers of the age. In the case of Stuart, evidence of anti-Semitism – in his 1924 account of 1921 Vienna – predates published evidence of a specifically fascistic politics; but it may be that the anti-Jewish riot Stuart seems to have witnessed in Vienna at the age of nineteen was a seminal event with regard to both strains in his thought. The degree to which Stuart might have absorbed anti-Semitism from his family and from the Irish republican movement – to say nothing of Irish society generally – must remain a matter of conjecture, not least because in his writings and interviews Stuart projected the persona of a man radically alienated from such everyday influences.

Jewish characters figure in several of Stuart's novels of the 1930s. In his first novel, *Women and God* (1931), there is a lunch scene in Paris during which a Russian character called Laura speaks and thinks anti-Semitic thoughts about a fellow Russian called Madame de Solanges ('Russian – hell. She's a Jewess. A Russian Jew.'). There is nothing ambiguous about Laura's anti-Semitism, but the import of the scene as a whole is difficult to discern. Laura is a sympathetically drawn character, but her behaviour in this scene is out of character, probably because her husband has just left her. To complicate matters further, Laura's anti-Jewish outburst is preceded by a conversation between the lunching group and a black man called Paul, whom Laura knows and views with disgust. Paul, sensing her hostility, speaks his piece:

'Where do I belong? I live here in Paris. I was born here. Where should I go? Into the jungle, you think? Back to the jungle. Ah, you too despise us niggers. We are worse than the Jews. They have a bad time too.'

37. For a discussion of Eliot's anti-Semitism (and other things), see Christopher Ricks, *T.S. Eliot and Prejudice*. On the cultural roots of German fascism, see Fritz Stern, *The Politics of Cultural Despair*.

This exchange seems to feed Laura's rising anger:

She felt over-taut. At a white heat. And cold at the same time. Her breasts were paining. She felt their points press against her dress. She put her hand to her left breast. Touching it with her hand made her tremble. She had to talk. She had to say something to take her mind off the way she was. If only that Jewess weren't sitting staring at her. God! What a woman to be with! To be with, and to be feeling like she felt![38]

The lunch scene in *Women and God* does not admit of any unquestionable interpretation; but it might be read as a study in the way private pain can give way to public expressions of latent bigotry, rather than an exercise in such bigotry itself: it seems to take anti-black and anti-Jewish feeling as its subject rather than its purpose. Madame de Solanges, though a complicated and not wholly sympathetic character, is not depicted stereotypically or with particular hostility.

Of the six novels Stuart published between 1935 and 1939, three have important Jewish characters. While Stuart attributes to these characters traits that are wholly consistent with anti-Semitic stereotypes, as well as traits that most people would find repellent, Stuart himself, in two of the three cases, attaches positive value to these traits and paints the Jewish characters in a mostly sympathetic light. Máire Mhac an tSaoi has argued that this is 'a common and not very subtle form of deniable racism':

Mr Stuart professes to like Jews; his works tell you why. He has an affection for them because they are pimps, smugglers, even quasi-collaborators; he likes them, as an old-time Southern colonel liked blacks, for their defects.[39]

Mac an tSaoi is justified in seeing Stuart's apparent affection for roguish Jews as problematic, but she fails to notice that Stuart's novels are filled with sympathetically drawn characters who possess such 'defects', and that these characters are usually not Jews.

38. *Women and God*, pp. 175–82.
39. Máire Cruise O'Brien [*sic*], 'Why Francis Stuart's Stance Outrages Me', *Sunday Independent*, 30 November 1997.

If there is anti-Semitism in any of these books, it does not reside in the fact that some of the criminals and rogues who inhabit Stuart's pages happen to be Jews.

Stuart's three major Jewish characters of the 1930s are the film producer Sam Salmon in *In Search of Love*, the penniless South African teenager turned corrupt London fire assessor Ben Goldberg in *Julie*, and the Liverpool workhouse orphan turned successful Dublin banker Ike Salaman in *The Great Squire*. Sam Salmon, unlike the other two, is depicted in a wholly negative light: he is an unscrupulous manipulator who exploits those around him and makes fatuous speeches about being a common man. (This is in sharp contrast to Ben Goldberg and Ike Salaman, who are resolutely plain-spoken.) It is not impossible to imagine a character of Salmon's traits being depicted in a positive light in a Stuart novel; but in fact Salmon is a pure stereotype, and in portraying him Stuart neither questions nor transcends, but simply replicates, the garden-variety anti-Semitism of the day.[40]

Ben Goldberg and Ike Salaman are more difficult to assess as Jewish characters, because in creating them Stuart does a number of seemingly conflicting things: he perpetuates stereotypes; he calls attention to the anti-Semitism of other characters; and he comes close to inverting the value system from which the stereotypes derive their hateful power. Goldberg, a South African teenager on the make in London, sets up as a fire assessor and quickly decides that in order to get ahead he will have to collude in arson. The novel's central character, Julie Harben, idealizes Goldberg, telling him that he could 'be something grand':

'Not me, Julie. Not grand; that's not my line.'

'Yes, it is,' she answered stubbornly. She was regarding him with serious brown, wide-apart eyes and out-thrust underlip.

---

40. The commonness of such anti-Semitism at the time is perhaps reflected by the fact that Elizabeth Bowen's short and sniffy review of *In Search of Love* in *The New Statesman and Nation* of 14 September 1935 does not mention the depiction of Salmon.

Goldberg laughed. He had no illusions about himself.

'What else is there but to make money?' he asked.

'Lots of things,' she said.

'Not for a fellow like me. That's the only way I have of being somebody, see? I don't want to remain just a third-rate little Jewboy all my life.'[41]

Goldberg's obsession with making money chimes, of course, with anti-Semitic stereotype and is inimical to Stuart's hatred of materialism, a hatred that is voiced by Julie. Yet Julie loves Goldberg, and her scruples about his scam are balanced by a sympathetic understanding of his rationalization for what he does:

You think because I'm a fire-raiser I'm the lowest of crooks, an enemy of society, eh? [...] But I'll tell you something. I'm a benefactor of society compared to most factory owners, big store owners. I don't defraud the poor and squeeze the last ounce out of them. I go for the rich, Julie; for the Insurance companies and for the banks.[42]

This couldn't be further from the anti-Semitic lie that Jews are the controlling conspirators in a rapacious global financial system; Goldberg's few co-conspirators are not, to judge by their names, Jewish, and his enemies are, as he says, the big banks and insurance companies. There is, of course, a large dollop of casuistry and bad economics in Goldberg's rationalization – banks and insurance companies will always simply pass on the costs of fraud to their customers – but Stuart clearly means it to be taken seriously.

Stuart describes Goldberg working at a fire scene:

There he was, playing this game with the actual pieces in his hands. Not doing it in a remote way only, with figures, watching tape-machines. He had to have something solid he could handle or at least kick over with his feet. Such abstractions as 'Pig iron steady' or 'Industrials easier' would have meant little to him. But when it came to the real stuff of the big-town game behind these symbols, then he was in his element, then his genius got to work. His small blue eyes had only to glance at a bit of cloth, a piece of furniture, a fragment of china, and he knew all about it, that is, all he needed to know about it. Its value to a shilling.[43]

41. *Julie*, pp. 52–3.
42. Ibid., p. 116.
43. Ibid., p. 92.

Here, again, Stuart attributes to Goldberg a stereotypically Jewish trait: a belief that the monetary value of an object was 'all he needed to know about it', and a 'genius' for reckoning that value. As against this, though, Goldberg is unable to relate to the 'abstractions' of international finance. Most importantly, perhaps, Julie sticks by Goldberg, even when he is sent to jail, and the book ends with Julie dreaming of being reunited with him and going back into business. The whole logic of the book depends on the reader feeling sympathy for Goldberg; and if Stuart's intent had been anti-Semitic the book would have had to end differently.

Ike Salaman, the Jewish character in *The Great Squire*, is in several respects very similar to Goldberg. He is even more fanatically obsessed with making money:

His keen swarthy face glowed with the cold passion that consumed him as he bent over the grey parchment. Figures. How secretly beautiful they were! What delight in getting them to dance to one's own tune! Ah, that was the real happiness: this secret mathematical dance of figures, in rows, in spidery waltzes, in formal gavottes, to that thin maddening tune that he had long dreamt of but only heard for the first time to-day, the clink and clank of a great number of sovereigns.[44]

As with Goldberg, this obsession with money appears to arise primarily, if not wholly, from the fact that Ike Salaman is a Jew; and in this, Stuart is guilty at the very least of a sort of abdication of the fiction-writer's duty to create fully human characters, and at worst of perpetuating a stereotype that, in 1939, the year of the novel's publication, was being used to frightful ends in Europe. At the same time, as in *Julie*, the whole logic of the novel depends on the reader feeling an essential sympathy for this roguish Jew, and Stuart goes to some lengths to engender such sympathy. If Salaman's almost mystical love of money appears to be attributed to his 'race', his desire for success has roots in terrible memories of the orphanage from which he escaped:

44. *The Great Squire*, p. 169

He thought of the two little boys murdered in the outhouse of the Galilee Home. That sobered him. It was his sign, his secret banner; for it he was ready to suffer and to make suffer. They had been tortured to death because they had been born into the world paupers. There had been seared into his mind the terrible injustice of society. He accepted it; he had nothing of the reformer in him, no urge to alter it. But he would, accepting the rules, see if he could play the game better than almost any one else. In that queer way he also felt that he was revenging those two innocent victims whom he had sworn never to forget.[45]

The reasoning here may seem incoherent, but it is consistent with that of other sympathetic characters in Stuart novels, most obviously General Porteous and Mairead O'Byrne, who wish to 'shatter the smugness of the world' using its own tools. And just as *Julie* ends with an invocation of the fruitful reunion of its spiritual female protagonist and a materialistic Jew, so *The Great Squire* ends with *its* spiritual female protagonist going to a ball on the arm of Ike Salaman.

It is perhaps impossible to arrive at any ironclad reading of the three major Jewish characters in Stuart's novels of the 1930s. Stuart unquestionably traded in stereotypes, and Anthony Cronin's claim that 'there are in fact no anti-Semitic sentiments expressed anywhere in all the millions of words' Stuart wrote is unsustainable, even if we restrict ourselves to the fiction.[46] The history of anti-Semitism is, among many other things, the history of a

---

45. Ibid., p. 243.

46. Anthony Cronin, 'Stuart an Innocent Abroad', *Sunday Independent*, 30 November 1997. Cronin appears to be paraphrasing a comment made by Stuart in an interview with Eileen Battersby, published in the *Irish Times* on 14 November 1996: 'I have spoken and written several million words in my life. No one could ever point to a sentence of mine that was or is anti-Semitic.' Hugo Hamilton adopted this unfortunate approach to the question in a letter published in the *Irish Times* on 4 December 1997, in which he wrote of 'a writer who has been shown repeatedly not to have uttered a single line of racial hatred in his entire works'. Besides the fact that this has never been 'shown' – it is difficult to imagine how it could be – the idea that anti-Semitism can or should be reckoned in an isolated 'word' or 'line' of prose is ill-fitted to the nature of racism, and indeed to that of fiction. Ironically, this 'not a word, not a line' claim may have played into the hands of those who attacked Stuart for a 'line' of *prima facie* anti-Semitism in a 1997 television documentary, discussed below.

demonization that has often gone hand-in-hand with an idealiza-tion: the Old Testament image of a spiritual people is held up against the perceived decadence of modern Jews. With Ben Gold-berg and Ike Salaman, Stuart might have been trying, however unconsciously and problematically, to dissolve this fictive binary by imagining a spirituality of materialism. (In some of his post-war novels, however – most notably *Victors and Vanquished* (1958) – the binary is intact. Stuart's use of 'spiritual' Jewish characters to mouth a critique of modern Jewry seems enormously presumptu-ous in a way that the pre-war novels never are, and is unconvinc-ing as either social commentary or fiction.[47])

It is natural that post-war readers, knowing of Stuart's collabo-ration with the Third Reich, would look with a sharp eye at Stu-art's depiction of Jews in his pre-war novels. If they expect to find a degree of anti-Semitism commensurate with that of the Nazi state, they will be disappointed – but they should not be surprised. As that state has come to be identified, understandably, with its greatest crime above all its other deeds, so we expect those non-Germans who supported that state to have been motivated pri-marily by hatred of Jews, and we may be predisposed to detect murderous implications in milder anti-Semitism. This expecta-tion overlooks the degree to which anti-Semitism was a wide-spread and even respectable form of prejudice in Ireland and in

47. For an examination of the depiction of Jews in Stuart's fiction, see Raymond Patrick Burke's M.A. thesis, 'The Representation of Jews and "Jewishness" in the Novels of Francis Stuart'. Burke's research is impressively vast, and his conclusions often compelling – partic-ularly with regard to Stuart's idealization of Old Testament Jews as against modern Jews; but Burke goes to frequently untenable lengths to find anti-Semitism (or sinister philo-Semi-tism) even in books that lack Jewish characters or references of any sort to Jews. In 1997 Conor Cruise O'Brien argued on the basis of Burke's thesis that *In Search of Love, Julie* and *The Great Squire* were proof of Stuart's anti-Semitism; a riposte by Anthony Cronin skew-ered O'Brien for failing to read the books themselves and for suppressing the closing sen-tence of a quotation from *Julie* that utterly undoes the seeming anti-Semitism of the preceding passage; but Cronin protested too much when he said it was 'arrant nonsense to describe [*In Search of Love*] as anti-Semitic in any way'. For both pieces see *Sunday Inde-pendent*, 10 October 1999.

Europe generally during the 1930s,[48] and also ignores the much broader appeal exercised by fascism upon many artists and intellectuals in that decade.

There is no evidence that anti-Semitism was a motivating force in Francis Stuart's decision to live, teach and broadcast in Nazi Germany. At the same time, it is difficult to avoid the conclusion that some strain of anti-Semitism was a necessary enabling factor in that decision. We know that Stuart was willing to write in the mid-thirties of how unmoved he had been by an anti-Semitic riot in Vienna. And we know that in the late thirties Stuart was reading the papers, which were increasingly filled with accounts of the persecution of the Jews by the Third Reich. On 9 December 1938, a month after *Kristallnacht*, Stuart wrote the following letter to *The Irish Times*, which published it on 13 December:

Sir,—For some months past there have appeared in the European situation features that may gravely affect us in Ireland. I am going to take up a little of your space in the belief that a recognition of these is a matter of considerable importance.

First, there has been a widespread tendency to identify religion with democracy. Without going into the relative merits of varying forms of government and social organisations (a thing, however, that badly needs doing), it must be remembered that no Church can, by its nature, affiliate itself to any social ideology. It is true that its individual members, not excluding the Pope, may do so.

It was a very remarkable fact, and one responsible for not a few converts to Catholicism, that the Vatican remained completely independent of, and unswayed by, the new scientific theories of the last century, many of which were later jettisoned. It would be all the greater pity if it were to show any tendency to be influenced by one of the several sociological theories of the present age.

Whenever this has happened before, as in the case of the Divine Right of Kings, a later age has found such advocacy unjustifiable. So I am certain that a time will come when any too whole-hearted advocacy of democracy (as

48. One sign of the status of anti-Semitism in Ireland is the fact that Charles Bewley, who had made no secret of his virulent anti-Semitism as far back as the early 1920s, was allowed to serve as Irish Minister in Berlin from 1933 until 1938. For Bewley's career, see Andreas Roth, *Mr Bewley in Berlin*.

experimentally practised in the English-speaking countries) on the part of the Vatican or any large portion of the Hierarchy will seem to future Catholics equally strange.

My second point (there are others which I must forego for the present) is in connection with the Irish plans to aid refugees published in to-day's papers. This has a direct bearing on what I have already written. With slums such as we have in our large towns, with nearly one hundred thousand unemployed, with many of our fellow-countrymen living on, and even over, the border line of starvation, such an appeal for funds must seem ironical to an unprejudiced observer. I suggest that those most closely connected with the scheme are not unprejudiced. It seems to me that this plan is calculated to prove the humanitarianism of the democracies compared with certain countries where such an idea does not prevail. True charity begins at home. In the parable of the Good Samaritan we learn that our neighbour is he who is nearest at hand. Thus I cannot help feeling that until democracy has proved its humanitarianism more thoroughly in the spirit of the Gospel it scarcely enhances its appeal by these gestures on behalf of suffering foreigners.

It is worth pointing out, once more, the divergence between the tone and mode of thought of this letter, and the disengaged consciousness described in *Black List, Section H*: this letter alone should be enough to put an end to the oddly persistent tendency among Stuart commentators to explain his German sojourn in the terms established by that novel. More surprising is the divergence between Stuart's view of Ireland as a sort of haven, or ark, in a chaotic world, as expressed in *Women and God* and *Pigeon Irish* (and also in the wartime broadcasts), on the one hand, and his opposition to a modest plan for receiving refugees in Ireland on the other.[49] Perhaps most disorienting, for anyone who has read Stuart's meditations on suffering and pity, is that in 1938 Stuart opposed letting refugees into Éire because such a scheme *would make democracy look good.* Here Stuart's political beliefs trumped all other considerations. He had whipped himself into believing that hypocrisy (which, needless to say, was present in Éire's derisory refugee programme) and what General Porteous calls

49. On Irish policy and practice with regard to refugees from Hitler, see Dermot Keogh, *Jews in Twentieth-Century Ireland.*

'organised benevolence' were greater evils than state-organized racial persecution. He was thus capable of declaring with a straight face that 'True charity begins at home' (a banal cliché in any context, a brutal one here), and of missing the point of the Good Samaritan parable (which, not surprisingly, was what most exercised the *Irish Times* readers who wrote in protest).

In a letter published in the *Irish Times* on 19 December, responding to critics of his first, Stuart concluded:

When democracy has found some solution to the pressing problems observable in the countries where it is practised, which I would define as, among others: Unemployment, slums, the tyranny of money, and the appallingly low level of general culture, then let it sit in judgment on other forms of government. But, in my belief, our bureaucratic democracies can never of their nature find such a solution, being themselves largely responsible for these evils.

Here Stuart reveals what might be the kernel of his pique: the idea that in preparing to accept refugees from Nazi Germany, Éire (like other democracies) was 'sit[ting] in judgment on other forms of government'.

Stuart, it appears, had made his own judgment – or had decided to suspend it. Within two months of the publication of these letters, he would be asked to give a series of readings in Germany, and in April 1939 he arrived in Berlin.

II

The invitation to give readings in Germany came through Helmut Clissmann, a friend of Stuart's wife Iseult and head of the German Academic Exchange Service in Ireland. Clissmann saw Stuart off on the mail boat from Dún Laoghaire, a fact that did not escape the attention of G2, the intelligence branch of the Irish army.[50]

50. Clissmann was being watched by the Irish authorities at this time; his presence at Stuart's departure led to the onset of surveillance of the Stuarts, as recorded in the file on Francis and Iseult Stuart, G2/0214, housed in the Military Archives, Dublin.

The tour, sponsored by the Deutsche Akademie, brought Stuart to Berlin, Munich, Hamburg, Bonn and Cologne. After the tour was finished, the head of the Akademie's English faculty offered Stuart a position as a lecturer in English and Irish Literature at Berlin University, beginning in the autumn. Stuart was inclined to accept, and wrote to Iseult asking her to come to Berlin with their children. She refused, and it appears that this, along with bureaucratic difficulties in Germany, prevented Stuart from accepting the offer for the time being.[51]

Stuart had some free weeks in Berlin following his tour. Geoffrey Elborn quotes a letter to Iseult in which Stuart wrote of seeing

framed pictures and articles exhibited here and there in the streets depicting types of Jews and the writing dealing with their activities in the past and present. These are mostly pages from newspapers – especially *The Sturmer* the special anti-Semitic one. Also I think from the *Schwarze Korps* the official paper of the S.S.

Also I have heard something of the Jewish activities prior to 1933 here and in cooperation with the communists – they were in many instances appalling. As for the presence of Jews now: They are scarcely to be seen in this part of Berlin (central) or the West End. But in the East End – beyond Alexanderplatz – where I penetrated one day there are still a good many to be seen. It is an extraordinary thing to see the busy, fashionable streets of a big city, without Jewish faces. It is something one realises gradually [...][52]

Stuart also wrote to his wife of a 'Midsummer's Festival' at the Olympic Stadium:

Such a spectacle and organisation! Thousands of the S.A. with torches. The Hitler Youth Movement in regiments circling the centre of the enormous arena that was floodlit, about 120,000 people there [...] As for the fireworks with which the celebrations ended, I have never seen anything like them. [...] At the end thousands of rockets burst and down from them floated huge Swastika flags from rockets [...][53]

51. This account is taken from *Francis Stuart: A Life* by Geoffrey Elborn. Elborn's information on the 1939 trip appears to come from interviews with Stuart and from letters Stuart wrote to Iseult. As Elborn does not list his sources, his account and transcriptions must be taken on trust.
52. Quoted in Elborn, *Francis Stuart*, p. 113.
53. Ibid., p. 116.

In early August Stuart returned to Ireland. In September, shortly after the German invasion of Poland and the ensuing declarations of war, he wrote to accept the position at Berlin University. On 29 September, he sent the following letter to the *Irish Independent*:

Sir—I wish to congratulate Deputy Esmonde on the very pertinent remarks he made in the Dail, as reported in your issue of September 29. Especially would I like to associate myself with them as regards his question about the functions of the representative being sent to us from the British Colonial Office and the somewhat one-sided character of our radio news.[54]

I am not suggesting that the appointment of a British representative to Ireland is not perfectly justifiable at the moment. It is simply that there appears to be a certain Governmental secrecy about the whole business that is not reassuring. Yet the Government would keep the loyalty of the public— so necessary to it at the moment—far more, surely[,] by allowing no suspicion of anything in the nature of a contravention of the strict neutrality it has set itself to be even rumoured. A clear and frank statement on this question is needed.

As to our news on the wireless, I am quite aware of the difficulties— owing to our geographical position largely—of collecting much independent news on the war. May I say here in parenthesis that the *Irish Independent* alone among the Dublin dailies seems to me to have kept reasonably impartial?[55] Could not our Broadcasting directors make some special efforts to put

54. Deputy Esmonde, speaking in a Dáil debate, was quoted as inquiring of Sir John Maffey, newly appointed United Kingdom Representative in Ireland: 'Is he coming here to serve the best interests of the country? He is coming here from the British Colonial Office. I hope he is not coming here to tell us to be good boys during the war.' The *Irish Independent* also reported: 'Mr. Esmonde said that the people wanted news, and the more news the Government gave them the fewer rumours there would be. Owners of wireless sets got no news about their own country, which might not exist for all that is heard on the radio.'

55. The verb 'kept' is somewhat misleading. The editorial stance of the *Irish Independent* in the first month of the war was indeed impartial in that neither the British nor the German side received preferential treatment in news coverage, while the leading articles were more likely to rehearse retrospectively the atrocities of the Republican forces in the Spanish civil war and praise Franco's qualities as a statesman than to advance any opinion on the war then underway. This reticence with regard to Germany was not, however, consistent with pre-war coverage in the paper: a leading article of 11 November 1938, for example, called the *Kristallnacht* pogrom 'unparalleled in modern history for its cruelty and fiendishness' and declared that these 'revolting attacks on a helpless minority will shock even a world grown used to Nazi excesses'. The paper's coverage of *Kristallnacht* was equal in extent and identical in tone to that of the *Irish Times*; less than a year later, the *Independent* offered no political opinion of the German invasion of Poland, while the *Times* took

before their subscribers a little more of the German and neutral view-points[?] At present it seems to me an undue amount of time is given to the statements of British Ministers.

Having spent the four months immediately preceding the outbreak of war in Germany, I know that there is much in the German case to interest the average Irishman. Conversely, I was often asked while there questions about this country, both cultural and political. Other neutral countries find it advantageous to have broadcasts in foreign languages at the present time; might we not follow suit with a regular broadcast in German? I know it would be eagerly listened to.[56]

To evade wartime travel restrictions, Stuart obtained a doctor's certificate falsely testifying that for health reasons he needed to go to Switzerland; from there he would cross into Germany. The visa arrangements took some months; he eventually travelled in January 1940. Shortly before departing, he published an article in *The Young Observer* entitled 'Ireland a Democracy? The Real State of Affairs'. The piece appears to have been hastily written and badly edited, but its critique of democracy is consistent with that of previous and future writings:

… both Universal Suffrage and the Freedom of the Press have lost even the shadow of semblance of signs of a people guiding its own destiny, that these catch-cries once claimed they were. Let us in Ireland refuse to be taken in any longer by these and the other democratic clap-trap, and begin to concern ourselves with examining other and more efficient methods of using what national freedom we have so far won.[57]

The circumstances of Stuart's 1939 German tour and of the several months he spent contriving to return, his letter to the *Irish Independent*, and the piece in *The Young Observer*, should be borne in mind when considering what is perhaps the most implausible

a staunchly pro-Allied line. It would appear that the consistently pro-British *Irish Times* was far less influenced in its editorial policy by British war propaganda than the *Irish Independent* was by de Valera's line of neutrality and by Irish censorship, which seem to have had a chilling effect on coverage that might influence readers to support the Allies.

56. *Irish Independent*, 5 October 1939.

57. Francis Stuart, 'Ireland a Democracy? The Real State of Affairs', *The Young Observer*, 1 December 1939. A clipping of this article is kept in a scrapbook assembled by Iseult Stuart and now part of the Francis Stuart Collection at the University of Ulster, Coleraine.

claim that has been made about Stuart: that he went to Germany because he wanted to experience defeat. The Germany he saw in the early months of 1939 was not, needless to say, a defeated country, nor showed any signs of being defeated any time soon; and all that happened between September and December was the swift dismemberment of Poland followed by the 'phoney war' during which Britain and France ventured little. Any lingering belief that Stuart had pitched his tent in Berlin and was waiting for the bombs to fall and the armies to march in, however long it took, is quickly scotched by a perusal of his broadcasts, which he started making more than two years after arriving in wartime Germany. On 5 August 1942, he told his listeners:

[...] it was not the chances of war that brought me to Germany; I came during the war of my own free will [...] My main reason was the very same one that has driven millions of other Irishmen to leave their native land: the necessity of earning a living. [...] My second reason is that, like I daresay a good many others of us, I was heartily sick and disgusted with the old order under which we've been existing and which had come to us from the great financial powers in whose shadow we lived. If there had to be a war then I wanted to be among those people who had also had enough of the old system and who moreover claimed that they had a new and a better one – about all that I shall try to speak in later talks.

This is almost certainly not the whole truth – difficulties in his marriage seem to have been an important factor in Stuart's move – but it appears to be truthful as far as it goes: living in Germany appealed to Stuart both economically and ideologically.

Before leaving Ireland, Stuart met the IRA acting chief of staff, Stephen Hayes, and another high-ranking IRA man, Jim O'Donovan, at the latter's house. He was asked to make contact with Abwehr II – the branch of German military intelligence that specialized in colluding with disenchanted nationalist groups abroad – and to ask them to send a new radio transmitter to the IRA, whose previous German transmitter had been seized. There is no evidence that Stuart had performed any active service for the IRA between the civil war and 1939; the circumstances whereby the IRA came to approach him to act as a liaison with the Abwehr are unclear, but as Stuart had contacts in both republican circles and among the small German community in Ireland, it is not surprising that he should have been approached.[58] That he agreed to act in this capacity suggests that he believed collaboration between the IRA and the Third Reich might bear fruit. (One of Stuart's students in Berlin, Hilde Poepping, who was also involved in broadcasting to Ireland, recalled in an interview that Stuart 'stressed wherever he went that he had come on a mission for the IRA'.[59])

In addition to the IRA message, which he delivered to the Abwehr on 4 February,[60] Stuart came to Germany armed with a letter of introduction from Eduard Hempel, German Minister in Dublin, to Ernst von Weizsäcker, State Secretary at the Foreign Ministry. From the Ministry – which he vistited on 26 January, and where he later claimed to have discussed with Weizsäcker the effectiveness of the propaganda broadcasts to Britain by William Joyce, popularly known as 'Lord Haw-Haw' – he received documents allowing him to move freely around Berlin.[61] It appears that it was not long after this initial meeting that Stuart was asked by

58. According to Carolle J. Carter, Sean MacBride, Iseult Stuart's half brother, told Stuart that the IRA wished to use him as a messenger: see Carter, *The Shamrock and the Swastika*, p. 105. Stuart's acquaintances among the German community in Ireland included Eduard Hempel, the German Minister in Dublin; Franz Fromme, an academic and Abwehr agent who met Stuart in Ireland in 1939; the anthropology student turned Abwehr agent Jupp Hoven; and Helmut Clissmann.

59. Quoted in David O'Donoghue, *Hitler's Irish Voices*, p. 40. Stuart's Kashubian lover Gertrud (Madeleine) Meissner, who later became his second wife, recalled in her memoirs that 'Himself [Frank Ryan] and Francis loved to talk about politics, Ireland and the I.R.A., all subjects that ... I had little interest in.' See Madeleine Stuart, *Manna in the Morning*, p. 28.

60. I am grateful to Mark Hull for providing a translation of the reference to Stuart on 4 February 1940 in the Abwehr 'war journal' (*Kriegstagebuch*).

61. Several accounts have said the letter of introduction was for Weizsäcker, and that Stuart met the State Secretary himself; the account of the meeting that is given in *Documents on German Foreign Policy* (vol. VIII, p. 546) has him meeting only the Under-Secretary, Ernst Woermann. Andreas Roth, in a paper forthcoming in *Irish Historical Studies* that makes use of previously untapped German archival sources, says there is no sign of Stuart's having met Weizsäcker.

a Foreign Ministry officer to write talks for Joyce and to translate German news into English; he agreed.[62] He wrote few talks for Joyce because the latter soon redefined his role as a broadcaster and began writing his own scripts; but Stuart did continue his translation work for the broadcasts to Britain.[63]

In April Stuart was introduced to Hermann Görtz, an Abwehr agent preparing to parachute into Ireland in order to make contact with the IRA. Stuart gave Görtz his family's address in Laragh, Co. Wicklow, and after Görtz landed in Co. Meath, in May, he made his way towards Laragh, which he reached four days later. Iseult did her best for Görtz, helping him to hide and buying him new clothes. The police eventually became aware that a German agent had landed – though they did not apprehend him until nineteen months later – and traced him back to Iseult, who was arrested on 23 May. She was eventually charged with concealing the unidentified German agent and dissembling when questioned about him; after being held for over a month in Mountjoy Prison, she was tried and found not guilty.[64]

62. According to the selection entitled 'A Berlin Diary' from Stuart's 1984 book *States of Mind*, Stuart was asked on 18 February by Dr Haferkorn of the Foreign Ministry if he would 'write some talks for William Joyce'. This selection – which appeared in slightly different form in the *Irish Times* in 1976 – is often cited, but it should not be treated as a 'diary'. Stuart rewrote and made wholesale additions to entries from surviving diaries, changing both their style and their substance. He also reconstructed entries from diaries that did not survive. Although the original diary for February 1940 does not appear to survive, there is no reason to doubt the truthfulness of Stuart's account of Haferkorn's approach; for an example of how Stuart's rewriting of his diary might create an inaccurate perception of episodes from these years, see n. 77.

63. For William Joyce's broadcasting career, see Cole, *Lord Haw-Haw*. In an interview with Emmanuel Kehoe in 1978, Stuart stated: 'I had written some broadcasts for William Joyce, though very few, because he soon began writing his own.' See *Sunday Press*, 23 July 1978. It is also possible that Stuart had some role in broadcasts to America: Horst J.P. Bergmeier and Rainer E. Lotz note that in a radio play called 'Lightning Action', about the 1940 German invasion of Norway, one of the speaking parts was played by 'Henry Stuart' – Henry being Francis Stuart's first name (Francis was a middle name). See Bergmeier and Lotz, *Hitler's Airwaves*, p. 49.

64. Eduard Hempel's dispatches on the case from Dublin to Berlin are recorded in *Documents on German Foreign Policy*, vol. IX.

The Görtz episode is revealing about Stuart's political stance and his importance within German efforts to collaborate with Irish republicans. Just as Stuart had been willing to carry a message from the IRA to the Abwehr, he was willing to volunteer his family home in Wicklow as a safe house for an Abwehr agent seeking to contact the IRA. It is thus not surprising that in August 1940 Stuart was approached by Kurt Haller, a liaison officer between the Foreign Ministry and the Abwehr, who asked him if he would be willing to sail with a German captain to Ireland on a craft that would pose as a Breton fishing vessel, in conjunction with the return to Ireland of IRA chief of staff Seán Russell and Frank Ryan aboard a U-boat.[65] Again, Stuart said yes; but this part of the mission was eventually called off.[66] Russell and Ryan did sail in the

65. Russell had travelled from America to Germany via Italy in May, and was an enthusiastic collaborator with the Nazis. Thanks to German intervention, Ryan had been allowed to 'escape' from a Francoist prison in Spain, where he had been fighting for the Republic, and was brought to Germany, where he lived an ambiguous existence, torn between irreconcilable political commitments and weakened by ill health, until his death in 1944.

66. The earliest surviving reference to the aborted fishing-boat scheme appears in Stuart's diary for 30 April 1942, where he noted that he had met the would-be captain for the mission at a party. (An account in the extract from Stuart's diaries published in the *Irish Times*, dated 'Early Summer, 1940', is one of the entries he later reconstructed from a non-extant diary.)

The scheme was also referred to by William Joseph Murphy, a Co. Armagh native who lived in Germany during the war and for a time did translation work for the Irland-Redaktion; he was arrested by Allied forces in Luxembourg in September 1944. In a statement made to MI5 in January and February 1945 in Brixton Prison, London (PRO, HO 45/25839), Murphy said that Stuart had described the scheme to him as follows: 'he and two other Irishmen named Shaun [*sic*] Russell and another whose name I cannot remember [*i.e.* Frank Ryan], had undertaken to run guns to Ireland. The other two were to go by submarine and make the arrangements for the reception of the cargo. These guns were for the I.R.A. as far as I understood. Upon the arrival of Russell and his colleague they were to advise him and he (Stuart) was to follow with the cargo.' As a result of Russell's death 'the scheme fell through'.

According to Murphy, Stuart in the summer of 1944 'suggested to me that perhaps [Murphy's Reichswehr contacts in] Bremen would take up the matter again in order to establish contact with the I.R.A., which Stuart said had been broken off since that time. He thought it would be a good idea if Bremen took us both to Ireland by submarine equipped with signalling apparatus.' In his diary for 30 June 1944, Stuart wrote: 'Murphy turned up yesterday – I was not so very surprised to see him – nothing, I think, would much surprise me these days – though I thought he was in Ireland. Made a suggestion to him which has a very

submarine, but Russell died en route, apparently of a perforated ulcer, and the mission was aborted; Ryan returned to Germany. Shortly after Ryan's return, he and Stuart visited a prisoner-of-war camp near Frankfurt to investigate the possibility of forming a pro-German 'Irish Guard' comprising Irishmen who had been fighting for the British. Nothing came of the scheme, which, according to Ryan's biographer, was conceived by Russell.[67]

Also in 1940, Stuart published two pieces on Irish nationalist heroes, Eamon de Valera and Roger Casement. Stuart's essay on de Valera for a book called *Irische Freiheitskämpfer* (Irish Freedom-Fighters) took broadly the same line as his 1935 essay on the same subject.[68] In *Der Fall Casement*, a short book translated into German and published in Hamburg, Stuart propounded the theory that Casement's 'black diaries' had been forged by the British. Its final paragraphs, translated into English, read as follows:

He often spoke of the future. Although he had suffered a failure – and how complete this failure must have looked to him at that moment – he knew nevertheless that the cause for which he died could never go down in the

---

slight chance of coming to something – it if is to, it will.' On 5 July, Stuart noted: 'No news from Murphy which probably means that our plan has not been accepted.' Murphy told MI5 that one of his Reichswehr contacts 'thought Stuart's proposition was nonsense'.

Murphy also stated that 'Stuart suggested that I should take up a job with the people with whom he was working, which turned out to be a secret radio station under the control of the German Foreign Office', and went into some detail about being trained as a news reader for the station. Murphy referred to the station as the 'Büro Concordia'; this was in fact an umbrella organization that operated several 'secret' radio stations purporting to be based in Britain and broadcasting 'black propaganda'. The claim that Stuart, who had by this time ceased broadcasting via the Irland-Redaktion, was involved in the secret stations is intriguing; in a letter to David O'Donoghue in 1992, Stuart firmly denied it. Bergmeier and Lotz mention in passing that Stuart 'occasionally contributed' to the 'New British Broadcasting Station', one of the Concordia stations, 'until about 1942'; in the context it appears they mean he was a speaker on the station. Unfortunately they do not give any further information on this, nor do they supply a source; see *Hitler's Airwaves*, p. 208. As for the 1944 affair, it is possible that Stuart misrepresented his relationship to the station to Murphy, or that Murphy misunderstood Stuart, or, indeed, that Murphy was correct. It is perhaps worth noting that on 3 May 1944, the Irish legation in Berlin reported to the Department of External Affairs in Dublin that Stuart 'does not at present propose to resume broadcasts but could not guarantee he might not do so at a later date' (NAI, DFA A72).

67. Sean Cronin, *Frank Ryan*, p. 196; see also Carter, *The Shamrock and the Swastika*, p. 124.
68. See Andreas Roth, *Mr Bewley in Berlin*, p. 63, for discussion of this piece.

end. His trust had already been largely justified. Ireland stands today on the verge of real freedom and unity; Casement's name is today immortal in the history of Ireland – raised high above the reach of the offensive slanders of English forgers. And the German victory on which he placed so much is, at the moment I am writing these words, almost complete.

Perhaps there will be a day, which lies not too far distant, when Irish and German soldiers will stand together before the unmarked grave in Pentonville Prison and honour the great patriot who did so much to advance friendship between the two peoples. And in that hour, hopefully, for what Roger Casement suffered, all will be richly repaid.[69]

According to Elborn, Stuart claimed that he 'never saw the finished book, and believes that this final paragraph was inserted either by the translator or the publisher, for he rather ingenuously declared later, that he did not consider what would happen if Germany won the war'.[70] It is not clear whether Elborn means 'disingenuously'; in any case, Stuart's claim that he, too, was the victim of a forgery is irrefutable in the absence of his original English manuscript. What is clear is that, whether or not Stuart wrote that final paragraph, it is in no way inconsistent with the positions implicit in his work for the Germans and the IRA at this time – or, indeed, with the rhetoric of the penultimate paragraph. The Germans believed they could use the IRA to get at the British, and the IRA believed the Germans could be of use in bringing about a united Ireland. There is nothing in Stuart's actions while in Germany, nor in his broadcasts, to indicate that he had a quarrel with the logic or morality of either view; and there is much to suggest that he agreed with both. If the Germans had won the war – and this looked entirely possible, even probable, in 1940 – an observance such as that conjured in the final paragraph of *Der Fall Casement* might very well have taken place, and Stuart could hardly have objected to it.

While the German Foreign Ministry and the Abwehr were collaborating, in however inept and desultory a fashion, with the

69. Stuart, *Der Fall Casement*, p. 110. I am grateful to Mark Hull for his translation.
70. Elborn, *Francis Stuart*, p. 137.

IRA, those responsible for the programming of the Irland-Redaktion recognized that the best Germany could hope for from the Irish state was a continuing policy of neutrality.[71] A neutral Éire could deny Britain the use of Irish ports; an Éire allied with Germany – never a real prospect, and almost inconceivable after the Battle of Britain – would have given Britain a pretext to occupy the twenty-six counties.[72] Support for Irish neutrality was the staple of the Irland-Redaktion following its expansion in August 1941 from two fifteen-minute broadcasts per week to nightly transmission.[73] Adolf Mahr, an archaeologist who was simultaneously director of the National Museum in Dublin and head of the Nazi *Auslandorganisation* there during the 1930s, worked in the Foreign Ministry in Berlin during the war; he put the matter very clearly in a lengthy 1941 report on the subject of broadcasts to Ireland, stating that Irish neutrality 'is of advantage to us'.[74] This view was adhered to in German wartime propaganda to Ireland, which took pains to praise Irish neutrality directly and reinforce it indirectly.

The first of Stuart's talks to be picked up by Irish and British monitors, and very possibly the first one he ever made to Ireland, was broadcast on St Patrick's Day 1942. The initial point he made in this talk, and one that he would return to frequently over the ensuing two years, was that he was 'not trying to make propaganda'. Whether this was aimed at his ordinary Irish auditors, at Irish officials who might take a dim view of an Irishman making

71. The Irland-Redaktion was a tiny branch of Germany's enormous radio propaganda apparatus, which was presided over by Joseph Goebbels as Reich Minister for Propaganda. Foreign broadcasting was under the dual control of the propaganda and foreign ministries. The latter seems to have had the upper hand with regard to the Irland-Redaktion; Hans Hartmann, head of the Irland-Redaktion from the end of 1941 until 1945, was appointed by Adolf Mahr of the Foreign Ministry. For a study of the Irland-Redaktion, see David O'Donoghue, *Hitler's Irish Voices*; for a study of German radio propaganda more generally, see Horst J.P. Bergmeier and Rainer E. Lotz, *Hitler's Airwaves*.

72. On the politics of Irish neutrality, see Robert Fisk, *In Time of War*; J.P. Duggan, *Neutral Ireland and the Third Reich*; J.J. Lee, *Ireland 1912–1985*; and Eunan O'Halpin, *Defending Ireland*.

73. O'Donoghue, *Hitler's Irish Voices*, p. 59.

74. A full translation of Mahr's memo is provided in ibid., pp. 186–93.

propaganda for the Germans, or at his own soul, is not clear; perhaps he had all three in mind. For Stuart in these broadcasts, 'propaganda' is a wholly pejorative term, and it is a term he connects exclusively with the Allies: he positions himself as an antidote to 'English', 'Anglo-Saxon', 'Anglo-American' propaganda. He could not, of course, have used the German airwaves to denounce, or even to cast doubt upon, German propaganda, and here is the rub. Stuart vigorously supported Irish neutrality, but this was not a 'neutral' position, nor, coming from the airwaves of the Third Reich, could it have been. If Stuart had wanted to urge the Irish state to ally itself to Germany – and in March 1942 nobody outside the ranks of the IRA seriously supported this – he would not have been allowed by his employers, who wanted Éire to remain neutral and knew that a call for Ireland to join Germany would only annoy de Valera's government. Éire's continuing neutrality was the *raison d'être* of the Irland-Redaktion; in this context, for Stuart to call himself 'a neutral', as he did on 5 April 1942, was a largely meaningless formulation. Similarly, while Stuart's denial of propagandistic intent seems to have been heartfelt in some confused way, it only muddies the water. What Stuart was making, in these broadcasts, was propaganda, and while the significance of the broadcasts is not limited to their status as such, we cannot begin to understand them unless we recognize that this is what they were.

Stuart's early talks echo one of the central themes of his 1924 *Lecture on Nationality and Culture*: the need for Ireland to engage culturally with continental Europe, rather than with Britain. This theme became less pronounced in later broadcasts, and in light of this it is relevant to observe that some of Stuart's early ventilations of it allude obliquely but unmistakably to a German victory. Such a victory still seemed a possibility, if not a probability, in 1942, and Stuart's tone was sanguine rather than resigned. On 29 March he spoke of witnessing 'something in the nature of a world revolution' and declared:

[…] once we take our place within the European system that is coming, we shall be ready to do all that is within our power towards the common good as we did long ago in the past. Do not ask what has all this to do with us – that, for all I know, may still be the attitude of a few of you. It is the attitude of fools. It is everything to do with us. Mark my words well: if some of the peoples in those European countries that had got what they wanted after the last war had not looked around […] and exclaimed, What has it to do with us?, they would not see their homes destroyed today.

The shift in register is striking: from a benign invocation of 'the common good' to a denunciation of 'fools' who fail to see the broader implications of the war and a harsh conclusion that countries like Poland and Czechoslovakia had got their due reward for choosing the wrong friends. Rather staggeringly, Stuart followed this observation with the following:

I do not know the various political currents, intrigues and secret alliances that went on between the last war and this. I am no politician and all that is quite beyond me. I'm interested in people, in individuals and their lives.

The naked conflict here between two impulses – a cultural and political view that Ireland had better distance itself from Britain and embrace 'the European system that is coming' rather than become another Poland, on the one hand, and an apparently genuine belief that all that mattered were 'individuals and their lives', on the other – was more marked in the earlier talks, when Stuart could plausibly allude to the coming of a new order in which Ireland's place in the world would change utterly. As the prospect of such a change ebbed, he placed less emphasis on European politics and more on Ireland's local political difficulties.

The necessity of a united Ireland was Stuart's dominant theme. Sometimes he placed Irish irredentism in a European context – comparing the Irish claim on Northern Ireland to the German claim on Danzig, for example – but more often he stressed the perfidy and decadence of Britain. The latter emphasis, of course, had clear implications for Irish attitudes towards the war: true Irish patriots could not contemplate supporting an empire that was occupying six counties of Ireland. Stuart was keen that Irish friendship with and respect for Germany not be confused with slavish submission to the German system. On 23 September 1942 he noted that some of his friends in Ireland,

Peadar O'Donnell for instance, are afraid that Irish friendship with Germany would mean accepting and copying German social and economic ideology. This is certainly not so. While I believe that we have much to learn from Germany and that our ties with the European continent must be made much closer, I am neither such a fool nor such a bad nationalist as to imagine that a foreign form of government can ever be imposed on us from without. What kind of state we build up on the whole of our island is a matter for ourselves to work out once we've got the whole of our island in our own possession.

This assumes that a united Ireland would be brought about through Irish efforts alone, or that, if it came about due to German assistance, the Germans would happily leave the Irish to sort out their own affairs. Stuart here was up against the problem always faced by collaborators from small nations, who may find themselves forced to imagine an implausible degree of munificence on the part of their putative sponsors – or else to be 'bad nationalists'. Even so, it is clear from these talks that Stuart certainly wasn't such a bad Irish nationalist or such an ardent Nazi sympathizer as to fail to realize that National Socialism was culturally and politically rooted in Germany; he may have hoped for a Nazi victory, but there is no sign that he ever hoped for a Nazi Ireland.

The talks are also preoccupied with what Stuart calls 'the great world financial system' – from which, he asserted improbably on 6 January 1943, 'Germany and Italy had broken away'. For Stuart, the enemy was the 'modern money states' (22 May 1943), primarily Britain and the United States. In his broadcast of 16 December 1942, he told his listeners that his admiration for Hitler sprang from the Führer's opposition to the prevailing system of international finance:

I began to find out something about Hitler and the new Germany and then of course I was completely fired by enthusiasm, for here was someone who

was freeing life from the money standards that dominated it almost everywhere that I had ever been, not excluding my own country; here was someone who had the vision and courage to deny financiers, politicians and
bankers the right to rule. Nor did the word dictator frighten me – I saw that
as it was. Our lives were dominated by a group of financial dictators and it
seemed to me at least preferable to be ruled by one man whose sincerity for
the welfare of his people could not be doubted than by a gang whose only
concern was the market price of various commodities in the world markets.

Fintan O'Toole, a sympathetic reader of Stuart's fiction, has
argued that Stuart in such utterances was employing 'the central
underlying notion' behind the forged *Protocols of the Elders of Zion*:

While not explicitly anti-Semitic, this talk of a gang of financiers ruling the
world is entirely in line with the *Protocols*. In a culture saturated by the *Protocols* and their offshoots, talk of 'a system whereby international financiers
hold sway' was in an easily broken code.[75]

O'Toole is correct to note this parallel and to point to its implications; but it is also worth examining the implications of the fact that
these references were, as he says, 'not explicitly anti-Semitic'.[76] The
Nazis rarely failed to connect their attack on what Stuart calls the
'financial dictators' with their stated belief, almost axiomatic in
National Socialist propaganda, that those dictators were Jews; and
even over the relatively tranquil airwaves of the Irland-Redaktion,
uncoded anti-Semitism was an occasional if by no means central
element of the programming. Stuart's avoidance of explicit anti-
Semitism is thus notable. Even so, it is difficult to escape the conclusion that Stuart allowed a principled disdain for materialism to
be infected by a conspiracy theory for which he could have had no

75. Fintan O'Toole, 'The Survivor', *Writing Ulster* no. 4 (1996), p. 80. The phrase 'a system whereby international financiers hold sway' comes from the edited transcript of Stuart's talk of 29 March 1942 prepared by the BBC, in which Stuart's words are sometimes
changed for the sake of brevity; in the parallel and verbatim transcript prepared by G2, Stuart speaks of 'a state of affairs in which international financiers wield political power over
the destinies of countries'. This is perhaps a slightly milder formulation, but O'Toole's argument is not affected: there are numerous passages in the transcripts that employ this 'code'.
76. The exception is the German transcript dated 9 February 1942, unknown to
O'Toole, which contains a derogatory reference to 'London Jews': see the Appendix.

evidence, and that the anti-Semitism that was intrinsic to this conspiracy theory did not disqualify it in his eyes. As for his listeners, it is reasonable to assume that many of them would have taken Stuart's references to the evils of the global financial system as coded anti-Semitism, if only because this accorded with their own prejudices. Any argument that Stuart's intent was not anti-Semitic must reckon with the likelihood that his remarks would have reinforced or flattered a strain of anti-Semitism among his listeners.

The impossibility of 'neutrality' for a broadcaster in Stuart's position is perhaps demonstrated most clearly in his treatment of the German defeat at Stalingrad. After the war, Stuart often said that early in his German sojourn he seriously considered moving to Russia; this has been taken as evidence that he was disillusioned with the Nazis, or that he was a sort of equal-opportunity adventurer, or that his politics were essentially left-wing. We can never know whether Stuart seriously entertained the possibility of such an improbable move, but we know from his writings that he had a genuine, if essentially literary, affection for Russia and that he admired the USSR's Georgian leader. His broadcasts contain not a hint of anti-Soviet rhetoric; he conserved all his bile for Britain and America. There is not a single reference in the surviving transcripts to communism, socialism or Stalin, and after the war Stuart claimed that he stopped giving talks because he was coming under pressure to include anti-Soviet material.[77] In light of all this,

---

77. It is worth noting that when publishing extracts from his diaries Stuart rewrote the passages dealing with this subject, and also invented two wholly new sentences for the entry of 2 May 1944: 'They won't arrest me as long as they think there is some chance of my resuming the broadcasts to Ireland, perhaps even agreeing to denounce the "Asian hordes". Luckily, I have some fairly well-placed protectors.' See *States of Mind*, p. 41. The original diary contains no reference to disagreement over Stuart's attitude to Russia being the cause of his giving up broadcasting, no reference to the possibility of arrest, no reference to threats. It is conceivable that Stuart was being careful lest the diary be seized, but this seems unlikely as the diary does refer to 'coercion from the Rundfunk [Broadcasting]', to which he referred scornfully as 'damned weakness' and 'dirty tricks'. The impression given by the original diary (which is held with Stuart's papers at Coleraine) is that the 'coercion' was mild and that Stuart was not particularly worried; the published version gives a rather different impression.

Stuart's comments on the battle of Stalingrad make for fascinating reading. On 6 February 1943, Stuart began his broadcast as follows:

On Wednesday morning the German people heard the last news from the small base of the Sixth Army still holding out at Stalingrad. The end was already very near, ammunition was almost all gone, most of those who still survived were wounded [... T]he fight in Stalingrad was over. If I was a German I should be filled with the deepest pride; as it is, I am glad to be living among such people – glad to be here in a country that can produce such men, men who still can overcome all human limitations and not one or two such only, but a whole army.

At this point, saying 'mere words are useless', Stuart turned to another subject; but he returned to Stalingrad at the end of the talk:

I know that you at home will have no difficulty in understanding what the German people have been feeling during these days of mourning; at certain moments in our history the whole of Ireland too has been stirred by a wave of sorrow and pride. [... N]ot even great victories like the taking of Paris [have moved Germans so much], for those might have been accounted for by the superiority of the German war machine. This is an affair of human beings, a triumph of flesh and blood.

Stuart's evocation of the 'triumph' of the vanquished German army arose out of a genuine belief in the value and nobility of suffering and defeat – a belief that he rather implausibly attributed to the German people as well. The 'blood sacrifice' school of Irish nationalism, of which Stuart in these talks and elsewhere showed himself to be a member, had similar beliefs. Nowhere, then, are the necessary evasions of propaganda more clearly on display than in Stuart's hymn to the German dead at Stalingrad; for as he and every moderately intelligent person in Germany knew, the greatest blood sacrifice was the USSR's: German news reports gleefully tallied the millions upon millions of Soviet dead on the eastern front.[78] Stuart may have felt emotional sympathy for the Soviet

78. For a first-hand account of the German reporting of the Wehrmacht's early victories in Operation Barbarossa, and an extraordinary account of life for a Jew in Nazi Germany generally, see Victor Klemperer, *I Will Bear Witness: A Diary of the Nazi Years, 1933–1941* (published in the UK by Weidenfeld & Nicolson as *I Shall Bear Witness*).

casualties, but he could not, of course, speak of them. He repeatedly told his listeners that he was speaking his conscience, that he was not the mouthpiece of any government; and insofar as the words he spoke were his own, this appears to be the case.[79] But the necessary silences of propaganda are an enormous obstacle to truth-telling, and it is thus impossible to read Stuart's remarks on Stalingrad as anything but a lie: a lie in which the German dead are heroic, the Soviet dead are unmentionable. This is the essential lie of wartime, and everyone who takes sides in war connives in it to some degree: our dead are always worth more than their dead. The privilege, and the responsibility, of the neutral is freedom from this lie. When Stuart sat at the microphone of the Irland-Redaktion, he was not neutral, and he was not free.

The second of Stuart's two years as a broadcaster unfolded against a backdrop of Allied victories on every front. He did not abandon the idea that a German victory might bring about a united Ireland, but he recognized that the prospect was fading:

> The fact that we are neutral cannot be taken as meaning that whichever end this war has is a matter of indifference to us. [...] A decisive victory for England and America would, I believe, mean [that] the last chance of winning the lost province in the North would greatly recede. (21 August 1943)

An increasing theme was that of Ireland's own virtues – virtues that would be all the more necessary if the war did not bring about a change in her constitutional status. It would appear that the years away from home had caused Stuart to imagine an Ireland that his own listeners might have had a hard time recognizing:

79. David O'Donoghue has argued in a newspaper article that the Stalingrad material was the result of a directive from Goebbels; Stuart, he writes, 'had little choice but to toe the line'. However, as O'Donoghue notes in his book *Hitler's Irish Voices*, Goebbels issued his directive on 3 February; Stuart's first eulogy of the Sixth Army was broadcast on 30 January. In light of this, the claim that Stuart was toeing Goebbels' line in the Stalingrad talks should probably give way to O'Donoghue's observation in *Hitler's Irish Voices* that Stuart 'broadly followed Goebbels' directive to describe the defeat at Stalingrad in terms of German bravery and triumph', which recognizes correlation but not necessarily causation. It seems probable that this was a theme to which Stuart gravitated of his own accord. See O'Donoghue, 'Francis Stuart – The Truth', *Sunday Independent*, 14 December 1997; and *Hitler's Irish Voices*, p. 107.

Our whole life outlook is quite different to the Anglo-Saxon one. We have never been poisoned by commercialism and no Irishman in his heart of hearts has anything but a slight contempt for money. Nor are we a people easily moved by popular catch-cries and publicised sentiment. We read the leading articles in even our own leading newspapers with as much scepticism as belief. Our opinions and our outlooks are formed neither by material ambitions nor by newspapers but in a quite different way, sometimes even in quite hidden ways which [are] hard to describe. I know that I myself as a boy was deeply affected by something in the Antrim landscape where I lived and I know that for many of you it has been the same. The fields, woods and villages where you grew up were the first and perhaps the strongest causes of your nationalism. This is the nationalism which is hard to undermine or pervert. It will withstand any amount of propaganda or financial pressure for it springs from the soil and it will remain as long as the soil remains and will see empires rise and fall. (28 August 1943)

Stuart seems to have reconsidered this flattery of the Irish nationalist spirit; in his broadcast of 8 January 1944 (of which the BBC transcript quoted below is clearly an edited version) he questioned the basis of the claim on Northern Ireland:

After the last war a group of comparatively small nations was created by the politicians and financiers of England and France. Poland, Czechoslovakia and Yugoslavia had governments based on the old capitalist system. The creation of these countries was hailed with a lot of shouting about freedom and nationalism. Yet their freedom was purely one of prestige and brought no blessing to the lives of their peoples. We in Ireland must never make that mistake.

Irish nationalists must see that Ireland does not become another of these little republics in which the old order reproduces itself. It is of no importance at all that the Tricolour should fly from the City Hall in Belfast instead of the Union Jack if Belfast workers are to find it as hard to live and support their families as before. Such freedom is merely illusion and such nationalism a farce and a danger. English politicians will be ready enough to let us have back the Six Counties if they are sure that the whole of Ireland will remain closely tied up to the old system.

We Irish have still very much to do to bring our social life on to a level with our national life. The first thing to do is to face the truth. Until Dublin becomes a much better place for the average working family to live in than Belfast, we lose more than half the force of our claim to Belfast.

This is the strongest expression of such heresy in Stuart's surviving talks. It is not, however, divorced from the broader view of the war that informs the broadcasts: Stuart's argument depends on a claim that the Irish state has not made and must not make the 'mistake' of accepting independence without creating social and economic justice, as the new states in central Europe had done. Yet it also recognizes that this is precisely what the Irish state had *already* done. This is not just a sloppily presented argument: it is a reflection of Stuart's unwillingness – and, indeed, inability, given that he was speaking under the auspices of the short-lived Nazi empire – to apply uniform standards to the various weaker nations of Europe. In a broadcast of 14 September 1943 he attacked those national movements that were dependent on the Allies rather than the Axis:

For the last four years they [British and American politicians] have received all their information from exiled politicians still waiting to play the old game of financial intrigue. I will only take one instance. There is Mr Benes, the leader of the Czech people. Incidentally, they include, in what they call the Czechs, people who are no more Czechs than I am. That is not the point. I had the opportunity of talking very frankly to several Czechs in the past few years, and whatever views they may have had on their own future, not one of them had the slightest belief in Mr Benes or desire to have him as their spokesman or leader. For them Benes belonged to a regime that was dead and could never, under any circumstances, be re-established; but the English and American politicians have not the slightest real interest in the Czechs, or in any other of the peoples of Europe. They simply wish to get those governments into power who will co-operate with them in their political and financial intrigues. [...]

I, as an Irishman, have had opportunities to get to know something about the different peoples of Europe during this war such as very few other private individuals can have had. As an Irishman I have always been met with friendliness and frankness, whether it was in the former Poland, the former Czechoslovakia or other countries now under German administration. I naturally cannot in a broadcast repeat many of the things that were said to me confidentially, but this much I can say: in some of those places where one might have expected to find a good deal of turning towards England and America, there was a very sceptical attitude towards the great financial powers [...]

One can only wonder whether Stuart expected his listeners to believe his claim to be a well-informed and fair-minded reporter on national sentiment in what he calmly calls 'the former Poland,

the former Czechoslovakia [and] other countries now under German administration'. This broadcast may be an example of what
has often been seen as Stuart's political naïveté, but if so then it is
naïveté with a hard edge. Stuart's willingness to see the national
aspirations of the Czechs in 1943 as a matter of 'political and financial intrigues' may simply reflect the fact that nationalism is not a
universalist ideology, but it is also indicative of the cognitive perils
of collaboration: while Stuart could see that 'the English and
American politicians have not the slightest real interest in the
Czechs', he still voiced a belief that the Germans had some such
interest in the Irish – and in the peoples they had conquered. Stuart's own professed interest in the fates of small nations other than
Ireland could not transcend his pro-Axis partisanship.[80]

Stuart never abandoned this partisanship, but in the later
broadcasts there existed alongside the hard sentiments an enduring belief that the war would somehow bring about a fundamental, and salutary, transformation of human consciousness. There is
a degree of pathos in this, because by this stage of the war it can
only have been a sort of religious expectation, unconnected to
real-life politics and events on the battlefields:

80. It should be noted that such views required neither naïveté nor collaboration: at the
height of the German military ascendancy in June 1940, Joseph Walshe, the Secretary of
the Irish Department of External Affairs, took a similarly cold-blooded view of Germany's
victims and a similarly unrealistic view of Germany's willingness to help Ireland, as J.J. Lee
has shown: 'Walshe would have liked to use the German victories in 1940 to have Hitler
deliver the North to Dublin. Purporting to be more afraid of Britain than of Germany, he
chose to see Nazi victories partly from the "England's danger is Ireland's opportunity" per-
spective, hoping that Hitler's declaration that he had no intention of destroying the British
Empire "did not mean the abandonment of Ireland". The problem was that if the Germans
ever came to be in a position to destroy the empire, or to deliver the North, they would by
definition be in a position to deal as they wished with Dublin. It took no great imagination to deduce who would use whom. But Walshe seemed curiously oblivious to the fate
of small and neutral continental countries.' It should be borne in mind that the remarks on
which this passage was based were made to the German minister, Eduard Hempel, and may
have arisen in part, as Lee notes, from what Hempel identified as an Irish tendency 'to say
agreeable things without meaning everything that is said'. Even so, Lee is right to note the
incongruousness of a Irish public servant failing 'to take cognisance of the fate of other
small neutral states before concluding that one of the weakest of all could bend Berlin to
its will'. See Lee, *Ireland*, pp. 247–8.

[…] there is a new stage coming, a new outlook after four years of war which has no use for empty phrases or sentiment, false righteousness and all the other stock-in-trade of the old-time politicians. On a long train journey at night a short time ago I had for a companion a young German soldier who spoke of his experiences at the front, not of the events which he had gone through, but of what he himself had felt, of the faith that had sustained him through all the worst dangers and hardships. […] As we travelled through the night, which incidentally was once lit up by shells from the anti-aircraft guns as we passed through an air-raid, I knew which of them I put my trust in, this young German soldier or Mr Roosevelt. I knew which of them was thinking of real and vital things and which of them was going on uttering the same old stale nonsense, and I believe you at home know the difference too and that when you discuss the war and the future of the world your ideas are much more like my companion's than like Mr Churchill or Mr Roosevelt, and it is these ideals of ours, this new outlook, that has got to have a chance, and it will have a chance. It is not only in Germany that the people have seen through the kind of world that Roosevelt and Churchill stand for. All over Europe the people are turning away from the old shams and looking for something simpler and truer. (2 October 1943)

This was not a coded evocation of the Nazi New Order, in whose victory Stuart can have had little faith by this stage. The transformation described here is, of course, couched in partisan terms – the new consciousness is that of the German soldier as against that of FDR – but it does not depend on a German victory. It is of a piece with the psychic journeys described in pre-war novels such as *Glory*, and it is a direct anticipation of the preoccupations of Stuart's post-war trilogy – *The Pillar of Cloud*, *Redemption*, and *The Flowering Cross*. What rings most false in it – the fantastic assertion that this transformation will be general, at least in Europe – is largely jettisoned in the novels, where Stuart hymns the flowering of new forms of consciousness and fellowship among small, isolated groups of people.

Those novels were born of Stuart's experiences in the years after he ceased broadcasting, when he and his companion Gertrud (Madeleine) Meissner became refugees from Allied bombardment of Berlin; then entered a post-war stateless limbo near the Austrian border with Switzerland; then became (apparently uncharged) prisoners of the occupying French, who eventually released them into a further limbo in Freiburg, Germany, that lasted until 1948. After a lean decade in Paris and London, during which Iseult died and Stuart married Madeleine, the couple moved to County Meath in 1958, and Stuart lived in Ireland for the rest of his life.

In the two autobiographical novels in which Stuart re-imagined his time in Berlin, *Victors and Vanquished* and *Black List, Section H*, the years of collaboration are transformed. Luke Cassidy, the central character of *Victors and Vanquished*, is an exact replica of Stuart in almost every respect, except that he refuses to carry the IRA message to Germany, refuses to get involved in collaborationist schemes while in Germany, and refuses to make propaganda broadcasts; he spends most of his energy looking after a Jewish family, a wholly imagined (and deeply unconvincing) plotline. The novel is a fantasy of the war Stuart perhaps wished he had had.

In *Black List*, the facts of H's life are far closer to those of Stuart's, but, as we have seen, Stuart depicts the consciousness and attitudes of H in ways that are almost impossible to square with Stuart's own contemporaneous writings and actions. H does not collaborate with the IRA or the Abwehr – the IRA message, the Görtz episode, the mooted sea-mission to Ireland and the idea of setting up an Irish Guard do not figure – but he does write talks for William Joyce, translate news into English for the radio, and write his own broadcasts:

What was he to say in these talks? [...] He could condemn such Allied atrocities as he'd heard of—the indiscriminate bombing was only just beginning—but that would involve him in the same deception as the propagandists who presented the war as a moral conflict. [...]

Could he express his belief that the only possible good that could now arise out of [the war] was if it ended by bringing the whole structure, ideological, cultural, moral, crashing down about the heads of whoever was left with whole ones? Hardly.

[...] He could try to stress the other reasons, besides material advantage, for Irish neutrality. One of these was that those who thought for themselves were free to come to certain conclusions about the war without feeling they were letting down their fellow countrymen who were taking the risks and doing the fighting.

They could question the Allied posture of moral grandeur, and in particular Churchill's, without giving comfort to the enemy. And they'd be able to dissociate themselves, in spirit, at least, from whoever proved the victors, and to forego participation in the celebrations ushering a peace that, not being the chastened kind born out of near-despair, would soon turn brash and complacent.

Dr Zimmerman asked H to come and see him and suggested he might not be laying enough stress on Hitler's war against communism—H had purposely never mentioned it—which, he said, must have much Irish support.

'Not from the sort of people I'm talking to,' H told him, 'some of them may be anti-British but none are anti-Russian.'[81]

There is a recognizable link between what Stuart tells us of the content of H's broadcasts and what he said in his own broadcasts – Stuart didn't attack communism, he did attack 'the Allied posture of moral grandeur', and he did lay much stress on the importance of Irish neutrality – but there is also much in Stuart's broadcasts that deviates from H's vision quite fundamentally. It is impossible to imagine H making comments of the sort that Stuart made in nearly every one of his talks, whether praising Hitler (H had stopped admiring Hitler during his first visit to Nazi Germany in 1939); railing against the global financial system (of which H takes no notice); condemning the Allied bombing that H says he wouldn't condemn; or attacking conquered nations such as Czechoslovakia for having chosen ideologically unsound allies. The point, once again, is not that there is anything intrinsically remarkable about deviations between an autobiographical novel and the life on which it is based, but simply that we cannot and should not look to Stuart's fiction to supply a reliable account of his life.

In an interview published in 1976, Stuart described the content of his broadcasts as follows:

81. *Black List, Section H*, pp. 354–6.

These broadcasts didn't usually deal with politics; they dealt very often with literature, both English and Irish, and even with other literature. When they were political, they concentrated on the internal situation in Ireland. Several of the talks, for instance, criticized the then government of de Valera for executing several Republican prisoners and allowing one or two others to die on hunger strike. This I was very much against and said so. There were also two or three prisoners in Ulster who had been condemned to death, and I mentioned them, though I'm not sure now whether they were actually executed. Then there was an Irish election, a general election, and I advised not to vote for de Valera.[82]

This account is wildly inaccurate. The broadcasts *did* usually deal with politics; they hardly ever made reference to literature; their political content was not restricted to 'the internal situation in Ireland'. Stuart might conceivably have criticized de Valera for executions, but he did not do so in the surviving transcripts and such comments would have been contrary to German propaganda policy. The reference to the 'two or three prisoners in Ulster' is probably a garbled allusion to the events culminating in the execution of Thomas Williams, to which he did refer repeatedly. In the broadcasts that deal with the Irish general election of June 1943, Stuart advised his listeners not to vote for *Fine Gael*, while his comments on the election could perhaps be read as tacitly supporting minor parties more uncompromisingly irredentist than Fianna Fáil, he never said a word against de Valera (whom he wished 'further success in his great task' on 14 October 1942). The unmistakable message of his pre-election comments was that Fine Gael was too soft on the national question: 'The overwhelming majority of you are at one in your wish for a free and united country and as far as I know there isn't one who'd ever threaten this except a handful of so-called Irishmen either belonging to or in touch with the Fine Gael party.' (These talks gave rise to a diplomatic complaint by Éire to Germany.)

It is not remarkable that a man in his mid-seventies would have inaccurate memories of things he had said more than three

---

82. J.H. Natterstad, 'An Interview [with Francis Stuart]', p. 27.

decades earlier; what is a little bit odd, though, is the level of detail in these inaccurate recollections. Stuart had obviously given some thought to the broadcasts in the intervening years – certainly in the early 1960s when he was writing *Black List*. In 1978 he noted that 'only very lately I was shown some transcripts of those broadcasts'; this was presumably not before the 1976 comments quoted above.[83] It would appear that Stuart had not forgotten the broadcasts, but had re-imagined them. What is unfortunate – although not surprising, in light of the enormous personal affection that the elderly Stuart inspired – is that so many writers and scholars have been enthusiastic participants in this re-imagining, creating a myth of Stuart that is far more palatable to contemporary sensibilities than the literary and political persona of the man who wrote and delivered the talks printed herein.

III

Of the five post-war novels that arise directly from Stuart's experiences on the Continent during the 1940s, three – *The Pillar of Cloud, Redemption* and *Black List, Section H* – are in print and effectively constitute the Stuart canon.[84] The other two are rarely mentioned, *Victors and Vanquished* having been forgotten presumably because it is so embarrassingly inferior to *Black List*, *The Flowering Cross* perhaps because it is a quieter, less arresting treatment of themes and scenarios explored in *The Pillar of Cloud* and *Redemption*. The three canonical novels are praised for their literary merits, but they are also widely viewed as constituting some sort of personal and artistic redemption. Fintan O'Toole, who has

83. See Emmanuel Kehoe, 'The Life and Times of Francis Stuart', *Sunday Press*, 23 July 1978.
84. Some of Stuart's later novels – *Memorial, A Hole in the Head, The High Consistory* – are among his most accomplished works, but they are out of print and have only a peripheral place in the Stuart mythology.

written eloquently on this theme, has been perhaps the only Stuart commentator to recognize that a redemption story has force only if we face the full truth of what, precisely, requires redeeming. Pursuing this truth is not an exercise in delivering a moral or political judgment, in the manner of a war-crimes tribunal; but it is, given the content of Stuart's pre-war and post-war fiction, necessary for a full understanding of his art, and of his singularly strange position in twentieth-century Irish history and culture.

Francis Stuart had been all but forgotten as a writer when in 1971 the Southern Illinois University Press published *Black List, Section H*. Over a decade had passed since Stuart's previous novel, and as he was almost seventy years old this new book from an American university press might have seemed a dying gasp. In fact, it was the beginning of a new phase of productivity, and of recognition that would last until Stuart's death nearly three decades later. *Black List* was well reviewed in America and Britain, and it inspired many younger Irish writers.

Almost everything that has been written about Stuart in the past thirty years has been admiring, and much of it has been produced by some of Ireland's most distinguished writers and critics. Yet even before the controversy of 1996–7, sympathetic readers tended to portray Stuart as a demonized figure – which, undoubtedly, in certain pubs and over certain dinner tables, he has been. A mythology of Stuart as ostracized because of his German sojourn ignores the fact that his immediate post-war novels were published by Victor Gollancz in London and by leading houses, including Gallimard, in Paris: if there was any blacklist, as has been claimed, it wasn't terribly effective. In the post-war years Stuart struggled with low sales and, in Ireland, with censorship – just as he had before the war, and just as almost every serious Irish writer of the era did. Gollancz continued to publish Stuart through the fifties, despite the low sales, finally rejecting a novel called 'A Trip down the River', which has never been published.[85] Overall, despite the difficulty Stuart had publishing *Black List*, it would be closer to the truth to say that he lived a charmed literary existence after the war than to call him an 'outcast', as many have done.

Towards the end of his life, Stuart was the subject of two separate, but essentially linked, controversies, the first surrounding his election to the honorific position of Saoi by the Irish arts academy Aosdána, in 1996, the second a year later arising from comments he made on a television documentary. The debate that spanned these two linked controversies was coherent insofar as it involved expressions of conflicting values: Stuart's admirers and critics wrote from fundamentally different assumptions about art, soci-

85. One of the persistent oddities of Stuart commentary has been the suggestion that Stuart couldn't have been a Nazi sympathizer or an anti-Semite because many of his books – his first five novels in the 1930s and his first eight post-war novels – were published by Victor Gollancz, a man of the Left and a Jew. Such a suggestion betrays a misunderstanding of the nature of publishing, particularly fiction publishing; and it also ignores Gollancz's well documented independence of mind, not to say eccentricity of judgement, and his ambivalence on the question of literary anti-Semitism. Gollancz did not publish *Things to Live For*, nor any of the three pre-war novels, discussed above, that contain problematic portrayals of major Jewish characters; the two books of Stuart's that he published that might be most troubling to a man of left-wing beliefs, *Try the Sky* and *Glory*, both came out in 1933, and were, coincidentally or not, the last books of Stuart's that Gollancz brought out until after the war. Interestingly, another book Gollancz published in 1933 was George Orwell's *Down and Out in Paris and London*, which is infused with a casual anti-Semitism. In her official biography of Gollancz, Ruth Dudley Edwards notes that Orwell's book gave rise to a heated correspondence between the publisher and one S.M. Lipsey, who was appalled that 'a book, containing insulting and odious remarks about Jews, should be published by a firm bearing the name "Gollancz"'. Gollancz did not defend Lipsey for his 'Jewish patriotism'. Edwards also writes that Gollancz was 'untroubled by the embarrassing anti-Semitism of Dorothy Sayers'.

It should also be noted that Gollancz made himself into a pariah among large elements of English public opinion after the war by his sympathy for Germany, and his insistence, against the general cry, that not all Germans were guilty. Edwards writes: 'Victor's work for defeated Germany was rooted in his particular passion for the moral underdog, not forgetting his sheer enjoyment of the drama and excitement of being seen to take up an unpopular cause. ... Later, he was to champion murderers against society's condemnation. Now the Germans were at the mercy of a world long trained to hate and despise them, it was quite consistent that he should move in their defence.' It is against the backdrop of his brave campaign on behalf of defeated Germany, which made him a national figure of love and hate in Britain, and which, incidentally, was characterized by a rather strident articulation of Christian ethics, that Gollancz's publication of Stuart's post-war novels must be understood. See Edwards, *Victor Gollancz: A Biography*, pp. 215–17, 401.

[55]

ety, and the theory and practice of redemption, and it was easy enough for readers to identify this basic split. But the debate was incoherent on the level of fact: accurate information about Stuart's collaboration with the Nazis, the ostensible subject of the debate, was scarce, and a number of old myths and red herrings resurfaced.

The second round of the controversy was sparked by a comment made by Stuart on a television documentary on anti-Semitism in Ireland.[86] On 22 October 1997 Kevin Myers in the *Irish Times* rendered the offending statement as 'The Jew is like the worm in the rose.' On 15 December, in a letter to the *Irish Times*, Ronit and Louis Lentin gave Stuart's remark as 'The Jew is the worm that got into the rose and sickened it.' Kevin Myers had another try on 17 December: 'The Jew was always the worm that got into the rose and sickened it. Yes, but of course I take that as praise. I mean all those so-called healthy roses, they need exposing – many of them are sick.' Paul Durcan, for the defence, claimed in a letter to the *Irish Times* on 31 October that Stuart had been 'quoting from himself', specifically from a passage in *Black List* in which he describes the 'Jewish idea' as 'a worm that could get into a lot of fine-looking fruit' – fine-looking fruit being the enemy. If Stuart was quoting the novel he was doing so rather liberally, no matter which version of what he said on the documentary we prefer; but Durcan's essential point was that the 'worm' metaphor was not meant to be hateful. The additional lines quoted by Myers ('I take that as praise') would appear to confirm this: what might for a standard nonagenarian anti-Semite have been a clumsy retreat seems, in the strange world of Francis Stuart, to have been a straightforward explanation of his dubious metaphor.[87]

86. The documentary, entitled 'A Great Hatred', was shown on Channel 4 on 15 October 1997. It was not seen by this writer.

87. The relevant passage from *Black List* concerns Mr Isaacs and reads as follows: 'When he told Iseult about his new [Jewish] friend she was indignant. Like her mother, who, through Iseult's father, had belonged to the anti-Dreyfus, Boulangist faction in France, she disliked the Jews. H sensed that this hostility was more than just political, especially with

Meanwhile, Máire Mhac an tSaoi brought a motion at a meeting of Aosdána on 26 November whereby the organization would
'reprobate' the sentiments expressed by Stuart in the documentary
and Stuart would resign from the body. Amidst what journalists
and Aosdána members described as procedural chaos, the motion
was overwhelmingly defeated.[88]
Some of those who wrote in defence of Stuart based their arguments on dubious claims about the nature of art and the artist.
Hugo Hamilton wrote: 'Stuart is no racist. He is not hiding anything, because writing novels and poetry is not the place to hide
anything.'[89] Such empty formulations only give credence to the
claim, made by Declan Kiberd and others, that Stuart's admirers
have relied on a romantic and essentially trivialized idea of the
moral status of art.[90] Hamilton went on to write, quoting Samuel

Iseult. She lived too much in the mind, by moral or spiritual judgments, not to distrust
what he was beginning to see was the Jewish character: humble where she was proud, real-
ist where she relied on abstract principles, revelling in the senses which to her were tire-
some. If there were a Jewish idea, which was surely a contradiction, it was a hidden,
unheroic, and critical one, a worm that could get into a lot of fine-looking fruit.' It is difficult to know where to begin in interpreting this passage; here it will suffice to say that H's
conception of the 'Jewish character' is transparently a product of Stuart's imagination, and
perhaps of a certain enduring hostility to Iseult, rather than of any particular attempt to
understand Jews. It is also an application to H, in 1921, of views Stuart could not conceivably have had at that time, as the *Lecture on Nationality and Culture* makes clear. For a
writer who had belonged to the pro-Nazi faction in Ireland to have his nineteen-year-old
alter ego mentally dismiss Iseult's parents as having belonged to 'the anti-Dreyfus,
Boulangist faction in France' is rather a bold imaginative stroke.
88. For newspaper reports of the Aosdána meeting, see Mic Moroney, 'Aosdána Rejects
Call for Stuart Resignation', *Irish Times*, 27 November 1997, and Gene Kerrigan, 'Aosdána
Make a Show of Themselves', *Sunday Independent*, 30 November 1997. See also letters to
the *Irish Times* from, among others, Val Mulkerns (1 December 1997), Aidan Higgins (17
December 1997) and Louis Le Brocquy (2 January 1998), claiming that anti-Stuart feeling
was stronger than the vote suggested (Moroney reported that Mac an tSaoi's motion
received only one vote – her own).
89. Hamilton, Letter to the Editor, *Irish Times*, 4 December 1997.
90. See Kiberd, *Inventing Ireland*, p. 610. See also Terry Eagleton's comment that Stuart's
'Romantic anarchism can also be a squalid cult of the artist as demonic immoralist, a superior form of slumming ... Stuart's self-destructive urge to put himself beyond the social
pale, his masochistic wallowing in self-abnegation, can simply be the reverse side of the
artist as state lackey, which is just what he became for a while in Nazi Germany.' (*Crazy
John and the Bishop*, p. 245.)

Beckett, that 'the greatest curse that can befall anyone is "an honoured name". Nobody understands this better than Francis Stuart.' The argument is self-defeating: why would Hamilton or anyone else bother to defend Stuart if 'an honoured name' – the very thing the Aosdána award conferred, and the very thing that Stuart's critics objected to – was really a curse? Hamilton can't possibly believe it is a curse; and neither did Francis Stuart, who willingly bowed his head to the President of Ireland to receive the gold torc that comes with the position of Saoi.[91]

Colm Tóibín has commented that 'Stuart makes no secret of his pleasure at our discomfort' over his 'need to betray'; but reading the corpus of literary-critical and journalistic writing on Stuart over the past three decades leaves one with the sense that there is something about him – or about H – that actually makes us feel quite comfortable indeed. Stuart has become a synecdoche for art, and for all of the romantic-cum-modernist clichés that artists in weak moments spin around themselves: the artist as outcast, the artist as sufferer, the artist as witness. Of course artists can be, and have been, all of these things; but in an age when Irish writers are blandly revered, and blessedly (if modestly) subsidized by state and super-state, the idea that we had still among us a writer who had been ostracized, blacklisted, reviled, was strangely reassuring. Thomas Kilroy has suggested that this phenomenon has origins far earlier than the dawn of the age of Aosdána:

91. In a 1977 essay, Stuart complained about the neglect of writers by politicians in Ireland: 'Even the United Kingdom expresses more public regard for its artists than is the case here. Writers are invited, along with prominent sportsmen and entertainers, to lunch at Buckingham Palace. More serious are the contacts between writers and political leaders in France. De Gaulle was continuing a long tradition when on his return to a liberated Paris he consulted Mauriac, Malraux and others about the kind of new Republic to be built from the ruins. In West Germany artists figure among the distinguished citizens entertained by the President, besides the close ties some writers, Günther Grass and Heinrich Böll come to mind, have had with members of the government.

'Writers in Ireland are much in the position Spanish and Portuguese ones were in under Franco and Salazar, or those in the United States under Johnson and Nixon. To my knowledge none of our best writers have ever been asked to Aras an Uachtaráin.' See Stuart, 'Literature and Politics', *The Crane Bag*, vol. 1, no. 1, Spring 1977, p. 73.

The modern declaration of freedom, of which it [*Black List, Section H*] is typical, rose out of the clutter of an over-ripe nineteenth century middle-class society. ... for all its immense achievement, its subversiveness has been effectively assimilated by the remnants of that same society and has become, in effect, one of the ornaments of that society's culture.

Kilroy goes on to write of the 'illusion that the society in which we live is in any profound way touched by extreme individualism in the writer. Quite the contrary, such individualism, however outrageous, is curiously consoling to the society of liberal aspirations.'[92]

The society of liberal aspirations was not much edified by the sad little controversy that surrounded Stuart during 1996–7, in which important issues were repeatedly gestured at but rarely explored. Regarding Aosdána, it was no clearer at the end of the furore than it had been at the beginning whether the organization recognized non-artistic criteria for membership or for election to the elevated post of Saoi – a question perhaps complicated by the fact that the word 'saoi' connotes wisdom, not just artistic achievement. Fintan O'Toole was the only defender of Stuart who displayed any detailed knowledge of Stuart's wartime activities and made no effort to sanitize them. Hostile critics had an easier brief, because they could make telling arguments without having any knowledge of Stuart's fiction, and with only the barest knowledge of Stuart's activities in Germany: the mere fact that Stuart had willingly propagandized for a state that, among greater crimes, suppressed the arts and persecuted artists, provided, for some, a *prima facie* case against his being honoured by an official arts organization.[93] But the hostile critics could never explain how a body like Aosdána might go about establishing and enforcing criteria for judging the political activities and opinions of members; and it was telling that in some cases their response to the disputed

92. Thomas Kilroy, 'The Irish Writer: Self and Society', pp. 185, 186.
93. Perhaps the most cogent articulation of this viewpoint was Kevin Myers's *Irish Times* column of 24 October 1996, which seems to have ignited the debate.

'worm' remark betrayed glee at having been proved right about Stuart rather than hurt at the supposed slur.

Through it all, hardly anyone seemed to have any idea of what Stuart had actually said over the German airwaves. The present book aims to remedy the primary cause of that ignorance: the relative inaccessibility of the transcripts in archives. This introduction has explored aspects of Stuart's work that provide a background for Stuart's wartime broadcasts. The political content of Stuart's writings and activities in the twenties, thirties and forties gives the lie to the established view of Stuart as a blind betrayer, an anarchic neutral. That that view arises primarily from a work of fiction, *Black List, Section H*, is ironic and unfortunate: unfortunate not only for our understanding of Stuart's life, but also for our understanding of his art. Only by reading documents such as the *Lecture on Nationality and Culture*, the essay on de Valera, the letters to newspapers, and the wartime broadcasts, is it possible to recognize that the consciousness of H is a literary construct. It is, to be sure, an autobiographical construct; but the aspects of it that have been most compelling to readers are precisely those that prove impossible to square with what we know of Stuart's life and thought. We must therefore re-examine everything we thought we knew about the book, and about its author.

It has been comforting for many to think that this accomplished writer with his questionable past has, by a literary alchemy misleadingly called 'honesty', turned those questions into the stuff of art. The wartime broadcasts, so incompatible with the spirit of H, raise new questions and cast Stuart's art in a new, and fittingly crepuscular, light.

B.B.

Acknowledgments

This is not in any way an 'official' edition of Francis Stuart's wartime broadcasts, but I am very grateful to his literary estate – Paul Durcan, the executor, and Finola Graham, Stuart's widow – for granting permission to publish without restriction the surviving transcripts.

Without the indulgence of my colleagues at The Lilliput Press – Antony Farrell, Siobán O'Reilly, Liam Carson, Marsha Swan, and Sarah Bannan – this book might have taken a decade to produce. An offhand remark by Antony Farrell was largely responsible for guiding my rather aimless research on Stuart into the form of an edition of the broadcasts, and I am grateful to him for keeping his nerve when I proposed the project.

I wish to acknowledge the staffs of the libraries and archives I consulted. The late director of the Military Archives in Dublin, Peter Young, and his successor, Victor Laing, were particularly helpful and encouraging. Thanks are also due to the staffs of the National Library, Dublin; the National Archives, Dublin; the Public Record Office of Northern Ireland, Belfast; the library at the University of Ulster, Coleraine (especially Kay Ballantine); and the British Library and Imperial War Museum, London. Although I was unable to visit the archive of the German Foreign Ministry, which is in the process of moving from Bonn to Berlin and thus closed to researchers, I am grateful to Dr Peter Grupp for his vital assistance.

Many fellow researchers generously shared their knowledge with me; three in particular were enormously helpful. David O'Donoghue took a friendly interest in the project from an early stage, shared the fruits of his work on German wartime broadcasting to Ireland, and commented on a draft of the introduction. Mark Hull translated German documents and provided valuable source material and advice. Andreas Roth made me aware of relevant documents in the archive of the German Foreign Ministry and allowed me to read pre-publication versions of two relevant works: his book on the politics and career of Charles Bewley, published by Four Courts Press, and his paper on Francis Stuart's broadcasts, forthcoming in *Irish Historical Studies*.

For the provision of research references, accommodation, and good advice (not always followed), I offer my warm thanks to the following: Brian Barrington, Kevin Barry, Neil Belton, Terence Brown, Elizabeth Clissmann, Catriona Crowe, David Dickson, Martin Fanning, Roy Foster, Kathy Gilfillan, Vivienne Guinness, David Hayton, Ann Marie Hourihane, Vincent Hurley, Declan Kiberd, Sinéad Mac Aodha, Donna Monroe, Síofra O'Donovan, Karin O'Flanagan, Eunan O'Halpin, Colm Tóibín, Robert Towers.

Finally, thanks are due to the Arts Council of Ireland and Aer Lingus, whose Artflight programme facilitated a research trip to London.

Note on the Text

From the early days of the Second World War, German propaganda broadcasts to Ireland were monitored by G2, the intelligence branch of the Irish army. The vast bulk of the text that follows is based on the transcripts of Stuart's talks that are kept in file G2/X/0127 in the Military Archives, Cathal Brugha Barracks, Dublin. A few G2 transcripts that no longer survive in the Military Archives are preserved in the file kept by the Department of External Affairs on German broadcasts to Ireland, now held in the National Archives in Dublin, which consists largely of transcripts of talks by Stuart that were forwarded to the Department by G2.

The G2 transcripts were prepared from tapes of the broadcasts. Between two thirds and three quarters of Stuart's broadcasts were transcribed by the G2 monitors, although some of these transcripts are far from complete because of poor reception. The G2 file contains several notes referring to broadcasts that could not be transcribed at all for this reason; and in a few instances, the file contains no sign of a broadcast by Stuart on dates when he would have been scheduled to speak.

German broadcasts to Ireland were also monitored by the BBC as part of its enormous monitoring programme during the war. BBC monitoring reports are held by the Imperial War Museum and the British Library in London, and reports prepared for the government of Northern Ireland are kept at the Public Record Office of Northern Ireland in Belfast. The BBC reports on Stuart's talks take various forms. Some are complete verbatim transcripts.

Others are compressed versions of verbatim transcripts in which Stuart's words, but not *all* of his words, appear (in several cases I have been able to compare such reports with the G2 transcript for the same broadcast). Still others are third-person summaries written in the words of the summarizer, occasionally giving passages verbatim in inverted commas. The job of distinguishing these three types of transcript was made easier by the distinctiveness of Stuart's diction and the rambling rhythm of his sentences. In several instances, the BBC file has allowed me to fill in gaps from the G2 transcripts (presumably because on those nights the BBC monitors enjoyed better reception than the G2 monitors). Because it contains relatively little verbatim transcription, I have made conservative use of the BBC file, particularly when there was no transcript of any sort in the G2 file for the date in question.

A transcript of a talk by Stuart dated 9 February 1942, held in the Politisches Archiv des Auswärtigen Amts (the archive of the German Foreign Ministry), is printed in the Appendix, along with a discussion of why I have not included it as part of the main text. I am grateful to the historian Andreas Roth for making me aware of the relevant file; and also to Dr Peter Grupp of the PAAA for providing me with photocopies from the archive, which is currently in the process of moving from Bonn to Berlin and thus closed to researchers.

The earliest talk by Stuart that was picked up by Irish and British monitors – and possibly the first propaganda talk he both wrote and delivered himself – was broadcast on 17 March 1942. Stuart's talks followed no apparent schedule until August 1942, when he began broadcasting on a weekly basis. He began speaking twice weekly in September 1943, and he made his final surviving talk on 5 February 1944. The broadcasts were made from Berlin until August 1943, when the Rundfunkhaus (Broadcasting House) was bombed and the Irland-Redaktion moved to Luxembourg.

In editing the transcripts I have tried to be as unobtrusive as possible. The monitors who prepared the transcripts clearly paid more attention to getting the words right than to punctuating Stuart's talks properly, and I have followed common sense in editing punctuation while trying to preserve Stuart's characteristic cadences and the oral character of the talks. Whereas the G2 transcripts reproduce every word or sentence fragment that was audible to the monitors, I have replaced fragmentary passages with bracketed ellipses whenever such passages are incomprehensible or highly ambiguous. For example, an ellipsis has replaced the following passage from the G2 transcript of Stuart's broadcast of 18 November 1942:

Sometimes I feel afraid that .... discussions we had by the fireside before or in the early days of the war .... strange to me personally in a farmhouse in Meath or in a Clare village in which tonight you can hear the sea.

No cuts have been made for the sake of tightening sentences or eliminating repetition, or for reasons of space. Sometimes, I have summarized long fragmentary passages in which no individual sentence makes sense but from which it is possible to discern the thrust of what Stuart was saying; such summaries appear between square brackets and in italics. In other cases, where it is clear that Stuart mis-spoke or the monitor mis-typed (usually simply by missing a word), I have supplied the correct word in brackets.

In all of the situations sketched above, I have erred on the side of conservatism, particularly when inserting words in brackets: I have never inserted a word where there was any possibility that the interpolation might change Stuart's meaning.

Editorial comments are in italics and enclosed in square brackets. Notes made by the G2 monitors that might be of use to readers of the present volume are reproduced in inverted commas. A question mark in square brackets indicates that I have doubts about a transcription, but not strong enough doubts to justify deleting the word or phrase. Contemporary spellings have been retained; misspellings have been corrected.

The Broadcasts

17 March 1942

I'm glad to have this opportunity of saying a few words [...] I want to make it clear than by speaking to you I am not trying to make propaganda. You can hear as much of that as you want [...] and by now you have a good idea of what is true and what is false. I, the writer, do not want to add to this mass of propaganda; if I'd wanted to I could have done so during the two years [I have spent] here in Germany. But my only desire is to put before you very simply my idea of Ireland's place in the world and her future, which I am perhaps able to view with greater clarity from a distance. [...]

What a blessing it is that we are celebrating this [St Patrick's] day at peace, not having escaped war by dishonourable and cowardly means but by refusing – as far as lay within our power – to waver from a strict and fearless neutrality. As an Ulsterman it is galling to me that a large number of foreign troops are today occupying that corner of our country.[1] But though we have escaped the war, and I hope may be able to do so until the end without sacrificing anything of our national integrity, we cannot nor do we desire to escape taking our share in the building of the new Europe.

There are a few points which should be considered. Whether we like it or not, and personally I do not dislike it, there will be

1. Stuart would have considered the peacetime British army garrison in Northern Ireland to be 'foreign', but this is probably a reference to the American troops that had been based in Northern Ireland since shortly after the United States entered the war.

no such thing as complete isolation, political, economic or cultural. Nations will have to live as members of a group or family, with as much individual freedom as members of a family have but with certain duties and responsibilities towards the family. We do not fall clearly to any group, but I believe it is of the utmost importance that we follow our early tradition and turn towards the European continent. We have, as it is, been cut off far too long from that great source of life and culture. [...] I believe we can rebuild our country only [...] as a branch of the great European tree, and [belonging] neither to the British Commonwealth nor to the American sphere.

When I think of Ireland I think of Glendalough, where my home is, and thinking of Glendalough I cannot but think of Europe [...] [*Stuart refers to the travels of Irish scholars from Glendalough and other ecclesiastical centres 'in the Middle Ages to France, Germany, Italy, Spain, the Alps, to keep alight the flame of the spirit of Europe'.*] [...] To put it plainly, we have had too little contact with countries that have something to give us. We have on the other hand been surrounded by communities whose life is [based] on money and the power of money. Whether we turn to England or the United States we see the god of money. Perhaps, as in the case of America, we have sometimes been forced to appeal to this god, but all the same it was and always will be an alien god to us – just as it is a completely alien god to Europe. [...] When one European country, France, seemed to begin to believe in that modern heresy, then the life went out of her and she collapsed.

Ireland belongs to Europe and England does not belong to it. I believe that after this war our future should be linked with the future of Europe and no other.

[*The G2 monitor noted: 'speaker exceedingly poor, broadcast very good quality up to the start of the talk and announcer's remarks are very distinct. I am of the opinion that the talk was received very badly on all receivers, and that the fault may have been due to a faulty micro-*

phone'. The comment 'speaker exceedingly poor' may have been a ref-
erence to Stuart's abilities as a broadcaster, of which he himself had a
low opinion in the early days of his work for German radio. On 6
August 1943, by which time he had made a few sporadic broadcasts
and had just made the first of a weekly series of talks, he complained
to his diary that 'I do not yet know how to control my voice.' See
'Selections from a Berlin Diary, 1942', The Journal of Irish Litera-
ture V, 1, Jan. 1976, p. 87.]

29 March 1942

In speaking to you from Germany I do not pretend to know any
more about the war, in its military and strategic aspects, than you
at home do; but from here at the hub of Europe I am in a position to get a clearer idea of it, of something in the nature of a
world revolution, the great dividing line in history, a vital change
upon the face of life. [Just] because we have so far been able to
remain neutral, it would be a grave mistake for us Irish to think
that it had nothing to do with us. There is no good of saying, We
want our lost provinces back, we want freedom and security and
then we want to be left alone. No, if we hope to find national fulfilment after this war, in the new world, as I believe we shall, then
we must not be merely intent on taking, we must give too. I
believe the majority of you see this. So far we have been forced
into too much isolation. We were forced into a system to which
we did not belong and for which we had no feeling of affinity, and
therefore we rightly refused to cooperate in this system, called the
British Empire or the British Commonwealth. But I think that
once we take our place within the European system that is coming, we shall be ready to do all that is within our power towards
the common good as we did long ago in the past. Do not ask what
has all this to do with us – that, for all I know, may still be the attitude of a few of you. It is the attitude of fools. It is everything to

do with us. Mark my words well: if some of the peoples in those European countries that had got what they wanted after the last war had not looked around [...] and exclaimed, What has it to do with us?, they would not see their homes destroyed today.

I do not know the various political currents, intrigues and secret alliances that went on between the last war and this. I am no politician and all that is quite beyond me. I'm interested in people, in individuals and their lives. I've met and talked with members of several European countries in the past year or two – a thing which those gentlemen in America who sent their troops to Irish soil certainly have not done – and they none of them want the old Europe, or anything like it, back again. They do not want a Europe in which the struggle to live and keep alive one's children drains away all one's life. They want a Europe where they – and [I am] speaking of the common people especially – [can] earn a reasonable livelihood without slavery, have a home in peace, a wife, children, and be free from anxiety and have time for reading, going to a theatre or cinema and sometimes for holidays. Those are their personal desires and beyond that they want traditions free to be carried on and developed unhampered. On the other hand, what they do not want [are the] political affairs of the League of Nations – in what assemblies, by the way, one of the few honest speeches ever heard was that delivered by Mr de Valera when he acted as President[2] – nor do they want to return to a state of affairs in which international financiers wield political power over the destinies of countries as they did in the past. [...]

2. Ireland assumed the presidency of the League of Nations shortly after Fianna Fáil's rise to power in 1932, and Stuart may be referring to de Valera's first speech as chairman of the League assembly on 26 September of that year, in which he stated: 'In spite of the opinions you may have formed from misleading reports, I want you to know that our history is the history of a people who have consistently sought only to be allowed to lead their own lives in their own way, in peace with their neighbours and the world.' In this and in subsequent addresses to the League, de Valera suggested that the League was not living up to its Covenant; by the time of the Italian invasion of Abyssinia, de Valera was openly (and justifiably) pessimistic about the League's viability. See Michael Kennedy, *Ireland and the League of Nations, 1919–1946*, pp. 168–9 and *passim*.

Two things especially we have grown to hate or loathe: one is the system which made money the greatest power on earth, and the other is what I might call political idealism. We don't want any more fine-sounding words or League of Nations speeches. We don't want any more shouting about humanity, equality, freedom – the very words have begun to sting. No, we want a little warm-hearted realism, not a lot of cold ineffective phrases [...] We want to live at peace under our leader or leaders. [...] We must be living as part of the great European whole and we must learn to see that our own good is part of the European good and vice versa.

I'm aware that all this is but the briefest outline, but in the few minutes in which I have to speak to you anything more than general ideas would be out of place; besides, the time is not yet ripe for any more detailed survey of our position and future. When that time comes there will be other Irishmen better fitted than I am, I hope, to guide and advise us – for my own work lies elsewhere. All that I can do is put a few ideas that may be of interest and use before Irish nationalists at this hour of crisis.

5 April 1942

There is to me an aspect of Easter Week 1916 which has a special significance. It is a fact that never did a lost cause seem so completely lost, never was there a more final and complete defeat than that suffered by the handful of Irishmen at the end of that desperate week. Not only were they overwhelmingly crushed by the might of the British troops, but they had apparently failed to inspire any sympathy in the mass of their own fellow-countrymen. If ever in the eyes of the world there seemed a complete failure, that was it.

But what happened? Looking back we can now see clearly that in some mysterious manner the apparent fiasco was in reality an undreamed-of success, such a success, in fact, as the death of the comparative handful of men has seldom brought about in history. I do not think that modern history can show a richer harvest from the bloody sacrifices made in many countries and on many battlefields. In 1916 a fire was kindled in Ireland which for a long time before had been at a low ebb and which since then has never been permitted to die down. At the time it seemed that the loss of the best of the nation's sons must lead to another period of national deadness. But no, there has sprung from their blood a new Ireland […] In no other way could that new Ireland be born. […]

As this evening I walk about the Berlin streets as a neutral […] I know that had those few men not barricaded themselves into a few buildings in Dublin that day twenty-six years ago our position now would be a very different one. The final victories are not won by those who can boast of the most colossal rows of figures on paper nor even by the reality behind those figures. Mass production alone will not win a modern war without faith in the ideals of one's country. The men of Easter Week won a great victory because they had faith and passion. Had they had the war machines as well their victory would certainly have been achieved more quickly without the loss of their own lives, but without that faith and passion they would have achieved nothing […]

I believe that the spirit of Easter Week is the one spirit which will bring us through this world crisis and whatever the future may hold. By that I mean faith in our country and way of life and a warm heart towards the suffering world; and let us beware of the disease of political idealism and its counterpart materialism. Whenever you find the worship of money you seem to find this output of mental idealism that leaves the heart so cold. Please God we shall be able to remain neutral to the end, but if we were to fight it would certainly not be for any so-called ideal. We, knowing what lies behind them, have had enough of those to make us sick. God preserve us from all such cant. For us Irish there is only one reality, our own life on our own soil free from the tyranny of money. I hope and believe that the end of this war will give us back our national unity and that the struggle which began its latter phase on that Easter morning in Dublin will then be, at last, at an end. Then will begin a new phase in our life. The intense national isolation into which we have been forced must give way to our taking our place, not in some artificial form invented by politicians like the League of Nations but in the great organic European family.

25 May 1942

[*The G2 monitor logged 'Stuart missed' and 'Recording too noisy for transcription'. The BBC monitors evidently had better reception, and produced what appears to be a verbatim or nearly verbatim transcript; at moments the cadence seems uncharacteristically clipped, and here it is likely the transcriber did a bit of editing.*]

It is easier for me than for you at home to realise what a great thing it is that up till now, Ireland has not been caught in the war; but because we have been able to preserve our neutrality, it is no reason for looking at the war as a passing storm, after which all will be as it was before. The world will never be the same again. In the new world it will not merely be a matter of regaining our lost territory. The peace must bring a change of outlook. The last peace was made by professional politicians and financiers. We had twenty years of it and many of those years were as bad as any in our history. The next peace is going to be a more realistic and human affair, in which neither money nor political idealism will play any great part. We are not going to step out of some of the bloodiest battles in history into an earthly paradise. Great faith and energy will be needed to overcome the colossal difficulties. These qualities, I believe, we as a nation possess, for we can always be stirred by an appeal to the heart, where Wilson's Fourteen Points and the League of Nations left us cold. Our fight for independence was more than a fight for our country's freedom. It was a determination to have nothing to do with the whole political, social and financial system.

At the present moment our first concern is quite rightly to secure enough food[?], but a people themselves must justify their existence as a nation, and a nation which fails to do this must perish sooner or later. If we come safely through, there is a great obligation to play our part in helping to build up a new civilisation. This idea may seem strange at first, for it is a long time since we, as a nation, have had a chance to do this, so occupied were we in saving ourselves from the influence of an alien system. We have been surrounded so long by a civilisation so spiritually and culturally dead that we could have no possible communion with it.

This was true not only of England but also of the USA. At one time we hoped for a vital contact with America, but that never materialised. The closer America came in her outlook to England, the more impossible it became for Ireland to reach an understanding with her. True, Irish writers, myself among them, had a certain public in America, but our books were read as curiosities, rather than from any feeling of sympathy or kinship. I myself and many Irishmen felt the same about American literature. Sinclair Lewis, with his Main Streets and Babbits,[3] was alien and sinister. We had some sympathy with Eugene O'Neill, because we felt he had something to say which was of real value. This was probably due to his Irish origin.

Our future life as a nation is, I believe, going to be lived in closer contact with European nations. Maybe at the end of this war we shall be one of the few unscathed nations. What then will be expected of us? We must give up all traces of that outlook coloured by the old system, for one is not always immune from what one fights against most bitterly. The great majority of you have not been tainted by that creed which has its origin in indus-

3. Sinclair Lewis's novels included *Main Street* (1920) and *Babbit* (1922).

trial and imperial England, for I know too much about conditions at home to make the mistake of identifying the contemptible outlook of certain sections of the press with that of our people. If our faith in our own tradition is firm enough, we can later be of use in undoing the great harm done to religion by those who are making it a propaganda catch-cry. We must wipe away some of the filth that has been flung in the face of religion in Europe by those politicians who send their troops to defend the cause of money, to the tune of 'Onward Christian Soldiers'.

5 August 1942

This talk is a kind of introduction to a series that I hope to broadcast to you at weekly intervals. It is certainly not that I have any desire to join the ranks of the propagandists, but I believe that neither you nor I have the right to cut ourselves off from the storm that is raging around us no matter how much we may feel inclined to do so. Being neutral does not mean to remain unaffected by or insensitive to events that are going to determine the sort of civilisation that is going to develop in Europe. In this series of talks I hope to comment on some of these events and tell you some of my ideas as they affect Ireland, but first I think it would be no harm if I were to explain very briefly my motives in doing so.

To begin with, it was not the chances of war that brought me to Germany; I came during the war of my own free will, incredible as that may seem to the more unadventurous of you – so thank God I don't think there are many of you like that at home. My main reason was the very same one that has driven millions of other Irishmen to leave their native land: the necessity of earning a living. I had, unfortunately, little chance of doing that at home during the war. My second reason is that, like I daresay a good many others of us, I was heartily sick and disgusted with the old order under which we've been existing and which had come to us from the great financial powers in whose shadow we lived. If there had to be a war then I wanted to be among those people who had also had enough of the old system and who moreover claimed that they had a new and a better one – about all that I shall try to speak in later talks. I had begun to see that no internal policy for Ireland could ever be completely successful unless joined to an external one that re-established our ancient links with Europe and European culture.

I came here with these somewhat vague ideas or rather feelings, and since then they have become a great deal clearer to me and I hope to make them [clearer] to you; but I often [...] fear this relationship between Ireland and Europe, above all between Ireland and Germany, is a one-sided one. I not only want to bring something of Germany and German ideas to you but I also try, in the Berlin University and elsewhere, to make people here and especially young Germans conscious of Ireland and interested in her problems and outlook. Incidentally, it may interest you to hear that at the present moment there are two Irish novels being serialized in papers here: Liam O'Flaherty's great novel *Famine* in the *Frankfurter Zeitung* and one of my own in a Berlin weekly.[4]

Having given you these reasoned motives for wanting to speak to you, I see what in one sense is a quite irrational one: it is that at times I get such a longing for home, for that peculiar atmosphere that is symbolised in different ways for each of us; I see again the Antrim boglands where I spent my boyhood, a small farmhouse and a row of trees around one side of it for shelter and a bicycle leaning up against a whitewashed wall. I feel now that the very mud on the tyres of that bike is sacred, and at such times even to speak to you at home – some of you perhaps listening to me from that very bogland – is something. [...]

4. This may be *The Coloured Dome*, whose serialization by *Die Woche* Stuart referred to in his diary on 23 May 1942.

It is true that only a comparative few of us at home had a clear vision of Ireland as a nation; most of us have simply not that gift, most of us are too busy farming or shopkeeping or being politicians to have much conscious idea of our national destiny. All that matters is that there are always a few with enough vision and energy to plan for the whole nation, but it is not to this section or that that I want to address these talks; it is to as many of you as will listen to me, whether you have much interest or not in the problems of Europe.

There is only one thing that I take for granted in you – and to those who haven't it most of what I have to talk about will, I'm afraid, be meaningless – and that is that you think strongly about Ireland even if it is only a few small fields or a line of hills. I want to speak to all of you who have that feeling for some corner of our country. As to those comparative few who not only love Ireland but who are ready to sacrifice all for the freedom of Irish soil, I do not flatter myself that I can teach you anything. I will only say this, that you may now feel isolated and alone – but have patience: the past has belonged to the politicians and the financiers, the future is going to be yours.

12 August 1942

[*G2: 'Beginning missed.'*] [...] and I think that you will agree when I say to the arrest of Gandhi,[5] I do not claim that I have nothing but admiration for Gandhi's outlook. [...] One thing is certain and that is that he is no militarist. His arrest is therefore another fact hard to reconcile with the claim that this war is being fought by the democracies against militarism. Of course the truth is,

---

5. Gandhi, fearing the adoption by the British of a scorched-earth policy should India be invaded, had launched a 'Quit India' campaign in April, and was building towards a major civil disobedience movement when he and the rest of the Congress party leadership were arrested and imprisoned in early August.

though I'm sure it is not realised by the masses in those democracies, that this war is the defence of the system by which life is dominated by money. India has been made into a great link, perhaps the greatest, as Napoleon saw, in this chain that fetters the world, and yet [it poses] a vital threat to this liberal materialism.

You may wonder why I call it liberal. It was so called by its advocates and there is no reason to quarrel with the term if you remember that this liberalism consists in the freedom of any individual to make as much money as he can. The fact we in Ireland want from the coming peace is little more of this liberal materialism. We are sick of that civilization based on money [...] What we want is a very different kind of social philosophy, one that will bring real peace. Can there ever be such a thing, I hear you ask. I know well how you feel, a bit wary of the whole business, wanting to forget it. Many of you have already seen one war and one peace, and [are dubious of] what this one will be like when it comes. So would I be if I thought it was going to be made by the same sort of politicians as made the last. I don't want to exaggerate, I want to try to find the truth in all this [...] I think that some of those behind the League of Nations had a kind of ineffectual idealism [and they] were those who shouted for disarmament; the others of course saw that arms were the most effective means left to mankind to revolt against the god of money. So they could at the same time parade their idealism and see that the world was made safe for high finance. Now, disarmament alone can never secure a lasting peace. Not disarmament but the definancialisation of life can do that. [...]

The arrest of Gandhi, the great pacifist, is a concrete proof the great politicians are not interested in the cause of disarmament at all when it does not serve their purpose. Gandhi is now a threat to them as Hitler was a threat to them. But Hitler had a great army behind him, therefore they preached pacifism. [...] [Although Hitler and Gandhi] seemed to have so little in common, both find themselves in conflict with the great democracies. There is a proverb, 'Show me your friends and I'll tell you what you are'; in this case I say show me your enemies. What these two leaders have in common is that both deny the possibility of a civilisation based on money to be anything but a disaster for the majority of mankind.

This is exactly the point that affects us vitally. The path of civilisation [...] is also one in which money does not play the all-important part, but it did, and still does, in the old order. I would like to be clear [...] I do not say that Ireland should become a small replica of a National Socialist Germany any more than I'd say we should model ourselves on Gandhi's India, but I do say, over and over, that until we free ourselves from what I call the liberal materialist order, we cannot be a happy and peaceful community.

19 August 1942

I sometimes think that some of you at home may say, It's all very fine but what's all the talk about, the curse of war has overtaken the world, why not keep quiet till it's over, why all this talk and argument? This attitude would be very logical and understandable for anyone who had found the kind of peace, the kind of life that we had before the war, more or less satisfactory; but for those who didn't, and I am one, then we must see to it that this war marks the end of the old system.

Let us for a moment turn back and try and see what the old life was really like. I don't mean now the intimate personal lives which you led, for even in the midst of the most unfavourable circumstances people are usually able to make their own homes, their own personal existence, surrounded by family and friends, more or less as they wish; but I think you will agree that the whole trend of the civilisation under whose shadow Ireland lay was an extraordinarily bad one. It was not our civilisation but one which had begun to dominate us more and more. It was one which in place of culture took business, and in place of religion high-sounding phrases; a civilisation in which Christianity was twisted to suit a society of businessmen, and prosperity and respectability were made into the highest virtues. In such a society, who came to the top? Hollywood film stars, bankers, a few novelists of almost incredible worthlessness, politicians, professional idealists of the League-of-Nations brand and inventors of patent medicines. It was a society in which neither courage, art, moral virtues nor even aristocracy was respected or valued. Advertising had become a disease, an insane struggle for money went on in all the cities, and one of the few things thought more of was material success. I do not think that that is an unfair or exaggerated picture and I could go on and elaborate it, but there is no need; you know it as well as I. The only difference, perhaps, is that many of you accepted it as inevitable whereas I have come to see that it is not only not inevitable but that it was in its worst form limited to the great democracies. With the exception of France, which was fast following in the steps of England and America, things had not come to such a pitch on the continent of Europe. The great European tradition remained victorious over the onslaughts of modern materialism. I make this statement fully aware how you at home have been subjected day and night to propaganda that [claims] the very opposite: that it is this Anglo-Saxon form of civilisation which is the upholder of idealism against barbarism. [...]

I tell you what I've seen – I tell you the conclusions I draw from what I have seen. I've lived for long periods both in the midst of the civilisation just described and also here in Germany. I do not say that I find everything here in Germany perfect and marvellous – if I did you would certainly have the right to accuse me of being a propagandist after all – but what I do say is that materialism and superficiality have not eaten into the roots of life here as they have there. All human values have not been financialised. We in Ireland have our own way of life, our own outlook – and so we should, if we are to be worthy of freedom – but our way of life has not only been threatened but to some extent actually dominated by this alien civilisation in whose shadow we live. This of course is clearly seen by many of you, and the Irish language [survives despite] the great effort made to combat it, but even before this war it became obvious that that was not going to be enough. [...] the only way to disassociate ourselves from that alien civilisation is [...] to associate ourselves with the life and culture of the European continent. [...]

30 August 1942

Tonight, the first thing I want to do is to send you the sympathy of many many Germans who have spoken to me of the fate of the six Irishmen condemned to be hung in Belfast.[6] It is the first time that I have ever been asked to say something in these talks to you and I do it very gladly, because I know the people who have asked me and I know that their feeling comes from their hearts. I am not going into the question of the trial. The accused men all denied the only charge which would have given their captors the slightest excuse of legality to what they intend to do. [...]

I'm going to take it on myself to address some words to Mr Churchill on behalf of the millions of Irishmen in Ireland, in America, who have no way of doing this themselves. But I do not think I shall say anything which many of these millions would disassociate themselves from. Blood, tears and sweat: these words which have been lately linked to your name have always been familiar to us. We will credit you with believing in and understanding this language and we will speak to you in it. We will not talk of justice [...] or the rights of small peoples; we've long ago seen their emptiness and to use them is as ridiculous as using the

6. Six IRA men had been sentenced to death for the murder of RUC Constable Patrick Murphy. Appeals from de Valera and the U.S. government led to five of the six receiving reprieves; the sixth, Thomas Williams, was hanged a few days after this broadcast.

slang of the year before last. No, we will keep to your own famous phrase, and 'twas a good one. Indeed, it may well be for that one phrase, rather than your statesmanship or strategy, that you'll be remembered in history.

Ireland for its size has poured out more blood, tears and sweat than any other nation. We know what those words mean better than you do, but perhaps unlike you, we begin to see an end at last to this long tale of sacrifice. We don't know whether, having asked your own people for such endurance, you believe you can give them a final recompense; that is not our affair. What is our affair is that Irish blood, sweat, should not have been spilt in vain. And we tell you now that the blood of these six Irishmen will be about the last that you and your fellow statesmen will have the opportunity to spill within the seclusion of prison walls. Do you think that it can go on for ever? What do you suppose is enough – did you not find a few months' bombing of London enough, or if not, what limit would you set to it? For us, seven hundred years is enough. You must know as well as we do that the time is past when Ireland could have little or no effect on the money-dominated world of which you and your fellow statesmen were masters. [...] We neither appeal to you in the name of justice nor do we make threats. [...] the very name of justice and threats are mostly used by the weak, and we do not now feel ourselves weak.

We ask you to reprieve these six Irishmen, [but] we believe that the chance of your listening is very small. You may think the lives of six Irishmen are unimportant compared to the thousands being lost on the fronts, which you yourself are directing, but to us it is not yet the matter of six Irishmen – though God knows to us six are precious – but it is a matter of six more added to the thousands and the millions of Irish lives lost directly or indirectly through the domination of our country by yours. [...]

16 September 1942

While some of the greatest battles of the war are raging and news of the most sensational kind is pouring in, we Irish abroad still continue to search the papers and listen for the shortest references over the radio to affairs at home. And what little news comes through centres more and more around Belfast. To me, Belfast recalls many memories of childhood; to me then it was a mysterious and exciting place to which I was sometimes taken from my home in the north of Antrim. I am convinced that this city is still going to play a very important part in our history. Even now it is beginning to become the Irish Danzig.[7] The comparison may seem at first a strange one, for we must admit that outwardly Belfast has little in common with the beautiful old town on the Baltic. Yet for us the undoubted ugliness of much of Belfast is nothing. As Danzig became the focus of the German people's nationalism, so now is Belfast becoming for us the focus of the latest phase of Irish nationalism.

In the earlier days of the war, I think that many of you had no very clear idea of what it was all about. [...] Gradually, however, things became clearer. India, perhaps, was one of the clearest indications of the real aims and outlook of the democratic states. Even the least politically minded of you began to know where you were then; but now it is not only India, it is not only Bombay, Calcutta and Delhi, now it is Belfast. Belfast is an Irish city. Whatever the industrial stamp given it by the English occupation, it remains essentially Irish. The second city of our land. More important to

7. Germany had lost Danzig in the Treaty of Versailles, and between the wars the city was a League of Nations protectorate, adjacent to East Prussia but within the Polish customs area and accessible to Poland via a corridor of land leading to the Baltic Sea. The city's population was largely German, and Nazi influence there waxed at the expense of League authority after 1933. Hitler always intended to take Danzig back, and his demands for the reversion of the city to Germany provided part of the pretext for the invasion of Poland.

us than even Danzig was to Germany [...] not only to its citizens but to the whole Irish nation. You've probably been looking more at maps in the past year or two than ever before, gauging distances, drawing pencil marks as the tide of battle ebbs or flows. Now let us look at the map of Ireland for a change, look at Belfast on it: it stands less than fifty miles from the nearest point on the border. Fifty miles of occupied country between us and it – not much reckoned by some of the amazing advances made by the German divisions, but for us a great deal. Fifty miles too much between us and our fellow countrymen suffering there alone and cut off from us: that is a terrible thing, to have some of one's own race cut off from the rest and subjected to persecution. When a whole nation stands together it isn't so bad, but it is intolerable to think of those Irish people separated from the rest of us and at the mercy of foreign troops and police.

From now on our chief desire must be to break that space between. There can be no peace for us until that is done and they're united with us again. It is useless to think of peace before that is accomplished. Even before this war that was clear to me; it must be even clearer now. When Chamberlain stepped into an aeroplane on his way back from Munich, waved a piece of paper and said 'this means peace in our time', it seemed like a horrible joke. An elderly, complacent businessman without a drop of passionate blood in his veins, what did he know of the longing of a people to be united again with those cut off from them, of the determination of a people to face the fifty miles from the German border to Danzig or the determination of our own people to bridge the fifty miles from the Irish border to Belfast? Chamberlain is dead and forgotten. The German people have regained their lost provinces, all living passionate desires will in the end triumph, 'tis not the schemes and intrigues, the compromises and diplomacies of politicians and financiers that are going to create the postwar world. I say to our fellow-countrymen in Belfast, endure on for only a little longer; our hearts go out to you.

23 September 1942

To begin with this evening I want to say something about India. There are a good many Indians here in Berlin, typical exiles, who believe that only through a German victory can their country finally gain its freedom. They publish a monthly paper here called *Free India*. This paper is printed in German and English and is edited by Pandit Bakar. In the present number appears Bose's[8] statement made over the radio some time ago. I am going to read a short extract from this to you. Some of you may have heard it when it was given. I think this passage will have special interest to you:

It is high time that my friends and colleagues at home learned to differentiate between the internal and external policy of Free India. The internal policy of Free India is and should be the concern of the Indian people themselves. By standing for full collaboration with the tripartite powers in the external sphere I stand for absolute self-determination for India where her national affairs are concerned and I shall never tolerate any interference with the internal affairs of the free Indian state. So far as social-economic affairs are concerned, my views are exactly what they were when I was at home and no one should make the mistake of concluding that external collaboration with the tripartite powers means acceptance of their domination or even of their ideology in our internal affairs.

I have friends in Ireland to whom I would like to stress this passage. I know that some of them, Peadar O'Donnell for instance, are afraid that Irish friendship with Germany would mean accepting and copying German social and economic ideology.[9] This is

---

8. Subhas Chandra Bose (1897–1945), Indian nationalist who broke with Gandhi. In 1940 he escaped from prison and went to Berlin, where he organized a pro-Axis force consisting of Indian prisoners of war captured in North Africa; he was also a chess partner to William Joyce. In February 1943 he left Germany in a U-boat to take charge of the Free India force raised by Japan from Indian prisoners taken in the Malaya campaign. The force fought in the unsuccessful Japanese offensive against India in spring 1944.

9. Peadar O'Donnell, writer and republican who split from the IRA in 1934 to form the left-wing Republican Congress.

certainly not so. While I believe that we have much to learn from Germany and that our ties with the European continent must be made much closer, I am neither such a fool nor such a bad nationalist as to imagine that a foreign form of government can ever be imposed on us from without. What kind of state we build up on the whole of our island is a matter for ourselves to work out once we've got the whole of our island in our own possession.

I've many ideas on this subject but I'm not going to bring them into these talks because in the little time I have there are more immediate things to speak of, and also because I want to make the issue very clear. I have no aim in these talks except the one in which you can all share, that is to keep our thoughts fixed on a free and united Ireland in the midst of all the chaos, hostile propaganda and attempts at internal sabotage. There is only one supreme important aim for us Irish now: while Irish people are being hounded, imprisoned and persecuted in the north-eastern [counties] we outside them must do all in our power to end that intolerable situation as soon as possible. At the moment there may not be much that we can do, but the speed at which this war is being fought makes a rapidly changing position and the time when we had to reconcile ourselves to almost endless endurance and patience is over.

I want specially to speak to those of you in the Six Counties, if only to send you some words of encouragement and greeting in the struggle. Conditions forbid that the rest of the Irish nation can speak to you openly, but here I am free to send a few words to you, and while I am well aware the words are not much use to you, they may all the same give you an idea of how much you in the North are in the minds and hearts of us all. From the earliest days of the occupation of our country it has always been the aim of the occupying forces to divide us and so weaken us, but today that is more difficult. You in the North are an integral part of us, in spirit and in blood, and so you shall remain. I cannot make any prophecies, but this much I believe: if we stand together in firmness and for-

titude the time will come that the sacred soil of Ulster will once
again be free Irish soil.

7 October 1942

Today is an important anniversary in Irish history and I am going
to say something about it. But it is also a personal anniversary on
which I want to send a word of greeting to my son, in the only
way I can, and who I have constantly in my thoughts and especially yesterday on his sixteenth birthday.[10]

From time to time in the history of nations men arise whose
destiny is linked with the history of that nation. These are figures
who usually appear at crisis and turning points in the history of
their peoples [...] These figures are naturally rare but they are
never forgotten. Even those who have heard nothing of history
have heard of them. We have had one such man in our history and
I believe only one. We have had great patriots, men who led and
inspired the advance guard [...] but only one who inspired all sections and classes. I speak of him the anniversary of whose death we
celebrate today, Parnell.

Parnell was for a time the leader of the whole Irish people, the
only man who could ever be truly called by the people the
Uncrowned King of Ireland. Those who had the privilege to be
living at the height of his career saw that passionate devotion that
a great leader can inspire in a whole nation – one of the greatest
experiences in the history of any people. Most great nations have
had these leaders. Such were the Napoleons of France, the Abraham Lincolns of America, Gandhi today for India, Frederick the
Great for the Prussians and Hitler for the new Germany. All these
men in their own ways, in those ways particularly suited to the

10. Ion Stuart, Francis and Iseult's only son. They had two daughters: Dolores, born
1921, who died of spinal meningitis as an infant, and Catherine (Kay), born 1931.

peoples to which they belonged, lifted their nations on a great wave of fervour and heroism. Parnell, with a more limited material at his disposal, was one of these. He declared, 'No man shall set a limit to the forward march of a nation …'

The spirit of all these leaders [is] the spirit feared and hated by the politicians of the democracies and great financial powers who believe in a cold and impersonal political system because it is the one that suits them. The emergence of a great leader is one of those human miracles which cannot take place in England or modern America. Their system of government based on money destroys the possibility of such a wave of love and faith in one man […] These great leaders have in fact always been forced to oppose the British system, whether Napoleon, Lincoln, Gandhi, Hitler or Parnell. It is the conflict of two great conflicting outlooks, the personal and passionate as against the impersonal and mechanical. The whole mass of propaganda coming from the democracies in the past years, even long before the war, was aimed at bringing the idea of a leader into contempt. It was seen as being incompatible with their own system. Even at this moment of crisis the two great democracies cannot produce a great leader. Even their admirers would not claim that Roosevelt's or Churchill's destiny [is at one with] the destiny of their respective countries; it is even probable that neither will remain in power the length of the war.

Here in Germany I have had the opportunity to see how a great leader can inspire a whole nation. Whatever propaganda you may hear, one thing I will tell you: Germany is today an inspired nation. That is the main secret of her victorious armies; the source of that inspiration is rooted in one man, Hitler. So once were we too united and inspired by Parnell. This of all times is a fitting one to honour his memory […] We are in the midst of a struggle which will decide whether the new world will be one in which some highly developed system of finance, camouflaged by high-sounding phrases, will be the deciding factor in our lives or one in which we can return to the ordinary human values.

14 October 1942

[*G2: 'Beginning missed.'*][...] At that time [*i.e. at the end of the First World War*] the corpses of 250,000 men of Irish blood lay buried in the trenches and shell holes of Flanders and other theatres of war. [...] [They were] the poor victims of this imperial world war, many of them victims of British social maladministration of their native land; others came from abroad, from industrial districts of Lancashire and Scotland, from overseas, from the towns and cities of America, Australia and wherever their ancestors had gone, driven away from their native soil by Anglo-Saxon greed. They probably believed in what was England's greatest historical lie, namely that England wages war for the liberation of small nations. They knew no better; likewise thousands of Northern Irishmen fought and died for what they believed to be their duty, whilst others were given to understand that if they fought well a grateful England would give Ireland Home Rule once the war was over.

Wherever they fought they fought well, and the German soldiers had every respect for the military qualities of these victims of English policy. The Germans knew moreover that these misguided Irishmen were doomed to the most bitter disappointment when the time would come when Britain would have to honour her solemn pledge. All this is now history; Éire has won her place as a sovereign nation and has reasserted her right to stay out of [a] war which is not hers. The martyrs for Irish liberty of 1916, of 1918 to 1921, have not died in vain. But even so there is still a large part of historic territory of the Irish nation which no longer shares in the blessing of peace. Against the will of hundreds of thousands of its inhabitants it has been made a bridgehead for foreign interference with the destiny of the whole nation and a point of vantage for the English war effort in this imperialistic war waged by Britain against the Continent. In Northern Ireland too the British executioner can still put to death patriotic Irishmen like the late

Thomas Williams, who was legally murdered by the British administration on September the 2nd 1942 for no other crime than for being loyal to his nation. In this part of Ireland the claim of one of the oldest nations of Europe, the right of the Irish to live in liberty, in unity and in peace with the other nations of Europe, is to be denied for ever by the selfsame forces which are responsible for the first as well as for the second world war. But just as the present war is nothing else but the final act of the international tragedy of 1914–1918, a tragedy which the Germans and the Irish thought would never repeat itself, so the present struggle for the maintenance of Irish neutrality, and the rights it implies, is nothing else but a consummation of the heroic deeds of those Irishmen who died in Easter Week 1916 for Irish liberty and unity.

Mr de Valera was one of the heroes then condemned to death for his bravery by the English self-styled fighters for the small nations, but destiny willed otherwise and the hero of Boland's Mill and of Mount Street bridge will figure in history, not only as the undaunted fighter for liberty and unity of his nation but also as one of the very few really outstanding statesmen of our generation. It is the earnest hope of his admirers that he will also successfully master all that may lie ahead, in the interest of his country and of tormented mankind. In this spirit we too want to express on this solemn day our respect to Mr de Valera and to wish him further success in his great task.

21 October 1942

I know well that at home there is a wisdom that never gets into the papers, and rarely enough indeed into the speeches of politicians. Therefore I'm not at all despondent about the state of affairs with you or about your outlook. I'm quite certain that this very evening you are discussing events in the world by your fireplaces with a good deal of sense and justice – that is, those of you who are not discussing hurling, coursing, or the absorbing topic of horse racing. But all the same I'm glad that you are not left completely to the mercy of the propaganda that assails you at all sides, without some words of guidance and wisdom. Oh no, don't begin to laugh, I don't mean mine. There is one voice of great authority raised at home from time to time, which echoes far beyond Ireland's shores. And because this great personality speaks with extraordinary simplicity, and even humility, and says something like 'I know my words will have no influence on the course of events', his voice is all the more impressive. I'm sure that you know by now whom I mean: Cardinal MacRory.[11]

Here is a man who, being no politician, is not bound by the restrictions of a politician in a neutral country. A man who has obviously no other aims than the temporal and spiritual happiness of his flock, that is to say, of the whole people of Ireland. We've many things to be thankful for at present, and a few to deplore. But one of our greatest blessings is that at the moment of this great crisis in our history, we've also been given such a man as our spiritual leader. Cardinal MacRory uses no fine phrases, and obviously does not put much value on words at all. In a world of so many high-sounding phrases [...] he has remained for the most part silent. But on the few occasions when he has made a public pronouncement, his words by the very weight of sincerity and goodness behind them, have been carried far, far beyond the limits of his own fold. I think the Cardinal himself might be a little surprised to learn in what far lands and foreign languages some of his utterances have been read and pondered on. Here is a man who speaks only to his flock and does not presume to lay down the moral law to the rest of the world, for which reason, of course, the rest of the world is much more likely to listen.[12]

11. Cardinal Joseph MacRory, Catholic Primate of All Ireland. The tone and content of Stuart's praise of MacRory are reminiscent of his praise of de Valera in his 1935 essay.

12. Stuart may be referring to MacRory's anti-conscription stance. MacRory was openly nationalist, although it is difficult to judge the significance of Eduard Hempel's statement

Having begun to speak about Cardinal MacRory, it is more fitting than ever that I should keep this talk above the level of argument and denunciation. Indeed I try mostly to do so, though I think there are times when a little healthy denunciation is no harm. But there is something now more positive for us to think about. Those of you who have children growing up at home today will be the first to agree with me when I say that our aims be our future security from a foreign war, from unemployment, and from inner division. And this is similarly dependent on three things: first of all, a contented Europe, and not a Europe in which one group of nations enjoyed prosperity, so very unjustly distributed prosperity, at the expense of another group. Secondly, we must break from an alien social, cultural and financial system, which came to us from the great democracies and has been responsible for endless unhappiness. And lastly, we must have back once again that part of our soil and those of our people which are part of the whole nation. The first of these is out of our power to achieve, though we may help towards it indirectly. The last two, we can never rest until we accomplish.

18 November 1942

In giving these talks I always have a very concrete picture in my mind of you who may be listening. [...] I've learned that it is only thus by trying to keep a very definite and vivid picture of some of you whom I speak to before me that I can hope to say anything [...] When I think of you from here in Berlin tonight so peaceful and secure in your homes it seems to me impertinent for me to expect you to switch on the wireless to listen to more talk about security

---

to Berlin in May 1940 that 'the idea of possible German action for the return of Northern Ireland would now also find ready acceptance in nonradical nationalist circles, among others allegedly with the far seeing influential Irish Cardinal MacRory' (quoted in Fisk, *In Time of War*, p. 355).

through this war [...] I think of you tonight in those Belfast streets which I know so well and I want to be able to say a few words that would at least let you know that you [... have] not been forgotten amid the more sensational events in this conflict.

[...] We did not want this war nor did we have anything to do with the making of it, but now that it has come we've one great aim and that is that the end of it should not find part of our territory still torn from us. When I hear the vague and pseudo-idealist type of American and British statesmen [talk] about the setting up of European Councils and World Councils and heaven knows what, I'm not impressed. We have obviously nothing to hope for from such high-sounding inventions, no more than we had from the League of Nations. If these councils were ever set up they would concern themselves with enriching certain small nations at the expense of the former enemies of Britain and America. That in a nutshell would be the main activity of these so-called courts. When American troops landed on French territory in North Africa, a statement was issued to the effect that the Allies had no designs against the sovereignty of France in these territories. Without going into the value of this statement I only want to record the fact that when American troops landed in Northern Ireland naturally no such promise was given, but perhaps in the eyes of these statesmen France has more right to North Africa than we have to Northern Ireland [...]

I imagine how bitterly you smile over the propaganda that is being poured out through the propaganda machines of the great democracies, as their statesmen like to call the countries in which unemployment and starvation reached levels never known before in modern history.[13] When I say that you and your endurance have not been forgotten, I'm not speaking to you in my own name but also in the name of your fair countrymen in the Twenty-Six Counties. Remain steadfast as you are doing. I know well the great

13. This is presumably a reference to the Great Depression.

desire that keeps you true, that desire to have the lands and streets and fields you love once more recognised as part of a free Ireland. I have the same hope. [...]

2 December 1942

Tonight I'm going to speak about an event that may appear small in comparison with what is happening on the main front but one that concerns us very closely. It is a very good thing to turn our eyes sometimes from the vast battlefields of the world to our own small but urgent affairs. A few days ago news came of the sentencing of Hugh McAteer and two other members of the Irish Republican Army in Northern Ireland to long terms of imprisonment by a British court.[14]

When I began these talks I tried to make it clear that I was addressing them to no special section or party at all. I wanted to speak to any of you who would listen. I know well that there are some of you who have bitter feelings about these men and that there are at least a few of you perhaps [who] maybe feel some sort of hostility towards them because you think that the activities of them and their comrades threaten the peace and security that you and the rest of Ireland enjoy and value so much, and for that I certainly don't blame you [...] You want them to escape the horrors of war that they have done up to the present – but wait a minute.

Who must you thank for the fact that you in the Twenty-Six Counties have so far escaped these horrors of war? You know as well as I do that it is thanks to Pearse, Connolly and Casement, men who in their day were also looked on by some of their fellow countrymen as involving Ireland unnecessarily in bloodshed and danger. It is thanks also to the men of 1919 to '21, and thanks to men like Rory O'Connor, Liam Mellowes, Barrett and McKelvey,

14. Hugh McAteer was the head of the IRA's Northern Command.

the twentieth anniversary of whose execution we celebrate in a few days.[15] Yet these very men were, as I say, also looked on at the time by some Irishmen as dangerous disturbers of the peace; but now how differently we regard them. [...] Had it not been for these men there is not the slightest doubt that today, not the Six Counties only but the whole Thirty-Two would be involved in this war. We would have our harbours turned into naval bases, armament industries set up in our towns, and of course our towns and cities and ports would have been bombed, perhaps the whole country would have been a battlefield. These three members of the IRA sentenced for so-called high treason should also have Irishmen behind them in their fight for the return to us of the North. They belong to the same great tradition as the Irish soldiers of the past who made it possible for a part of our country to stay out of this war; and I say to any of you whom whilst agreeing with their aims may be inclined to blame them for not being more patient and waiting a bit: What would have happened if the others in the past had waited a bit? You know well what would have happened. This war would have found us still a part of Great Britain, or at least with our ports in British hands. As it were we only escaped this fate by a bare couple of years, which is not very much.

These men who have just been sentenced by a British court belong to the advance guard of our nation. Most of you who are listening to us have other work in the life of the community, but all of us are Irish with the same interests and the same goal in the end. McAteer and his comrades in a British prison, you on your farms or in your shops [...] The time is past when any of you [...] can look on these men without sympathy or understanding [...] The time is past for these small internal hostilities. We must stand firm in the face of all that threatens us as one people, and the

---

15. Rory O'Connor, Liam Mellowes, Richard Barrett and Joseph McKelvey were executed on 8 December 1922 in reprisal for the assassination of Seán Hales, a Free State major general and TD, on the previous day.

longer I am away from Ireland the clearer this becomes to me. Therefore tonight let us salute these three men, the latest […] to suffer for Irish unity.

16 December 1942

The wider this war spreads, the more territories become battle-fields, the more necessary it becomes for a small nation like our-selves to keep our own positive aims before our eyes. We do not believe that a negative policy of remaining out at all costs is enough. In these talks I put before you the things I believe to be the minimum on which we Irish can build our future. These three essentials are the end of partition, a break away from the system by which life is dominated by money, and a turning towards Europe. I see these three points as being largely dependent on one another and I believe that these and these alone are sufficient to make our island into one of the happiest lands on this earth. It is about the third of these three aims that I think it specially neces-sary to speak to you because it is the least understood at home – indeed at home it is very hard to see how completely we are dom-inated, as far as power and influence is concerned, by English and American outlooks.

I will tell you an experience of my own, or rather a series of experiences in the years before the war. It happened that I had to spend a large part of 1935 in London. Till then I knew very little of Germany or indeed of Europe at all – I spent a few months in Germany some years before that,[16] I had meant to go back but hadn't been able to – but now in London I kept having Germany and especially Hitler thrust at me in a very strange way. I could not go into a barber's without the fellow who cut my hair repeat-ing the latest gibe at the German leader. It was the same with

16. This is a reference to Stuart's travels in central Europe in 1921/2.

chance acquaintances, with men one spoke to in a pub, or waiters, hotel porters, cigarette-shop proprietors – everywhere I heard these jeers at Hitler, these jokes about the new Germany.

Like most Irishmen I have no use for secondhand opinions. My reaction to all this was to make me wonder what Hitler really was. Anyone who is the butt of these small city-made mentalities seemed to me to be probably someone of consequence. I began to find out something about Hitler and the new Germany and then of course I was completely fired by enthusiasm, for here was someone who was freeing life from the money standards that dominated it almost everywhere that I had ever been, not excluding my own country; here was someone who had the vision and courage to deny financiers, politicians and bankers the right to rule. Nor did the word dictator frighten me – I saw that as it was. Our lives were dominated by a group of financial dictators and it seemed to me at least preferable to be ruled by one man whose sincerity for the welfare of his people could not be doubted than by a gang whose only concern was the market price of various commodities in the world markets. I was under no illusion as to our position in Ireland; we might have a certain political freedom but very very little social freedom, and life in Ireland was largely based on money standards just as in England and America. When I returned home, however, I found that the whole cheap and miserable propaganda had spread there by way of the British press, of course. In Dublin barber's shops one heard the gibes and sneers that had been going round London a few months before. I'm ashamed to have to say this but it is only by facing the truth that it can once and for all be remedied.

One way to remedy it would be to cut off the import of English newspapers, but there is an even better way and that is to turn to the continent of Europe. I know there are going to be great difficulties in the way of this, some that I have not even the time to enumerate, far less to suggest how to overcome, in these short talks. As long as the main outside influence that comes to us comes from the gutters of London and Birmingham we shall never develop true social and cultural life. It is interesting that English statesmen are making a belated effort to patch up the wreck of their social life. They will probably later make a similar effort in regard to their cultural life, which, God knows, is in an equally hopeless condition, but that is not our business. What is our business is to take means in the future to protect the more impressionable members of our community from being continuously subjected to the propaganda of the two great English-speaking countries and being completely cut off from the rest of the world.

25 December 1942

[*G2: 'Broadcast picked up in the middle of a talk by Francis Stuart.'*] [...] As I walked here through the Berlin streets and saw people hurrying home with their last-minute Christmas trees, I thought of those Irishmen in the cells of Dartmoor[17] and tried to imagine what I should say to them if I knew by some miracle they could listen to this broadcast, or rather what you would wish me to say to them – for it is a question of the whole Irish nation and I believe that even those of you who at the time may have deplored the destruction and danger to civilian life resulting from their actions will now gladly join with the rest of us in this message for today.

Destruction and the loss of lives, even civilian lives, has become too common for us to look at it in quite the same way. Indeed the precaution that these men took to safeguard civilian lives during their campaign in England seems strangely pathetic in the light of after events. Yes, I try to imagine what our message to them would be, if even a few words, a sentence or two, could pen-

17. This appears to be a reference to IRA recruits imprisoned for their role in the 'S-plan', a campaign of sabotage in England that left several civilians dead in 1939.

etrate those walls. Strangely enough I think it would be nothing political, for men who have been through as much as they have leave politics behind; nor would it be religious, for I think at the moment Roosevelt and all the other democratic leaders have made us loathe the very sound of a public utterance which brings in religion. Our message would be very simple; I think it would be only something like this, to say to them: We do not forget you; when the other nations think of their men at the front we think of you; we can do nothing for you directly to help you but what we can and are doing is to make our aim the same as the one for which you fought, and please God we will achieve what you began.

I don't think I need apologise to any of you for devoting this short Christmas talk to a message to a comparative handful of our fellow countrymen who can never probably hear it, but I know well that there are many of you whose feelings today must be much the same as mine and if you had had a radio to speak over would have done what I have and I daresay less clumsily.

30 December 1942

Christmas is over and work begins again and wherever we are in Ireland or Germany there is the same natural feeling of regret, but there is also noticeable [here] that [...] energy and determination that all foreigners here remark on. I will tell you how I spent Christmas evening. I turned on Athlone on the radio; there was a Garda Siochána band playing hornpipes and jigs. You at home cannot imagine with what feelings we far away listen to these common tunes. They took away the taste of Mr Roosevelt's message to Mr Churchill, which I heard a little earlier. That piece of concentrated self-righteousness [...] was a worthy addition to the American President's utterances. It will stand beside 'Onward Christian Soldiers', 'American Crusaders' and all the rest; but as I say, our own homely tunes soon took the bad taste out of my mouth. I thought of Ireland and of all those I knew there, of the people in the cottages around my own little village of Laragh, of farmers, doctors, fellow writers, racehorse trainers, publicans, Civic Guards; I thought of friends in all these and many more callings and I saw how at this time and faced with this great world crisis we were all one. I do not say that any of you have to alter your own ideas about questions of government or national principles, just as I have no intention of altering mine, but at the moment we are a nation which will stand united. We are a nation gravely threatened with only one thing that concerns us, and that is the continued existence of that part of our island which we hold. We are a nation [...] with some of our territory overrun by foreign troops; we cannot afford the slightest appearance of disunion any more than can other nations today who are actually fighting on the battlefields, and I do not believe that there is any real disunion in your hearts. I do not attach any importance to the fact of the traitorous attitude taken by one or two Irishmen in public speeches some time ago; indeed the general reaction was a further proof of the essential solidarity of the country.[18]

And now let us turn for a moment to the coming year. Let me say at once that I have no startling prophecies to make; we must leave such further sensations to some of the democratic statesmen. I have no more idea when this war will end than you have; all I know is this, that the great nations of the European continent, Germany, France, Spain and most of the small ones, no more want American or British troops on European soil than we want them on Irish soil. Let these people stay in their own countries and look after their own affairs. That is the attitude of the average continental European and I think it is very much ours too.

I happened to see a party of American prisoners at a railway

---

18. Probably a reference to pro-Allied speeches by James Dillon, a Fine Gael TD who was forced to resign from the party in 1942 for his stance. A few other TDs spoke outside the Dáil against neutrality, but the policy had overwhelming political support; see Fisk, *In Time of War*, p. 169.

station the other day, a cheery, tough-looking lot. They did not seem to be regretting the fact that for them fighting the good fight was over. I daresay that I might have had a drink with any of them had we met in Chicago, but here they seemed terribly out of place and I could not help thinking sadly how the same crew, but complete with their rifles and bayonets, are swarming all over Antrim and five other Irish counties. This chance encounter gave me even a deeper sense of the closeness of the ties between Ireland and Germany than I had before, because whatever ideas one may have, ideas are a poor substitute for actual experience. I felt how European we Irish were and what foreigners most Americans are to us although they speak a language understood by us, at least with a little difficulty. As I say, we have no idea what the coming year will bring; but one thing I believe as this war drags on: we Irish will come closer and closer together. External partition may remain for a time but all internal [partition] will, and is, disappearing. And now the few of us here in Berlin want to join with all of you in Dublin, in Belfast, and all over Ireland in wishing for the continuance of peace in the Twenty-Six Counties and a final peace of the Thirty-Two Counties.

1 January 1943

[*G2: 'Just as Mr Stuart was announced the radio appeared to go off the air for two minutes. When next heard Mr Stuart was saying:'*] [...] I am only going to recall those events which concern us closely, which had a special significance for Ireland. This I will try to do in four or five brief pictures.

A grey cloudy day over Belfast Lough. Slowly past the Antrim coast steam transports camouflaged in streaks of blue, grey and green past the dark ruin of Shane O'Neill's castle and edge into the wharf almost under the shadow of Cave Hill. The latest Broadway and Hollywood melodies whine over the water. The conscripts from the culturist[?], money-mad American cities swarm ashore. They pack into lorries in their new uniforms and singing their metallic foreign-sounding songs they are driven off through the sad [...] haunted Ulster land.

Now another tune, this time from a battleship somewhere in the Atlantic. A few deck chairs in a sheltered corner; two men have just risen. The smaller and fatter extinguishes his cigar, the taller leans on his stick, the crowd of press men put away their note-books and disappear into the background behind a wall of berib-boned naval and military officers. They stand at attention while a band on the afterdeck plays 'Onward Christian Soldiers'. A look of self-righteousness settles on most of the faces. The fat pale face of the smaller of the two principal actors in this show flickers for a moment with a secret amusement. One or two of the less hard-ened press men look rather sick.[19]

A street in India. A brown-faced, dark-eyed crowd coming along it carrying banners and placards on which appear the names of Gandhi and others of their leaders in prison. The further end of the street is empty at first. Suddenly around the corner appear steel-helmeted troops who quickly spread out along the walls of the low houses on each side of the street and mount a couple of machine-guns. There are a few shouted orders, the line of Indians hesitate for a moment and then continue to walk forward. The machine-guns rattle and some of the brown-faced figures fall, some run down side streets but many stand quite still with their brown hands and thin brown wrists stretched upwards holding the banners high in the hot sunlit street. Others stoop and pick up the banners from the dead hands which still grasp them and once again they lift them up.

And now an early morning during summer in a Belfast street. A group are kneeling on the pavements under the walls of a

19. Churchill and Roosevelt met on a battleship off the coast of Newfoundland in August 1941 to sign the Atlantic Charter, a declaration of war aims and general rallying-cry.

prison; around them are passing buses, loaded carts and cars in the nearly streets. What a different kind of hymn this is to that other that had been blared out on the deck of a battleship two months before. Then there was the flash of the steel gun turrets, the walls of bemedalled uniforms, the flutter of two flags from the masts, but here none of the like which shows power. The power of endurance is within, it is hidden in the bowed bodies of those kneeling figures; their prayer goes on. A warder comes out and pins up a few lines of typed script on the big door of the wall. A few lines which tell that a young Irishman called Williams has just been hung.

The last picture is that of the great room of the Mansion House, London, and the time November. Mr Churchill speaking, he speaks of the news of North Africa and he is flushed with his first success.[20] And in the intoxication of his apparent success he speaks openly. There is only one sentence which need be repeated; it is this: 'What we have we hold.' It is greeted by a storm of applause [...]

That is all. I could go on recalling many other pictures from the past year; these are enough. I know what we have to do; even those of you who can do least can nevertheless remain faithful to that little group kneeling in the Belfast street, and in feeling at least you can ally yourself to that other group in an Indian street. We have an answer to Mr Churchill's challenge, 'What we have we hold.' The time has not yet come to give that answer. Meanwhile I wish you at home peace and happiness in the coming year; and [to] those of you in the Six Counties for whom such a wish would be empty, I wish you happiness not in peace but in endurance.

---

20. The tide of the war in North Africa turned in the favour of the Allies in the latter months of 1942, with Rommel's forces retreating from Egypt and Allied landings in Morocco and Algeria.

6 January 1943

As I have often said to you in these talks, we mustn't look upon this war simply as a disaster that has befallen the world, which we hope to escape as far as possible and after it return to our previous existence. For this war is in the nature of a world revolution and we must see to it that although we hope to escape its horrors we've also a share in its benefits. I do not believe that millions of men will have died simply that things may go on the same as they did before. We must never again return to conditions such as they were in the years before this war. The truth is that they were desperately bad and there's no good trying to hide that fact. When we look back at the position impartially and when we are not bound by loyalty to any particular political party but only loyalty to the whole nation, then surely it must strike us all that with all our natural resources we should have been able to provide for a comparatively small population, but in fact we could not do so. Some of you – the lucky ones – may never have realised how bad things really were. Others of you I know realised it only too well. It's only personal experience that makes one sure what sort of lives are being lived in any particular country. [...]

It so happened that on several occasions I had some experiences that brought vividly before me [the manner in which] many of my fellow countrymen were living. I have no time to tell you these in detail; some of them I would not like to speak of with so many others who are not Irish listening; but I do not think that these things should be hidden, although it makes me as an Irishman ashamed to have to speak of them. I will only tell you one [...]

One day five or six years ago I was walking along Molesworth Street, Dublin, when I met a friend who had been interned with me in Maryborough prison,[21] whom I had not seen for some time.

---

21. Stuart was interned in Maryborough during the Irish civil war.

A couple of years of unemployment had so changed him that I hardly knew him, but not only his clothes were in rags: there was also a change in his expression. His name is Larry Evans and I know he will not mind my telling it; there's certainly nothing for him to be ashamed of. It is for me and for those of us who were so long in realising how bad things were, who may feel ashamed.

Around his mouth were boils and sores. He opened his mouth to show me the same thing inside it. He told me what food he had been living on for the past month. Then I suddenly realized a very terrible thing: there was still famine in Ireland. Larry Evans, who had fought for his country, who had been in the Connaught Rangers from the time of the famous mutiny,[22] was suffering from the same symptoms as we read about those who went through the famine of 1848 experienced, and not only him but very many others right here under our noses in Dublin and in many more of our towns. I began to think very seriously about this whole position. Being no politician, I could not accept the argument that in modern industrial conditions such a state of affairs was inevitable and could only be remedied – if at all – very slowly and partially. This struck me merely as the echo of the argument used by those in control of the great world financial system, to which we were still in many ways linked.

I then saw that Germany and Italy had broken away from this system and that although Germany was not a wealthy country and had too little living space for her population,[23] yet in a few short years she had abolished this terrible thing – hunger – which was still lurking in Ireland. It was not my business, and still less is it now, to concern myself with the far worse state of affairs in the great financial powers England and America. They're beginning to

22. Two Irish companies of the Connaught Rangers mutinied in the Punjab in July 1920; they 'were influenced by service grievances as well as by indignation at coercion in Ireland'. See Bartlett and Jeffery, *A Military History of Ireland*, p. 399.

23. One of the tenets of Nazi ideology was the supposed need for *Lebensraum* – living space – in the East for the German people.

wake up to the fact, in England at least, that something must be done, and so we have the Beveridge report.[24] Personally I believe that the powers of big business and international finance are far too powerful in the democracies to let even such a half-hearted attempt as this make the slightest difference to them, but as I say, this has nothing to do with us. Luckily in Ireland the forces that bind us to the old system are not so strong; they can be broken and, if you wish it, will be broken. Once we are again a united nation we can turn towards the continent of Europe, where even outside of Germany and Italy people are everywhere realising that after this war want and hunger must never be allowed inside its borders and that whatever form of government they have, it must be one strong enough to protect them against the rule of money camouflaged as democracy.

13 January 1943

I wonder how many of you listened to Mr Roosevelt's address to Congress as relayed by the BBC, or perhaps read a report of it in the papers. It was as full of the same self-righteousness and pseudo-religion as ever. I have neither time nor inclination to go into it in detail. I will only look over one sentence. It is that in which Mr Roosevelt accused the Axis powers of breaking the Tenth Commandment and went on to the effect that the United Nations had the God-given task of punishing them for this, and ensuring that they had not the power to break this or any other Commandment in the future.

In every one of his utterances Mr Roosevelt dissembles more and more, one of those Pharisees so vividly described in the

---

24. The first Beveridge report, produced in November 1942 by an inderdepartmental civil service committee chaired by Sir William Beveridge, proposed a new universal social insurance scheme and also called for radical new policies on health, housing, education and employment for post-war Britain.

Gospels. These men who are always quoting the Lord and the prophets against their enemies, these whited sepulchres who pose in the public eyes as upholders of justice and religion on earth and yet are themselves rotten. I dread to think what would become of the world under the domination of Mr Roosevelt and company. There would be a rule of hypocrisy and Phariseeism such as would, to my mind, be far worse than any previous dark age in history. I believe that the principal cause of most wars arrives from this very Phariseeism, from a twisting of the truth. If the leaders of nations entering on a war would frankly and simply state the reasons for war, wars would not be so long or bitter as they are now because either it would be seen that the differences, if both had justice in them, could be settled, or else, if one side was obviously in the wrong, the people of that nation would, after a time, see it and the war would end. [...] When the people of a nation are told they are fighting to see that the Commandments are kept, there is obviously no hope of peace or understanding in the world.

As I said to you before, I never make myself the mouthpiece of official German views, indeed I don't suppose there has ever been an Irishman who has accepted all official views no matter whose they happen to be, but there is one German view that I recognise the truth of more and more clearly: it is that which declares that Mr Roosevelt is warmonger number one. As long as this kind of Phariseeism prevails there can never be peace in the world. For this reason I look on Mr Roosevelt as even more dangerous than Churchill, for on occasions Churchill can be truthful and natural, as when he said 'What we have we hold.' When we remember [the manner in which] much of what he refers to was got, we see that his statement is of course simply his expression of gangsterism. But such a gangster is not so dangerous or so hard to deal with as a Pharisee. The Axis leaders do not shout about the Commandments or religion or humanity. They have always had certain very concrete aims which they stick to. The peoples of their countries have too long and too deep a tradition of civilisation and religion in their blood to listen to a debasing of these things. Germany, Italy, France and Spain have given the Western world three quarters or more of its religion and culture, but the leaders of these nations do not find it necessary to set themselves up as champions of these things. That is reserved for the leader of the nation that has given the world three quarters of its motor-cars and little else. Not that I want to make gibes at America or the American people; it is easy to do that, but it is not constructive. If America has not yet added much to the real wealth of the world, that is probably because she is still too young a nation and also partially because money and the outward trappings of civilisation have become too important there.

Let us in Ireland be true to the great tradition behind us. I mean the tradition above all of taking some hold on truth in the midst of untruth and chaos. We did it in the Dark Ages and we must do it again. Over ten years ago I wrote a book called *Pigeon Irish* in which I foresaw the coming war and the part we would have to play in it, and although a few of the outward facts are different I still see our part very much as I saw it then. It is to keep to true and lasting values in the face of the war hysteria and diversion of truth and hypocrisy all around us. I believe that is exactly what you are doing. May you go on doing so till the end.

20 January 1943

The first thing I want to tell you tonight is the pride and thrill with which on Saturday evening we heard of the escape of the IRA men from a jail guarded by the whole might of the British and American war machine.[25] It was one of those exploits which stand out [...] and give heart to [...] a whole people. Such was the defence of the Alcazar and such too was the amazing exploits of

25. Hugh McAteer and three other IRA men broke out of Crumlin Road jail in Belfast.

the submarines at Scapa Flow.²⁶ I salute these men not only on my own behalf but on yours all over Ireland.

It can never too often be said that the main reason that this war is being fought by the democracies is defence of the great financial system on which the whole of their lives has become based. I believe that that will be the impartial verdict of history [...] [*G2: 'Remainder of talk useless owing to noise and fading.'*]

30 January 1943

In my last talk I spoke of the escape of the IRA men from Belfast Jail because I know that that made a very deep impression, but I ought to remind you that I'm no politician and I speak about what is most in my thoughts such as I would if you were neighbours who happened to drop in for a talk in the evening. Tonight and indeed for the past week there's been one main thought in most people's minds, and that is the men of the Sixth German Army at Stalingrad.²⁷ At first I had not meant to mention them in this talk: you might feel that it is a subject that has very little to do with Ireland, that there are more pressing things for me to speak about, and perhaps from a political or propagandist point of view that is true. But as I say, I care nothing for propaganda or politics in that sense. No one can be in Germany in the last few days without being deeply affected by what is happening in Stalingrad. I know you at home well enough to know how quick you are to respond to such things. It has always been in our nature to be comparatively unmoved by the qualities showing victory, but to be inspired

26. On 15 October 1939 the British ship *Royal Oak* was sunk by a German U-boat while docked in Scapa Flow in the Orkney Islands, with the loss of 834 men.

27. The Sixth Army attacking Stalingrad was encircled by counterattacking Soviet forces in November 1942; after lengthy efforts to extricate them, the Sixth Army surrendered on 2 February 1943. Their defeat was a foregone conclusion when Stuart made this broadcast, three days before the surrender.

by those who know how to fight a rearguard action against overwhelming odds. [...] been so degraded in this war that I do not
like to praise these men of the German Sixth Army. Besides, what
is praise coming from someone sitting comfortably [...] in front
of a microphone [...] I readily admit that when it comes to finding words, the publicists of the democracies can far outdo us.[28]
Only one thing I must say, the BBC [...] in its attempts to belittle the state of these men, says that if they were not defending their
own soil there was nothing heroic in their conduct. It was one of
the weakest attempts of the BBC that I've heard for a long time.
To the soldier, the ground that he is ordered to hold is his soil. The
soldier's outlook in this is a simple one and no subtleties of the
BBC can alter it. When an English army at war fights on to the
last man as the German Sixth Army is doing, then let BBC propagandists be contemptuous about the courage of its enemies. 'Tis
not that I want to belittle the courage of English soldiers – many
of them must have shown great endurance at Dunkirk and elsewhere – but I cannot say the same of their generals. But what the
men, officers and generals of the German Sixth Army are doing at
Stalingrad is altogether beyond the ordinary standards of bravery.
'Tis not something that one can set as a standard for the behaviour of other soldiers, however brave. But I'm not going to dwell
on it, I only want to give you a hint of what the German people
are thinking and feeling today. I am a foreigner, I cannot presume
to share fully in their emotions, but at the same time I cannot
remain unaffected by it. It is not that anyone talks much of this
topic, a word here and there; the Germans are not a demonstra-
tive people. But the feeling is there, it is in the air, and you too
would be affected by it if you were here. [...] [*G2: 'Remaining couple of sentences inaudible owing to noise; talk subject, throughout, to
interruptions and difficult to follow.'*]

28. Stuart's use of the word 'us' was not lost on the G2 officer who prepared a report on
Stuart's broadcasting dated 1 April 1943, noting that Stuart was 'more or less identifying
himself with pro-German propaganda'.

6 February 1943

On Wednesday morning the German people heard the last news from the small base of the Sixth Army still holding out at Stalingrad. The end was already very near, ammunition was almost all gone, most of those who still survived were wounded [...] The fight in Stalingrad was over. If I was a German I should be filled with the deepest pride; as it is, I am glad to be living among such people – glad to be here in a country that can produce such men, men who still can overcome all human limitations, and not one or two such only, but a whole army. Today is the third day of mourning here for the dead soldiers of the Sixth Army. I am not going to attempt to talk about them, mere words are useless; therefore I will turn to another subject.

If Ireland should grow up in closer contact with Europe, as I hope, then two things are necessary: a deeper understanding of Europe and especially of Germany, in Ireland, and on the other hand a wider knowledge of Ireland here in Germany, and these two things I am trying my best to bring about. I don't want you to think that my only efforts are speaking to you about Germany. Indeed you might well call me a poor patriot if that was so, and you might even accuse me of being a propagandist after all, but that is not so: although I speak to you every week for five or six minutes, and though some of these talks are about Germany, on the other hand I speak to a lecture room full of German students for an hour every week about Ireland. It is about these talks to the students of the Berlin University that I want to say a few words to you tonight, though I naturally feel a good deal of responsibility in trying to give these young Germans a picture of modern Ireland and I try to say only those things which I believe you who listen to these radio talks would agree to.

Among my listeners in the University there are always a few soldiers, either recovering from wounds or on leave from the eastern front, and to them, and them especially, do I speak. No one so well as they can appreciate the stories of our great soldiers of modern times, and only this week I spoke to them of Liam Lynch and of Cathal Brugha.[29] I also have something to say of some of our writers [... such as] Yeats and Synge and Patrick Pearse, for I believe that the spirit of a nation is best summed up in its soldiers and its poets and if these are understood then one has gone a long way to understanding the spirit of that nation. There is one aspect of the present situation that is followed with especially close interest by many young Germans, and that is of course the Six-County question. They see in it certain similarities with what happened here in Germany after Versailles, when large numbers of Germans and large tracts of German soil in the Saar, in Sudetenland, in Danzig and elsewhere, were cut off from the nation, and for this reason they feel a special sympathy for and interest in you Irish nationalists up in the Six Counties.

Before I end this talk I want your ear once again for a moment on what I spoke of in the beginning. I know that you at home will have no difficulty in understanding what the German people have been feeling during these days of mourning; at certain moments in our history the whole of Ireland too has been stirred by a wave of sorrow and pride. [... N]ot even great victories like the taking of Paris [have moved Germans so much], for those might have been accounted for by the superiority of the German war machine. This is an affair of human beings, a triumph of flesh and blood.

29. Liam Lynch was a leading Munster fighter in the Anglo-Irish war and on the anti-Treaty side of the civil war; he died of wounds received in action in 1923. Cathal Brugha was second-in-command at the South Dublin Union during the 1916 rising; IRA chief of staff 1917–19; Minister for Defence 1919–January 1922. He was killed in action on the anti-Treaty side early in the civil war.

13 February 1943

It is a good thing sometimes to turn away from the horrors and miseries of war and to dwell for a moment on the few good effects the war has had. As far as Ireland is concerned, there are several of these. To begin with [...] we are being forced to become self-supporting. I believe that this, quite apart from the war, is a very good thing. It is right and natural for a people like us, with our rich soil, to live on it; it binds us closer to it, makes us realise the preciousness of it and also does something towards giving back to country life and farming the value and importance it was losing to the modern mania of the towns and cities.

But I hope and believe that the war has had an even more important effect on us in Ireland than that, and that it is doing away with the inward partition amongst us that was even more disastrous than the outward border. That it must do if we are to survive this war and if we are to be fit to take our place in the new life of Europe afterwards. I look on Ireland from far away and I can see things clearly that are not so obvious when one is at home, and I see that of all the things that are necessary for our greatness as a nation and perhaps even for our very existence, unity is the first, I mean unity of heart and spirit among you all. I do not for a moment mean that we should all think alike: on all matters short of the life of the nation, the more different outlooks the better. When it is a question of Ireland, her freedom and unity, then we shall be, and I believe already to a large extent are, of one mind. In this we can afford no differences and no divergences from extreme and uncompromising nationalism, for it is only this great and united love of Ireland in the hearts of the Irish people that will save Ireland and bring her through all dangers. I believe that a nation passionately and self-sacrificingly loved by all her citizens is safe, whether that nation be large or small. Whenever in our history there has been this spontaneous unity among us, great things have been achieved, but it has been all too seldom.

We had it when the nation was united behind Parnell, but then came the split and all was lost. We had it again in the years 1919 to 1921, when the power of the English military machine in Ireland was broken, but then came 1922 and '23 and again it was lost; but now in this crisis we must have it and we must keep it. Some of you may be suspicious of any appeal for unity because in the past those appeals have too often been made by those who thought the best way of achieving unity was by compromise, by the most fiery and extreme amongst us toning down their national enthusiasm to the level of the majority, but this is certainly not my idea; on the contrary, it is more national spirit, more love of country we want, not less. I am not afraid of any disaster overtaking us because of the fiery spirits amongst us; if there were any large proportion of lukewarm people then we might be afraid. I do not ask you all to become outwardly ardent and active nationalists; for most of you the best way you can serve Ireland is by doing your own work as well as possible. What I say is that while you do this work remember sometimes that your own wives and families and the work itself is only safeguarded by the unwavering unity of you all as Irishmen. As I say, let us have divergences on all other matters, it doesn't matter much whether you believe in social credits[30] or in monarchies, in hurley or rugby football, whether you read the *Irish Times*, the *Irish Press*, or the *War News* or none of them, whether you speak Gaelic or only English or both, as long as you believe in Ireland above all these things and as long as your unity and brotherhood as Irishmen and women can never again be broken. When this is so and there is no longer any trace of inner partition amongst us, as I believe is beginning to happen, then the time is much nearer when outward partition will be swept away too.

30. A reference to the 'social credit' economics of Major C.H. Douglas. Stuart's denunciation of the global financial system suggests that he might have been amenable to Douglas's ideas, as was Ezra Pound, but there is no evidence that Stuart ever studied social credit or any other alternative economic model.

20 February 1943

When one begins to feel the first signs of spring in the air is the time, I think, when all exiles long to be back in Ireland most. It is just about this time when certain muddy little roads and wooded hills, and the few small fields that slope down to a lake, become so vivid in my thoughts that I [seem] at the moment to feel the peculiar soft air of home.

What partially reconciles me to not being there is the fact that it is only by my being here in Germany that I have this opportunity of speaking to you during these days of world crisis. And even if what I have to say is only a help to a few of you, that is enough. I am no great believer in numbers for the sake of numbers. Indeed I am suspicious of mass production in the human sphere as in the mechanical. That is why I do not believe that the sheer weight of numbers or even of machines, of which the American President is so fond of boasting, will be decisive in this war. [...]

I believe that there are at least a few of you listening to me because you feel that, in the whole mass of propaganda coming to you from the English-speaking countries, I as an Irishman have no axe to grind and will tell you the truth as far as I know. And because of this I feel a deep sense of responsibility and shall always avoid saying anything that I do not fully believe even though it would make a telling argument or be an easy score over the English or American publicists or statesmen.

In these weeks there has been one topic which you have probably been discussing at some length – I mean the situation on the eastern front. I daresay that you are capable of getting a pretty just appreciation of events unaffected by the only foreign newspapers that you see. There is no need to hide the fact that the German armies are fighting intense defensive actions and have fallen back on several parts of the front. The position is not disguised from the German people. For instance on Sunday evening the Russians announced the occupation of Rostov and in the German army communiqué this evacuation was given. The first news that the fighting had reached the outskirts of Kharkov came actually from the German High Command.

The German people have qualities of endurance and tenacity not yet realised by their enemies. It was thought that Germany was only capable of victories, but that is far from the truth; as Hitler himself wrote, any weakling can conquer, and went on to say that only in the face of adversity was the true spirit of a people tested. Nor does one here find the tendency to turn defeats into victory, an art in which the English publicists excel. The fact is being faced without illusion but also without despondency. The spirit of the German army shown at Stalingrad and also elsewhere at many unheard-of points has had the deepest effect on the people. But I have not the qualifications to speak in any detail about the military situation, which you can, in any case, hear discussed in other talks. What I wanted to say [is] that to us Irish it is Germany at this decisive and serious hour that it is almost easier to join with in spirit than at the great hours of victory. There may be some people whose enthusiasm for Germany was the enthusiasm that depended on rapid successes and sensational victories, but I think I can say in all sincerity that Ireland's sympathy and Ireland's friendship on the contrary increases at such times as these. We are a small nation, the friendship of our people cannot take any practical form, but at the same time I know many Germans who value it deeply and who marvel at us; surrounded as we are by the whole fury of the Anglo-Saxon propaganda we remain independent and unshaken.

6 March 1943

When I hear a report on the debate in the Dáil, as I did the other evening, on whether pubs should be open on Sundays at 1 or 1.30, I'm reminded more vividly than ever how peaceful life is in twenty-six counties of Ireland. I was making a joke over this item of news later with a couple of friends, a fellow Irishman and a German soldier. The Irishman said, 'Don't they realise at home that there's a war on?', but my German friend exclaimed, 'I'm glad they don't, it's a fine thing to think that [there is] at least one place in Europe from which the war is so far away.' To this soldier, who had been through the campaigns in France, Poland and Russia, peace was a precious thing, it was even a holy thing, and his feeling was not exceptional. It is these soldiers who had been through the most and were still ready to go through much more for the sake of peace, who value it most highly. This young lieutenant from the eastern front, with whom I sometimes have long talks about the problems of the day, said, Peace can only become real and permanent by everyone and every country in Europe doing something to contribute to it. There might then be total peace, like we now have total war.

How true this is. I wish that some of you from home could see as I did some parts of Europe over which the battles have been waged, and it appears what I saw was nothing to what my friend and his comrades have seen and experienced, but all the same I believe that most of you do really know how much you have to be thankful for and are ready and anxious to do all you can to help in the building of a lasting peace. It may not always be clear to you how you can help. I believe that Ireland can best help by setting an example of unity, peace and happiness within her own borders.

The more people that are happy and productive in Europe the less chance of war there is. It is [in] a nation's industrial, social, economic and moral chaos that there is danger to the peace of the world. Nations with a large percentage of unemployment, with a small dominating class of wealthy people, without any living culture of faith, these are the breeding places of war. We must never become like that. That is why I keep saying we must free ourselves from all traces of social and economic connection with the great financial powers. Let us in Ireland do all we can to show our gratitude for the peace that we have by making our small community into one in which there is no one without enough of the material necessities of life; and if any politician answers that that is impossible, I say to him, that is a dangerous and untrue thing to say. It reminds one of what the politicians of the great financial powers said before the war – now they daren't say so any more. We in Ireland must not wait until it is too late like they did. We must now make all the sacrifices, for building up peace and happiness, that other nations are being flogged to make for war. Let us on our own small scale do what we can to make the Twenty-Six Counties of Ireland one of the places in Europe where there is a chance of real peace for everyone; and that can only be done by giving everyone the chance to be productive in his own way.

The peace is really a matter of peace of mind and no one can have peace of mind who has not a feeling that he is of some use. That is why the whole system of the gold [standard] is a terrible one. Not only because that gold is inadequate but [...] because it is a degradation of the human spirit. The best way we can prepare for the peace that is coming is to lay the foundations of a lasting peace in our own lives and in our own community. I do not say that we have not already made a beginning, but we have still a long way to go. We have not only to improve the unity of our soil – and that is a hard task, and one which most of you cannot at the moment do anything about – but this other task, of making our social life happy and just, is one that all can even now share.

16 March 1943

[*G2: 'Broadcast not heard until 11.5 p.m. Francis Stuart speaking when picked up.'*] [...] Here in Germany, and in other parts of the Continent, cut off from our own country, we decided that this is not a time for sentiment and that you don't want us to talk about the harp, the shamrock, or the green fields of Erin. Indeed, we want to try to do something which is very seldom done and to speak a few words over the wireless which will be simple, sincere and from the heart. To begin with it should, of course, be you speaking to us, and not us to you. There is so much we would like to know that we cannot hear from newspapers or the speeches of politicians. How glad we would be if two or three of you from different parts of the country would tell us of what you are really thinking, what you fear and what your hopes are. Especially precious would be a few words from one of you Irish nationalists of the North. [...]

We know that in a sense we and you feel alike, we have shared with you all the anxieties, the hopes and the fears of the last years. Although we cannot talk things over with you, we know well what you felt when the first news of the American occupation of the Six Counties came through and during those terrible weeks when six men were condemned to death and later one hung in Belfast jail – we have shared all these emotions with you and we have shared the other events of this war which particularly affected our country. In all this we are one family, but if we know anything of home, tomorrow there will be many of you who for a few hours will forget everything in the excitement of a game of hurley, the first flat racing of the season, or whatever sporting event you may decide to celebrate the holiday by going to, and my God that is what we would like to be doing too, to forget this war and all the rest of it, at Croke Park, or Baldoyle, or wherever it may be. One day we will – one day we will have a great hurley match or a great race meeting to celebrate peace and hold it outside Belfast to celebrate the return of the Six Counties.

27 March 1943

The other day I spent some time looking through some old volumes of *Punch* dating from the latter half of the last century. At first I felt just a little guilty of wasting time in these days when there is so much to do, but it turned out not to be completely wasted time because it gave me a clearer glimpse of the outlook of those who have made England what she is. It was a political cartoon that I found especially interesting. There was a similarity about these which came from the fact that there was one figure that appeared in most of them. This was a tall, stately-looking woman dressed in something like a nightdress with a cord around the waist; she usually had a sword in her hand and a crown or tiara on her head. You have guessed of course that this figure represents Britannia. She was a heroine of these pictures, a lofty figure [...] The other characters in these cartoons represented foreign kings, emperors, soldiers, statesmen and others. They were shown as quarrelling [...] lying, waging war or rebellion; and always the figure of Britannia, calm and lofty, stepped between them and with a few words [of] righteous anger or calm wisdom restored peace and order. In one cartoon this was a priggish figure in white stepping between a ferocious Turk and a barbarous threatening Russian; in another she was in tears, having failed, it seemed, to reconcile a grotesque caricature of the German emperor and a French statesman. In another [...] she slightly raises her sword and an ape-like-looking creature with 'Fenianism' written on the [...] around his jacket slinks away into a ditch. In another she was majestically ordering the spectre of famine over India to retreat while a crowd of Indians were cowering in her shadow and touching the hem of her nightdress. In one she was calmly and bravely facing the menacing and brutal figure of Kruger, who appeared about to spring on her with a bestial snarl.

But I won't describe any more of these works of art; I only mention them because I think they reveal a great deal about English propaganda. It has not changed very much. The old-fashioned figure in the long white robe acting as a kind of angelic policewoman among a gang of murderers, thieves and other monsters, whether Irish, Turkish, German, Boer or Chinese, has simply been changed into a more modern figure. The central idea is, however, the same. British publicists still represent Britannia as a figure of lofty moral purpose and idealism who has been given the task of converting, correcting and punishing the evil world.

Well, it has taken a long time but at last the great part of this world has got sick of this stately woman in the white robe and has invented a rather vulgar but refreshing name for her. Nor are they more ready to be taken in by her more modern counterpart, the idealistic democrat. In fact they are thoroughly sick of the whole nasty business, though it took rather longer in most countries than it did us in Ireland. Lasting peace is not merely a matter of proper arrangement of frontiers; it is not even a matter of the equal distribution of the resources of the earth, though that has a lot to do with it. It is above all a matter of all people working together in friendship, recognising their common humanity, and no group trying to set themselves up as morally superior or as having some divine privilege to preach to the others. When all men feel these close human ties with all other men and when statesmen and publicists no longer try to make their people believe that the world was made for them alone, then there will be a chance of lasting peace. We in Ireland will never submit to any nation acting as international gangster and policeman or imposing its ideas on the rest of the world, and if that nation was Germany I would say the same. But it is not Germany who has ever attempted to do this, it has been England, and now it looks as if Mr Roosevelt intends to have a shot at it on behalf of America – but as I said, I think it is too late for this to happen again. The rest of the world is beginning to have ideas of its own.

10 April 1943

Tonight I'm going to say a few words about the coming elections. I have never in these talks taken any sides in party politics, and I'm certainly not going to do so now. As a matter of fact, until we are a free and united nation I don't see how we can have [...] party politics in Ireland, because there can only be one aim of any party, and that is the return of the Six Counties and independence of our whole island from foreign domination. If there is any party or any individual whose aim is less than this or different to this, then I hope and believe that you will show the true spirit of Ireland by rejecting these people. That must be, and I believe will be, the first consideration before you in the coming election. The second will, I think, be your desire to remain out of this war, and I share that desire with you. I've had a closer view than most of you have had of this war and I'm grateful for every day that we are spared from it; and whatever I say to you in these talks and in later talks in which I hope to speak more fully about the elections when the time comes, my aim will always be the same as most of my listeners' in these two ways.

I know well there are some of you whose views are more extreme and perhaps more logical. I know that this group, for whom I have the greatest regard, would say British and American troops occupied part of our country; therefore we should be at war with these powers. These Irishmen who hold this view are ready to suffer and die for it and have already proved this many times. But I, far away here in Germany, while honouring these men, am not advocating their policy. As I say, I've seen too many demolished towns and ruined homes. I want Ireland to remain out of this war as long as she honourably can.

That doesn't say that you should elect candidates who are going to take up a weak or compromising position. That indeed would have the very opposite result. [...] It is not my business to [...] in detail about who you will vote for, but, in general, I will only say that those who during the last years have shown themselves most determined to keep the Twenty-Six Counties of Ireland outside the influence of the great financial powers [...] are those best fitted to guide you through the rest of this world crisis.

We must not forget that an election confined to the Twenty-Six Counties cannot be the full and free expression of the people of Ireland [...] only a makeshift and not very satisfactory one at that. And secondly, I think that in voting you should also give special preference to those men who've shown themselves sincerely concerned for the welfare of the whole people of Ireland, and reject those who seem to look on the question of unemployment as a decree of destiny which is outside their power to do anything about. But above all don't think I am taking it on myself to try to dictate to you how to vote, I have no such idea. It is simply that the very fact of my having been at what I may call the centre of Europe during most of this war has given me a kind of bird's eye view of Ireland and events at home that may have a certain interest and value for you. I am far from Ireland and beyond the reach of all the opposing camps and party cries and I see clearly that in reality we have only need of one party, a party that stands for a free and united Ireland.

17 April 1943

A short time ago I listened to the report broadcast by the BBC of the proposal made by some official body or other in England for what is called 'The re-education of German youth after the war'. I doubt whether there is any other country in the world from which such a proposal could come quite seriously and with an obvious sense of the fulfilment of a moral duty. A very queer people, these English; listening to them one doesn't know sometimes whether to laugh or despair, but the idea made me think. I know something about both the youth of England, where I myself spent some years at a public school,[31] and the youth of Germany [...] From these reflections I went on to imagine that the war had ended [in Ger-

31. Stuart attended Rugby from 1916 to 1918.

many's favour] and [...] that I myself had been given the job of directing and re-educating the youth of England. Let me say at once that no one in Germany has any such ambitions for they do not share that sense of moral superiority which [...] England has. Continuing my daydreams, I began to plan how I should carry out my unenviable task [...] It seemed to me that one would have to start by undoing certain ideas which have been bred in them for generations and which have had the most disastrous effects on themselves and on the rest of the world. The first thing would be to make them get rid of what they look on as their high moral sense, this idea that they were the people best fitted to lay down the moral laws for the rest of the world; and that would, of course, mean a complete re-teaching of history to them, the history which would then look very different to them to the one they were accustomed to. The next task would be to get them to stop looking on money as, together with their own moral superiority, the most important thing in the world. This would, I think, be one of the hardest things of all, for to suggest to them that wealth gives no man or woman the slightest rights over any other man or woman, would be to them a kind of blasphemy. Then, after having disposed of this money god, one might begin on the more positive side, the re-educating of the youth of England. [*G2: 'Long passage inaudible owing to noise.*]

[...] one might even make them as interested in Shakespeare as the same German is. All this would be only a beginning, but at this point I lost interest in my daydreams and I saw that it was really a nightmare for which the thoughts of the very strange proposal that I heard on the BBC had been responsible.

8 May 1943

Tonight I want to say a few words to you about the coming elections in the Twenty-Six Counties. [...]

It is obvious that an election such as ours is going to cause a great deal of interest abroad. [...] It is no good believing that party [*i.e. Fine Gael*] protesting that they too have always advocated neutrality. [...] The small section that believe in a close co-operation between us and the great Atlantic powers should give Fine Gael their one vote. And the handful of Dáil members with this outlook are or have been members of this party. It is as well that this should be made quite clear. [...] Let me say though that I do not for a moment anticipate any [electoral] gains [for Fine Gael] but on the contrary I think that this party will dwindle into insignificance. [*G2: 'long inaudible passage'*]

The overwhelming majority of you are at one in your wish for a free and united country and as far as I know there isn't one who'd ever threaten this except a handful of so-called Irishmen either belonging to or in touch with the Fine Gael party. [*G2: 'Broadcast abandoned at this stage owing to noise.'*]

15 May 1943

Tonight I am going to speak to you my fellow Ulstermen in the Six Counties. I know that these are grave days for you. The new head of the puppet government is said to be contemplating conscription.[32] Whether Churchill will permit him to make such an attempt is, I think, very doubtful. It may well be, however, that the Northern government is becoming afraid of the growing strength of nationalism amongst you and wishes to precipitate the battle before your strength grows even greater. As we've all seen, there are men among you equal to the great Ulster leaders of old. They are lacking neither in courage nor in strategic ability, and I'm quite sure they will choose their own time and not be forced into

32. Sir Basil Brooke succeeded J.M. Andrews as Prime Minister of Northern Ireland on 28 April 1943. Conscription was never introduced in Northern Ireland.

anything against their judgement by any efforts on the part of Sir Basil Brooke and his colleagues.

But do not imagine that this is all I have to say to you on the subject. There still remains one very important point. If conscription is introduced and if any of you are forced into the British Army, even then all is by no means lost. It is just possible, though unlikely, that they will force you into their army, but it is quite impossible to make you fight their battles for them. They cannot make you fight for the continued occupation of your own corner of Ireland. For that is what, among other things, any military success for the British and American forces means. Therefore if the worst should come to the worst and any of you be conscripted and be sent to one of the battlefields, you have only to wait for a suitable opportunity and go over to the Germans. That has been proved to be not a very difficult thing to do in the latest form of warfare, where there are no very determined lines and where there is rapid movement. As I say, you have simply to submit to the training and all the rest and wait patiently until you are actually at the front and then, having arranged a suitable plan amongst your fellows, even if you happen to be only two or three who will probably be split up among different regiments, you can go over to the Germans or the Italians as the case may be. And I can promise you that you will be received as friends and well treated as soon as you've explained who you are. For the case of the Six Counties is well known here in Germany. It is true of course that you will be separated from your families and friends at home, but at least that is better than that you should get killed in fighting for the continuance of the enslavement of those families and friends under the government of Sir Basil Brooke. And I can say you will be treated with every consideration, both during the war and as long after it as you would have to remain away from your homes.

So far as this whole conscription business is concerned the position is quite clear. Your leaders will decide how far it is to be resisted. And even should they decide against open resistance at the moment, and should conscription be enforced, you still have the power to do as much harm [to] those who coerce you as by actual fighting in the streets of Belfast. And this you can do simply by not fighting at all. If the so-called Northern government think they can turn Ulster nationalists into British soldiers they will certainly be shown their mistake. The time is long past when they will find an Ulster division to fight and die for them as they did in their last war.

22 May 1943

[*G2: 'Beginning very noisy'*] [...] difficult to talk to you about it because I cannot help feeling that the few sober and few clear words that I can say cannot compete with the highly coloured phrases and exhortations of the professional publicists of the great financial powers. Indeed, when I hear or read some of the private propaganda issuing from the Anglo-Saxon stations and newspapers, I have a great wish to remain silent. When in the midst of all these references to freedom, humanity, civilisation and decency, what can I say? Well, I can only say what I myself sincerely believe, and that will sound very quiet and not nearly so idealistic as the speeches of the gentlemen I have referred to, but all the same I shall go on talking to you because I know that in the end fine phrases won't stand and what comes from the heart is what will be listened to, long after the huge propaganda machines have ceased to function. What would I doubt that there are some of you who listen to me in spite of the [...] far more high-sounding speeches that come to you from England and America, for when I speak of our own country I know that you will listen with interest.

Tonight I am going to say a few words about the war in general, and there is one thing which is very interesting and significant, and that is that this war has gradually developed into a war between Europe and a few great non-European powers. The English and

American publicists would like to deny this; they go to the greatest trouble to paint a picture of Europe longing for the hour when she will be freed by English and American troops. The truth, however, is very different. To begin with, what do you mean by Europe? You mean in the first place Germany, Italy, France and Spain. When we mention these four countries we have described Europe – not that I consider the smaller countries unimportant, but in a short talk I can only take the four outlined – and none of these countries wish for English or American domination of Europe. The people of these countries do not want to see an English or American soldier ever set foot on European soil. Even the French people who were dragged into this war on the side of England now feel that their destiny is bound up with that of the European continent and that the great European traditions to which they have contributed so much must be the basis of their future, and not the anti-European civilisation of the present England and America, for that is what it has come to. It has become a life-or-death struggle between the great European tradition and outlook and the new American and English outlook that is based on money.

There may be to the superficial observer much that is very attractive in these modern money states, whilst to those that can buy anything they want it can be certainly very pleasant for them. They do not say their type of civilization should be destroyed – perhaps an American wishes that America [would] produce something besides motor cars and skyscrapers, but when it attempts to dominate Europe then it will find every European [willing] to defend his own way of life. When Detroit and Pittsburgh are planning out bombers to destroy Nürnberg, Munich, Turin and other cities [...] our outlook and way of life makes it difficult for any European to feel neutral. Reading about these barbarians that are threatening Europe, they're trying to destroy something that they cannot understand, and whether we are actually in the battle or not, we must all feel, please God, they will never succeed.

29 May 1943

[*The G2 transcript begins with a garbled sentence referring to the question of 'what man should be officially responsible for the destiny of Twenty-Six Counties of Ireland during the very critical final phase of this war'.*]

[…] I say officially responsible, because, as every Irishman knows, the destiny of Ireland is not purely a matter of legislation but is very much to do with the state of the people. Therefore, even if these elections were to result in our most reactionary party getting into power, which however will certainly not be the case, it would not mean that Ireland as a nation would renounce her struggle towards unity and independence. It would simply mean that the struggle would become even more difficult and the ends be delayed.

Most of our politicians have made election speeches in which one might think that our existence as a nation depended on them remaining in power. That is certainly not so. The most that any political party can do is to remain faithful, in all their legislative activities, to the spirit of Irish nationalism, as […] suffered for through the centuries until today. They are not inventors of this spirit, they are not even the custodians, so to speak, of it, for you are that. The most that they can do is to see that the official policy of the Twenty-Six Counties, internal and external, does not contradict it. I say all this not to belittle our official leaders who have managed in spite of great difficulties to bring you all through the war till now without being involved, with the minimum discomfort. I am in a better position than most of you to know something of these difficulties. […] In many of your cottages over the length and breadth of our land, in Kerry and Galway, in Derry, Antrim and Wicklow, that spirit and that determination is as living and as strong as it ever was in the greatest moments of our history […]

And in all these cottages, in the small rooms of our towns and cities, live Irish men and women whose determination will remain completely unaffected by the result of the present elections. They are those who do more for Ireland […] than any politician can do. That may seem to some of you a strange statement, but I am convinced it is true […]

I believe in the destiny of the German people, of the Finnish people and our own people, the main three that come at once to mind. We have a great heritage, that heritage of an invincible spirit. You must value it as our greatest treasure […] and while I say no possible result in these elections can take that away from us, at the same time the elected men who value this heritage and [are] now ready to do what they can to acknowledge and preserve it, would be the very greatest benefit to Ireland at the present moment.

19 June 1943

[…] the longer the war lasts the clearer it becomes that the best way [any] one of us can ensure that the peace that comes after it will be a real and lasting one is by doing what we can to make our own little bit of Europe a place of peace and happiness – even if the place we can influence is no more than one small house and a few fields.

Thanks to the German government I have the privilege of speaking to you freely, which few people who are neither […] nor propagandists have today. I know the best way I can make use of this great privilege is not by vague and rosy promises and references to humanity and civilisation and so on, on the one hand, or hymns of hatred on the other. That I can leave to the publicists of the great financial powers. To us is to do all that we can [in order] that our small country enters a period of real peace after this war such as it has not had for a very long time – not since that almost legendary golden age in our history [... from] when St Kevin was in Glendalough to the death of St Laurence O'Toole. Let that be our aim, and if we can achieve it even in a small degree then we shall not only have achieved a great national triumph but we shall have done more for the building of the new Europe than we could in any other way. [...] If Mr Roosevelt would only act on this principle he would not have started a so-called crusade for saving the world but would have launched a far more realistic crusade at home to make America a country free of the worst horrors of unemployment, crime and [...] graft. In that way and in that way alone he would have done something towards the peace of the world. It will require a far greater president than Roosevelt to realise this very simple fact. [...]

What are the first conditions for bringing about this true and lasting peace within our own borders? I will try to answer that question in a few words. To begin with, we cannot hope to achieve the possibility of peace for all our people while some are cut off from the rest of the community and subjected to a foreign domination. [G2: 'Long indistinct passage']

The second condition is to see that none of the people living on our small island are in need of the necessities of life. That would be the primary task of any all-Ireland government and it is not necessary to say any more about it here. [G2: 'Further indistinct passage']

That is a subject that is impossible to go into in a short talk but there is one point that I will again insist on: it will be very difficult for us to make ourselves into a peaceful and happy community if we are to be surrounded by the English and American [...]

[The G2 transcript concludes with several incompletely transcribed sentences pursuing the theme of the necessity for Ireland to remain independent of Anglo-American influences.]

26 June 1943

The main topic of conversation this weekend at home will probably be the results of the election. I and a few other Irish here look forward to them with the greatest interest [...] But tonight I want to address a few words to any unionist in the North who by some chance may happen to be listening. To begin with, let me tell you I do not look upon you as enemies or with any hostility. No Irishman should be the enemy of any other, and if you are not Irish then I am not Irish myself, for I come of the same stock as you, I had the same upbringing in Antrim and share the same religion. People like yourselves were the companions and friends of my childhood. It is because I value the north-east corner of Ireland more than any other bit of earth that I wish it to return politically to the rest of Ireland.

[...] you know the people of it have nothing Anglo-Saxon in you. No doubt you know this very well. I do not suppose there is one of you who would like to be taken for English whether or not you may admire England and the Empire. I do not ask you to give up admiring England or the Empire. I've said over and over again in these talks, I do not wish to try and change the outlook, political, social or religious, of any Irishman – that is not my business. I only say to you, first be true to your own soil and blood and history and then think whatever opinions you like. You are Irish beyond any matter of opinion, and Ulster is Irish as much as Connacht or Munster. But I do not say that the people of Ulster have got the same outlook as the people of Connacht; on the contrary, once the whole of Ulster is once more part of Ireland, then anyone in Ulster who wishes to proclaim their admiration for England, or if they believe in cooperating with England or with any other country under the sun, would be perfectly justified in doing so; but while English troops occupy the Six Counties then anyone advocating this policy is a traitor to their own deepest tradition, to the very [...] even the soil under their feet. I do not ask you to become southern Irish, I do not ask you to become Catholics or IRA men or supporters of Fianna Fáil or pro-German or anything else. I do not ask you to become anything that you are not, I only say isn't it really time that you recognised that you are Irish [...]

Do you imagine that you are one of the anti-Axis nations? You know very well that you are not, you know quite well that Sir Basil Brooke is not taken seriously in London or Washington. General Smuts in South Africa or Mr Curtin of Australia have some weight in the Allied council[33] but Sir Basil Brooke has none. [...] Why, even Mr Benes and the leader of the Polish émigrés[34] are people of more importance in London than your Sir Basil Brooke, and not only in London but in the rest of the Empire. I'm quite certain and so are you that there are many Canadians, Australians and South Africans who have never heard of your prime minister.

[...] Before you can be of real help to any allies you must first stand on your own feet as Irishmen. If you had been part of Ireland at the beginning of this war there would have certainly been nothing to prevent any of you who wanted from going over to England and joining the British army [...] your attitude would have been respected [...] you would not have been the poor relation [...] you would have been free Irishmen [...]

33. Jan Christian Smuts began a second stint as prime minister of South Africa in September 1939 on a platform of immediate entry into the war. Smuts was close to Churchill and influenced Britain's African strategy. John Curtin, prime minister of Australia from October 1941 until his death in July 1945, was the head of the Australian Labour Party. Australia declared war on Japan separately from Britain, and during the war Curtin sought to achieve some autonomy as an Allied belligerent, rather than function as simply a subordinate dominion of the United Kingdom.

34. Eduard Benes was president of Czechoslovakia from 1935 until the Anglo-French capitulation to Hitler's demands over Czechoslovakia at Munich in September 1938, at which point he resigned. He then became the president-in-exile of the Czechs, first in France and then in England. After the war he was re-elected as president of Czechoslovakia; he resigned after the Communist coup of 1948. The leader of the provisional Polish government in London was General Wladislaw Sikorski, who was to die in September 1943.

17 July 1943

The battle of Sicily[35] is at its height; you may be interested in it. It may be that the battle raging in Russia will be claimed by history as the more important of the two but I have never attempted in these talks anything in the nature of military commentary and I have no qualifications for doing so except by that of natural common sense, which most of you listening to me have too. You are, I believe, well able to form you own judgement over all these military events having heard or read the experts on the different sides, but what is sometimes less easy to realise is the significance behind the battle.

In all the sensations of the last few days there is a very important aspect which has special importance. I will not call it the beginning of the American attempt to invade Europe, for that happened when United States troops landed in Northern Ireland, but it is the beginning of a powerful opposition to this American invasion. As long as these American troops were content to confine their aggression to our Six Counties they have had only to face the opposition of a handful of brave Irishmen, but now they are up against the might of the German and Italian armies. I believe it to have been one of the most significant days of this war in which American soldiers first set foot upon the continent of Europe; now has begun the [attack] of a money and machine civilisation on our old European civilisation in the building up of which Ireland took such a part. Now comes the attack of the civilisation of Detroit and Pittsburgh and Denver against the civilisation which had its beginnings in Rome, in Glendalough, in Salamanca and Nürnberg. Mr Roosevelt and all the propaganda machines of America and England cannot really hide this not very pretty fact, although I do not suppose for a moment there is much

---

35. Allied forces invaded Sicily on the night of 9–10 July.

good trying to argue against this British-American propaganda. Feelings are far too intense everywhere at this stage of the war for reasoned arguments to have much effect. Those who have the poison of Americanism in their blood, those who want to see the power of money dominate Europe, as it dominates America, are far beyond listening to arguments, but in speaking to you I do not have to use any arguments because I know pretty well what people here on the continent of Europe are thinking.

It is true that we Irish have many ties with the United States; it was a refuge for millions of our people in the worst days of our history. The Italian people also have ties with the United States and millions of Italians found a refuge there in their own bad times, but this does not for a moment obscure the real issue in the mind of any true Italian: they know that they are now fighting not only for the defence of Italy but for the defence of Europe and for the defence of a whole way of life. They are fighting for the small farmers that they may go on tilling their few fields and living happily in their small cottages with their wives and children without fear of their lands being bought up by huge combines and their cottages demolished, [of] great destructors towering unswervingly across the country, [of] themselves and their families tying their belongings on to an old cart and starting out down the road. They are fighting to prevent small shopkeepers and little traders from being ruined by chain stores and to defend Europe against gangsterism and graft and millions of unemployed and all the other things that are commonplaces under American civilisation – and do not believe this talk that the Italians cannot fight, or do not want to fight. The Italians may not be a military people, they may not be an industrial people, weapons and machines may be naturally strange to them, but the Italian regiments have already shown the greatest valour in this war, and when it comes to the defence of Italy and of Europe they are fighting and will continue to fight with valour surpassed by none.

I do not pretend to be able to change the hearts of the American soldiers, but I doubt very much whether any of them get much inspiration from thinking of themselves as crusaders. This attempt to invade Europe is simply an adventure for them [...] but the Italians are fighting for their homes [...] to live the lives they wish to live. They are fighting for Europe and incidentally for us too. There have been sneers and jeers at the Italians in England and America. There have been leaflets dropped over Rome, there have been messages from Roosevelt and Churchill to the Italian people, there have been attempts of flattery and bribery [...] but make no mistake about it, these Italian soldiers in Sicily and the west of Italy are good soldiers, far better soldiers than the American mercenaries, and wherever the failure comes in this immense struggle it is not going to be there.

24 July 1943

I believe that most of you who are listening to me are agreed long ago as to the advisability of Ireland remaining neutral in the present conflict. At the same time I think there are some among you who find it very difficult to simply look on whilst the troops of two foreign nations occupy Irish soil.

In spite of being cut off from you and so isolated from all real news from home, I am not blind to the fact that there have always been a few of you whom, as I say, believe that this is no time for us to be neutral, while other countries are fighting for their national integrity and freedom. I know that when you hear of the great Indian nationalist army being formed by Chandra Bose there are some of you who must feel very impatient while we appear to do nothing. I have never taken it upon myself to address this group of you at home; it is certainly not my place to do so. I have always looked upon you as those to whom our great tradition has been especially trusted and who know how to guard that tradition. But this much I must now say: in advocating neutrality I have never done so simply to be in agreement with the majority. I confess quite frankly that I have never been influenced by a majority, nor have I been influenced by any considerations of momentary policy. Indeed it would not have been difficult for me to have advocated a very different policy had I wished. But I have tried from the first to take all possible events and circumstances into consideration and to make up my mind quite independently what attitudes in this war would best serve not only our momentary interest but our future as a nation. [Our neutrality] in this war does not mean that we should remain in an attitude of indifference. This war is going to have vital effects on the future of Europe and on our future too.

While there may be some of you at home who think that I do not take a belligerent enough line in these talks, there are I daresay others who, as far as America is concerned anyhow, may think that I want to compromise our relations with one of our best friends amongst the nations. This last accusation would not be true. It was not we, it was the government of the United States, who made the continuance of these relations impossible when it ordered its troops into the Six Counties. If we were ready to sit down and condone their action we might very likely have come in for some words of praise from Mr Roosevelt, but what would have been thought of us among many of our fellow Irishmen in America? It is perfectly true that we should not lightly be ready to sacrifice the friendship of such a powerful neighbour as the United States, but does this friendship depend on the goodwill of Mr Roosevelt or on the ties between us and our own people in America? And these ties between the Irish in America and their motherland will only in the long run remain firm if the motherland herself remains true to her great traditions.

By our passive opposition to American policy in this war we may sacrifice a certain immediate popularity in that country. We may not be included amongst those small nations to be saved by Mr Roosevelt and his gang, but one thing is certain: in a few years there is going to come a reaction, both in England and America, to this war, to the whole policy behind it and to the whole hypocritical spirit in which it was waged. It will be a reaction even more violent than the one after the last war, that produced amongst other things a flood of pacifist literature. Roosevelt and his gang of warmongers are going to be swept into obscurity and discredited a good deal more thoroughly than even Wilson was. And [...] people in America and especially our own people in America are going to see very clearly that there was after all a great deal to be said for our neutrality.

Make no mistake, there will be many people then in the United States who will wish that they had never sent an American soldier to Northern Ireland or indeed to Europe at all. When they find out what the value of Mr Roosevelt's fine talk really is, as far as the living conditions of the ordinary American worker is concerned, there is going to be a very different outlook on the whole sorry business to what there is at this moment of war hysteria. I am far from saying, however, that we could calculate on all this. On the contrary, we should calculate on nothing but our own power of endurance as a nation. If we remain true to Ireland's great tradition during the present conflict we shall not lose any real friends by it. Do not be afraid of that. The only friends we will lose are friends not worth keeping, of which there are some in America and as many more in England. But in the long run we shall only gain by our refusal to be interested by the whole [...] which is raging in the Anglo-Saxon countries. A little more patience and endurance, especially for those of you in the North, and our place in the world will be securer than ever before.

14 August 1943

The enemies of Germany are making a supreme effort to overcome her. Encouraged by the retirement of Mussolini and the dissolution of the Fascist Party in Italy and the Sicilian campaign as well as events from the eastern front, their press and radio show they are fairly confident that victory is within their grasp.[36] It is certainly not my business to contradict them [...] All I want to do is to try to answer in a very general way the questions that I know must be in most of your minds. I am sure that many of you, and especially those of you in the North, are wondering whether things are really going so badly for Germany as the English, American and some neutral publicity is making out. Now, I can't go into military matters or make any prophecies about events in that sphere. Indeed I cannot, as I said, answer your questions in any detail, but a few words I want to say, because I believe it my duty to give you at home as true a picture as possible of the situation as it varies during the course of this war.

I believe that the increasing optimism in England and America at the present time, while being easily understood, is not justifiable. I do not think that things are going nearly so well for them as most of them, and perhaps even some of you, may be led to think. If it were so, I know of course very well, they would not make the slightest difference to you who listen to my talks. Your opposition to domination of the world by England and the United States is not formed by any desire to be on the winning side. It is an opposition that goes back to long before this war. Had there been no war it would have been there just the same. And furthermore, even if you were convinced of the probability of a German defeat, I know that your attitude would not change in the slightest, for we Irish are not of those people whose outlook changes with every favourable wind. While English or American

36. In late July, following the passage of a motion in the Fascist Grand Council critical of his leadership, Mussolini was dismissed as prime minister by King Vittoria Emanuele and put under arrest. A new government was formed under General Pietro Badoglio, who had led the Italian forces that crushed Ethiopia in 1936. Fascists who remained loyal to Mussolini would soon regroup to form the German-sponsored 'Salo Republic' in northern Italy, under the increasingly nominal leadership of the Duce, who was rescued from captivity by an SS commando unit on 12 September.

troops occupy part of our soil, we shall never lessen our opposition no matter what the course of outward events. Therefore, there is not the slightest reason for me to try to paint after events any different from what they are. Nor will I ever do so. If I were to think that things were now such as English publicists are representing them, well, I should simply not refer to them at all, but I do not by any means think so, and I do not want you to think so. I have not the slightest doubt that I can at any given time give you a far truer picture of the situation than you can get from most of the other sources available to you, which are unfortunately largely Anglo-Saxon sources of information. If you were in a position to hear all sides and see newspapers from the various belligerent countries, my task in these talks would be a far easier one, or at least it would be a different one to what it now is; but as long as English newspapers come into Ireland to the exclusion of all others, and as long as our own papers are dependent on English and American news-agencies, we here in Germany who speak to you must above all try to give you as much of the true situation as we can, and this is what I do and always shall do.

Just now Germany is passing through a difficult time; her western cities are being devastated from the air. No one who has not seen something of air-raids for themselves can really know what it is to have to endure such things. But endure they will. There is an immense power of endurance here, not only against air attacks but in all ways. It is easy to overlook this fact, especially for a foreigner, because this German endurance is quite a different thing from the English endurance. I do not deny that the English have endurance, in spite of the fact that they boast so loudly about it, but German endurance is much more strident. It is even accompanied by a certain amount of grumbling, rather like ours is, but it is something immense which I myself am only now beginning to fully realise. No, let us make no mistake, the present situation is not quite as it is seen in England and America. Let us wait a little before we form our opinions as to the course of events. Let us wait and remain confident in two things. First that English and American financial power will never again dominate the world, and secondly confidence in our own internal strength.

21 August 1943

[*The transcript begins with a number of incomplete sentences discussing the importance of understanding 'the deeper significance of the whole conflict'.*]

[…] The fact that we are neutral cannot be taken as meaning that whichever end this war has is a matter of indifference to us. […] A decisive victory for England and America would, I believe, mean [that] the last chance of winning the lost province in the North would greatly recede. It is fairly obvious to most of you but there is no harm in giving a few [facts] in support of this view [lest I be] accused of pro-German propaganda or baseless assertions. To begin with, we have the words of Mr Churchill himself: 'What we have we'll hold.' That is the false policy of the present English government and will certainly continue to be the policy of a government of a victorious England. Secondly, it stands to reason that having seen how vital [is] the Northern Irish state (doubtful those three words) in this war, a victorious England would not give them up. Thirdly, we have the precedent of the last war. The British government made promises to India, to the Arabs, and to ourselves which were never kept. Is it likely that, having this time made us no promises and received no co-operation from us, she [would] voluntarily give up the Six Counties? I could easily go on for the next half hour pointing out the reasons against any likelihood of a victorious English statesman saying to our representatives after this war, Here are the Six Counties, you can have them. I know no possible bargain we would be in a position to make as far as I can see […]

Let us be quite clear over this question. So much depends on it. And I know how all those of you up in the North realise this. Well, rest assured we realise it too.

[*The G2 transcript ends with a few incomplete sentences on the importance of Irish unity, followed by a reference to a 'long inaudible passage'.*]

28 August 1943

When this war began very few people outside Ireland believed that we would be able to remain neutral. Not only were we England's closest neighbour but we had the same currency. It seemed that England by her evil methods of financial pressure would be able to force us to give her all the help she needed. But much to everyone's surprise, except our own, and to the intense anger of the English politicians, we remained unaffected by propaganda and other pressure. It was largely to our advantage that we were an agricultural and self-supporting community and with little big business or industrialism through which England could try to coerce us. Wherever you find a great deal of money in private control you will almost certainly find a good deal of sympathy to the English outlook. [...]

Our whole life outlook is quite different to the Anglo-Saxon one. We have never been poisoned by commercialism and no Irishman in his heart of hearts has anything but a slight contempt for money. Nor are we a people easily moved by popular catchcries and publicised sentiment. We read the leading articles in even our own leading newspapers with as much scepticism as belief. Our opinions and our outlooks are formed neither by material ambitions nor by newspapers but in a quite different way, sometimes even in quite hidden ways which [are] hard to describe. I know that I myself as a boy was deeply affected by something in the Antrim landscape where I lived and I know that for many of you it has been the same. The fields, woods and villages where you grew up were the first and perhaps the strongest causes of your nationalism. This is the nationalism which is hard to undermine or pervert. It will withstand any amount of propaganda or financial pressure for it springs from the soil and it will remain as long as the soil remains and will see empires rise and fall.

It was only those that realised this that were prepared for our determined neutrality. You chose that neutrality and it has been kept scrupulously. I would like to point out here that there was a time after the fall of France in the summer of 1941 when that pledge of neutrality, given by those responsible for our policy at the beginning of the war, might have been broken. There was certainly not much then to have prevented us crossing the border and marching [...] [*G2: 'At this point Stuart was switched off the air and what seemed to be a programme of music from some other German station given instead. There was no formal closing of the Irish broadcast.'*]

4 September 1943

The war yesterday entered on its fifth year. We, almost alone of European countries, continue to live in a state very little different to that of peace. But that does not mean, as I am always saying, that the war is no concern of ours. On the contrary I think the longer it goes on the more our thoughts must be turning to the question of what will come after. One day it will come to a stop [...] and what then, you must often ask each other.

When you hear the views on this most vital of all questions which come from England and America you might well despair, for latterly the English and American publicists seem to have given up all pretence of a positive after-war programme and are more and more frankly admitting that they are simply out to destroy those peoples who stand in their way. And incidentally there is a message in their destruction. I believe that the devastation of Hamburg,[37] for instance, was carried out as much to eliminate what after the war would be once more a great rival centre of world trade than for any immediate results. The English and American politicians [are seeking] what they call the unconditional surrender of their enemies. It is illuminating to recall that when early in the war Herr Hitler gave his peace proposals he said nothing about unconditional surrender. It is obvious to a child that the unconditional surrender of those nations or indeed of any peoples imbued with national spirits is irreconcilable with lasting peace.

Let us examine this aim of England and America. The fact that they have not the power to accomplish it does not relieve them from the blame of cherishing it. Their aim apparently is keeping a hundred or so million people in Europe in a state of national subjection and ignominy, and in order to do this they must naturally have the agreement and support of their own people. That is to say many millions of people are to be kept in a state of dread and fear and hatred [...] so that the whole war mentality, with its semi-hysteria and wildest propaganda, would have to be kept going. And this will be called peace. This is the bankrupt notion of the peace that men like Churchill and Roosevelt think of entertaining. The fact is, of course, they do not know the first thing about peace, they're not interested in it, all they're really interested in is [...] victory for themselves and unconditional surrender for everyone else. I don't mind them for not seeing that this is impossible; that is simply their tactical error. But [...] as long as they have their few months of personal triumph their attitude is something more irresponsible and malicious than anything I can say can give you an idea of. If they had the power to accomplish their aims, which

37. Hamburg was devastated by seven days of Allied bombing in July–August 1942, during which incendiary bombs created firestorms that incinerated thousands of civilians.

thank God they have not, they would [...] be making quite certain of a third world war. But that wouldn't matter to them, they are both elderly men, as long as they win this second world war they won't worry very much over the third because they could probably postpone it to beyond their own lifetime.

No peace can be established on the basis of the unconditional surrender of any great and spirited people. That is my own greatest conviction and I want you to take special note of the fact that I am allowed to voice this personal opinion of my own from Germany. Would any speaker over the BBC be allowed to say it? I know very well he would not. The BBC has managed to create the illusion of free expression and of [...] tolerance. After listening to it for a long period I am forced to the conclusion that there is freedom in it for almost everything except the simple truth. The simple truth such as I have just expressed is something not permitted today in England or America. [*G2: 'The talk discontinued at this stage by the short-wave station but continued on the medium-wave band. Hopelessly indistinct on the medium waves.'*]

7 September 1943

[*The G2 transcript begins with a fragmentary sentence referring to 'the English landings on the mainland of Europe'.*]

[...] whatever the military consequences and developments, you may be sure of one thing: there will be an intensification of English and American propaganda, and you in Ireland, especially in the Six Counties, you are going to hear some of the most efficient propagandists in the world, for that is what they are, to justify the English and American invasion of Europe.

[*The transcript continues with several fragmentary sentences in which Stuart appears to be meditating on his role as an observer and com-*]

mentator on the war, and notes that he has been 'offered the opportunity of speaking to you in future twice a week'. There is then a 'very long inaudible passage'.]

The German people have a clear and sane idea of what they're fighting for. They are fighting for what they believe to be necessary for their own material existence as a nation. No one here has ever proclaimed as far as I know that they are fighting [...] in order to Christianise [England]. [...] And I certainly know by now the official viewpoint that these people are fighting [...] a holy war against the powers of evil represented by Germany and her allies. No, there is not the slightest chance for anyone to speak anywhere today with the least freedom, excepting here in Germany or perhaps from the broadcasting systems of some of her allies. From here one is not expected to adopt the righteous tone as though with one of the chosen people in a world of barbarians.

Now, [with] the landings in Italy, I clearly perceive that all this is going to get even worse. There is going to be less doubt in any Anglo-Saxon minds, at least in any official minds, as to the sanctity of their cause. More [...] are going to be blessed, there is going to be a lot more hymn-singing, and more distinguished people, many writers no doubt among them, are going to the microphone to tell their listeners what a blessing to humanity it is that there are such countries as England and the United States. Well, I've certainly no illusions that we can compete with all that, and I know that you don't need or expect to hear any attempt to contradict it all. All that is necessary for us is to quietly try to see the real significance of events as they happen and especially those that concern Ireland and their simple and true answers.

11 September 1943

English and American publicists have been triumphant over the events of the past week. But there are very few other peoples who feel like sharing their fun. The whole sorry business is not going to inspire anyone, even among their own people. We can be quite sure about one thing: the English defeat at Dunkirk is a far more inspiring thing to English people and their supporters than the English victory over Italy. At Dunkirk there was bravery and endurance, in Italy there was nothing but the law of [...] [*There follow two fragmentary sentences in which Stuart appears to be contrasting the respect with which neutrals viewed England in the early days of the war with the lower opinion held now.*] I am quite sure that even among the best of her own people, and among her supporters in the world, she will have lost all that she may have gained in the earlier days of the war. For her own people, and the neutrals, were waiting intensely as the hour drew near when English troops would be called upon [...] and land on the mainland of Europe. [...] it was a test which would give England the opportunity of revenging themselves and showing that their fighting spirit had not been undermined by the works of money and the social evil arising from that. It must have been a great hour for England, it must have wiped out not only Dunkirk but Malaya, Greece and even the Dardanelles.

And then what happened? The English leaders found a way out. By threats and bribes [...] with the Italian government to betray their allies. And when I say betrayed their allies I am not now referring to the Italian capitulation – that is a matter which I, as an Irishman, have no right to judge – but I am referring to the fact that they agreed to capitulate without telling their German allies until English troops under cover of this intrigue would be smuggled over to the Italian mainland. That would be the heroic way the English finally succeeded in putting foot on the continent of Europe. That was a miserable conclusion to these months of expectation.

The BBC announced that the surrender of Italy was a great day for the united nations. I think this is the most shameful day for England since the war began. These people have shown themselves very good at destroying some of the finest towns and cities of Europe. They have been bombed very thoroughly and well. In those ways they have shown themselves quite ruthless. […] But all that is not really what I meant to speak about when I began this talk. It is not our business. […] what is our business is to see that we learn this lesson well: there is no hope for any nation in the world today but their own national integrity and strength. Let no one deceive you on that point. A nation that loses its national integrity will lose everything. The most valuable people in any nation today are the nationalists. No matter what arguments may be used to the contrary, these people […] are a guarantee of the vital spirit of humanity. Thank God that in Ireland we are not lacking in this vital spirit and because of it we shall, I believe, overcome the trials which this war and whatever comes after this war may bring us, and emerge once more a great and united people.

14 September 1943

When will the war end? I'm sure that is a question often asked at home. Well, I'm certainly not going to try to answer it here, but there are a few facts that we must keep in mind in connection with this question. The official end of a war and the real end may be two very different things; that was the case with the last war, which officially ended in 1918. When did it end for us? That would be hard to say, but certainly not until a good few years later. The mere signing of peace does not necessarily bring about a world state of peace. I can at least say one thing quite certainly, that there will be no peace in our particular corner of Europe until you in the North are once again part of the Irish nation. I don't think there are many Irishmen who imagine they could solve the immense problems which have to be struggled with before lasting peace in Europe can be established; I certainly have no illusions on that point. I admit that there are many difficulties that seem to me insoluble, but I have no hesitation in saying that I have a good deal more idea of these problems than many of the politicians or responsible people in England or America seem to have. They know little or nothing about the real problems of Europe. In most cases they have never lived on the continent of Europe; if they have been on it at all, it has mostly been in large international resorts and cities. They have never been in any real touch with the ordinary peoples of Europe.

For the last four years they have received all their information from exiled politicians still waiting to play the old game of financial intrigue. I will only take one instance. There is Mr Benes, the leader of the Czech people. Incidentally, they include, in what they call the Czechs, people who are no more Czechs than I am. That is not the point. I had the opportunity of talking very frankly to several Czechs in the past few years, and whatever views they may have had on their own future, not one of them had the slightest belief in Mr Benes or desire to have him as their spokesman or leader. For them Benes belonged to a regime that was dead and could never, under any circumstances, be re-established; but the English and American politicians have not the slightest real interest in the Czechs, or in any other of the peoples of Europe. They simply wish to get those governments into power who will co-operate with them in their political and financial intrigues. It is this sickening old game all over again; all they want is the opportunity after this war to put their schemes into practice.

I, as an Irishman, have had opportunities to get to know something about the different peoples of Europe during this war such as very few other private individuals can have had. As an Irishman I have always been met with friendliness and frankness, whether it was in the former Poland, the former Czechoslovakia or other countries now under German administration. I naturally cannot in a broadcast repeat many of the things that were said to me confidentially, but this much I can say: in some of those places where one might have expected to find a good deal of turning towards England and America, there was a very sceptical attitude towards the great financial powers [...]

[...] there does not exist in England or America any conception of what the peace of Europe can be based on. The more they talk about peace the more obvious this becomes and the more obvious it also becomes that what they call peace is certainly not what we in Ireland are going to call it. If the war was to end with the partition of Ireland still in existence it would be for us only the beginning. I don't know whether it is part of their peace plans to hold on to Italy – to hold on to Sicily, I should say – but they just have the same right to it as to the Six Counties. But what their plans are is of no great importance; what [is important is] the determination with which they are resisted by the peoples concerned.

18 September 1943

[*G2: 'First few words missed'*] [...] nearly so much as does the fact that I must do all the talking and never hear anything from you. I know very well that most of you in Ireland are more interested in such things as the events of your own daily lives, in football, hurley, horse-racing, books and indeed perhaps even in your own work, than in politics or the European situation, and I think that is quite right. Any people that are really vital will find more to interest them in the life that goes on around them than in events that take place far away and which do not appear to concern them directly. I am very well aware that many of you on getting hold of the paper first turn to the sporting page, unless perhaps on those days when there has been something very sensational in the war news, and I also know very well that those of you of whom I'm speaking are just as good Irishmen as any others, but after four years of war you've become sick of it and want to forget it for a bit. Well, I thoroughly agree with you and I thank God [that] you, in the Twenty-Six Counties at least, can lead your own lives and forget about this war for most of the time. I feel that we owe that fact to an accident of fate or, if you like, a miracle.

The very fact that you can lead your own lives with a greater freedom than almost any other people in Europe imposes on us also a certain duty. We must do what we can to see that in the future in all countries people can lead their own lives in their own way, and that is the greatest and indeed perhaps the only real achievement of civilisation. The first thing that we can do about it is not to give expression to a lot of pious sentiments like the English and American politicians, but to work on our own small corner of the world. There is not nearly enough freedom, even in the Twenty-Six Counties of Ireland. There is freedom from war but not yet freedom from poverty. It is, as I say, a great thing that most of you can forget the war for most of the days, but it is a shocking thing that there are tens of thousands of you who can never for an hour forget the problem of money and how you are going to live and help your children to live. That is not my idea of peace.

You have got to realise two things: that the old pre-war money-dominated society was a rotten one, and [that] if this war doesn't destroy [it], it has been fought in vain. It may be that you and I have not suffered much personally under this system, it may be that we were lucky enough or clever enough to get hold of enough money to ensure our own personal freedom, but that doesn't give us the right to behave like the English and American politicians who have for twenty years consistently and callously ignored the sufferings of millions of their own people, simply because they, personally, were all right. These politicians believe in their hearts, although there are none of them dare say so, that those who have

not succeeded in getting money in the frantic commercial struggle for it, are in some way inferior and that it doesn't matter so
very much what happens to them. But here, on the continent of
Europe, there has never been any such idea and I believe in Ireland
such an idea never gained any real hold in spite of our close association with English and American civilisation.

[…] we must stand outside this war but we must not remain
unaffected by the revolution, and if this great revolution is successful, as I believe it will be, then it would mean that many more
people would be able to live their own lives in their own way; it
would mean for us Irish, not only that we become a united and
free nation, but also much more freedom for everyone within the
nation, for freedom is not just a political catch-cry, as it has been
made by propagandists, but is something so real for every one of
us that without it there can be no happiness and no peace.

25 September 1943

[*The transcript begins with several incomplete sentences stressing the
significance of the war for Ireland; Stuart states that 'In this coming
period our future will be decided.'*]

[…] We have seen great nations show themselves weak at the
moment of great crisis and we have seen other small nations rise
to great heights of endurance and of national heroism. France and
Italy started this war as two of the greatest armed forces in the
world, and today those armies are nonexistent. On the other hand
some comparatively small nations, like Finland and Roumania,
have shown an astonishing endurance in fighting spirit.[38]

---

38. Having lost territory to the USSR in 1940, Finland collaborated with Germany on
Operation Barbarossa, calling itself a 'comrade-in-arms' of Germany rather than an ally.
Romania functioned as a German puppet state during the war, and also joined in the Ger-
man invasion of the USSR.

India, which at the beginning of the war seemed hardly nearer her national independence than she has ever been, has come very perceptibly nearer to becoming a nation, while Burma, of which very little was formerly heard in Europe, has actually freed herself from foreign domination.[39] And what about Ireland? Whilst nations are rising and falling, how has our national status fared during this war? I think we can give a satisfactory answer to that question. The very fact of our neutrality has made our position much clearer in the world than it ever was before. The world now recognises the fact that we are not part of the British Empire. [...] this fact was quite clear before, but as far as most foreign countries were concerned it was actually by no means clear. The English point of view having much more publicity than ours, it was generally thought that we'd become a more or less contented member of the Commonwealth.

As I say, everyone now knows better. We Irish for the first time in modern history have been accepted as a free people determined to gain their full sovereignty over all their country. But it is not the purpose of this talk [to] congratulate ourselves on these facts. [*There follow a few fragmentary sentences invoking Irish history and ending with a reference to 'the men of 1916'.*] They re-started our fight for independence in latter days and in the middle of another war asserted Ireland's right to refuse to co-operate with England. What was done in 1916 has not yet borne its full fruit, but its significance can never have been so obvious as during these war years. Then we have the men of those years from 1919 on until the end of the civil war, men like Terence MacSwiney, Liam Mellowes, Cathal Brugha, Liam Lynch. Make no mistake about it, without these men and all the others you would not be rid[?] of this war today. Many of our towns would be devastated, many of our people slain on one battlefield or another; but that is not all, it is not

39. Burma, a British colony, was invaded in December 1941 by Japanese forces with the help of a Burmese nationalist army, and the British were expelled from the country in April 1942. The country was declared independent in August 1943.

simply for material advantages [...] it is above all the fact that we are a nation.

28 September 1943

I have not been in Ireland for over three and a half years and I am sometimes afraid that I am in danger of becoming as out of touch with the changing outlook at home as the emigrant politicians in England and America are with their own countries. And if I was to take seriously what writers of articles in the more exclusive weeklies have been saying about Ireland and especially about what they called the new outlook of the youth of Ireland, I would begin to wonder whether there was any use in speaking to you at all. But I know very well that in essentials neither your mien nor [your] outlook has changed since I was at home. [...]

[*There follows a long fragmentary passage discussing the evolution of Irish attitudes towards the war.*]

I do not believe for a moment in this new mentality that certain English observers try to attribute to [the Irish]. I am sure that there is a new outlook because none of us could have gone through four years of war without a change of outlook. But it is not [what] the English writers would like us to believe. There is, I think, a greater sense of realism in Ireland today [...] You have seen smaller nations like those of South America who were by financial pressure forced into declaring war on Germany and her allies, and then you have heard glowing accounts from the Anglo-American press of how even these nations have freely joined the crusade against barbarism.[40] You have seen [bombing of cities] described as being

---

40. Following the Japanese attack on Pearl Harbor, which precipitated the entry of the US into the Pacific war and Germany's subsequent declaration of war against the US, the

nothing but attacks on military objectives. You have heard of English bishops blessing bombing aeroplanes. [...] You have read and heard enough lies in the last four years to understand the meaning of this glorious fight for freedom and humanity, to ever want to hear the words 'freedom' and 'humanity' again. [...] it is not unlikely that there may have been a certain change of outlook in Ireland but it [is] of a very different kind to the one written of in the English weeklies. I have no doubt that by now it has become clear to almost all of you that this war is being waged by the big financial powers for one object, and one object alone, to keep their position in the world as great financial powers. [...]

There were only three nations who could have seriously threatened this Anglo-American money power in the world. These were, of course, Germany, Japan and Russia. [...] but what I am quite certain of is that the youth of Ireland have long ago seen through the whole empty sham of the Anglo-American attempt to pose as world saviours and world liberators. [...] Let us [...] cling to our own simple aim of an Ireland without partition and without poverty.

2 October 1943

There are many different ways of looking at this war. [Some people view it] purely from the military point of view and the question of strategy and armaments. To them it is simply a question of great armies ranged against each other on the different battlefields, and its course may be followed with the aid of maps and lines drawn on them [...]

But there is another aspect of the war which cannot be followed by moving pins on maps, I mean the war as it affects millions of people all over the world. It is too soon yet to say what the

---

countries of Latin America – with the exception of Argentina and Chile – broke off relations with the Axis countries and eventually became belligerents on the Allied side. Several countries effectively became US protectorates, and received financial assistance in recompense.

effect of this war is going to be on the world and civilization in general; it is certainly going to be very great, and nowhere is that realised more than here in Germany and especially among the soldiers at the front. After having had many talks with a German officer while he was convalescent from wounds received at the eastern front, I learned much about the outlook of the more thoughtful among the German soldiers; and here I must say that what I call the more thoughtful ones are the majority, not the minority, in the German army.

[... When they] talk about the bomb-pitted cities and the villages where they are billeted all along the eastern front, it is interesting and gives some idea of what is really going on, for as I said, it is not only the movement of troops that is important but also the outlook of those people who, because of their vitality and intelligence, are going to play a big part in the time which is coming. To me, it is of far more interest to hear the opinion of these soldiers back from the front than to listen to the latest pronouncements of Mr Roosevelt or Mr Churchill. What Mr Roosevelt and Mr Churchill have to say about the war and the future of the world is stale and dead. It is the same old stuff the politicians go on serving up generation after generation with a mixture of insincerity and hypocrisy. Whether there is any large public in their respective countries that still believe in it, I don't know; very likely there is, but whatever Mr Churchill and Mr Roosevelt are, they are astute enough not to go on talking in a way that even the majority of their own people have long [ago seen through].

The world after this war is not going to be greatly affected by the politicians of the great financial powers or even by those people in their own countries who still believe in them. All that mixture of sham idealism and money-worship is not going to survive very long; there is a new stage coming, a new outlook after four years of war which has no use for empty phrases or sentiment, false righteousness and all the other stock-in-trade of the old-time politicians. On a long train journey at night a short time ago I had

for a companion a young German soldier who spoke of his experiences at the front, not of the events which he had gone through,
but of what he himself had felt, of the faith that had sustained him
through all the worst dangers and hardships. What was this faith,
I cannot really tell you, I don't even think I need try to tell you –
it is something not unknown in Ireland. It is not so very different
from what gave us the power to carry on our own struggle in the
face of the greatest difficulties. It is a faith in the future, not based
on catch-cries but on something far deeper and surer; those that
had it never used fine phrases. As we travelled through the night,
which incidentally was once lit up by shells from the anti-aircraft
guns as we passed through an air-raid, I knew which of them I put
my trust in, this young German soldier or Mr Roosevelt. I knew
which of them was thinking of real and vital things and which of
them was going on uttering the same old stale nonsense; and I
believe you at home know the difference too and that when you
discuss the war and the future of the world your ideas are much
more like my companion's than like Mr Churchill's or Mr Roosevelt's. It is these ideals of ours, this new outlook, that has got to
have a chance, and it will have a chance. It is not only in Germany
that the people have seen through the kind of world that Roosevelt and Churchill stand for. All over Europe the people are
turning away from the old shams and looking for something simpler and truer.

5 October 1943

Before beginning my talk I want to send my love and best wishes
to Anne[41] for her birthday tomorrow. [*G2: 'The remainder of the
broadcast was so marred and distorted by noise as to render it impossible to reproduce it'*]

41. Unidentified.

9 October 1943

Tonight I want to speak to those of my fellow Ulstermen who may be feeling dispirited and disappointed. It must seem to you sometimes that you will never see the day when the last English and American soldier leaves the Six Counties. [...] We hear of [...] the declaration of independence in the Philippines,[42] we hear of the army which Bose is raising to fight for Indian independence, but you do not seem to see the day of your own return to a united Ireland coming any nearer. I am very well aware of your disappointment, impatience and anxiety, indeed I sometimes feel it too, but not for long, for I still believe as firmly as ever that final peace will not be established without the whole of Ulster being part of a free Irish republic.

This is not just a pleasant dream on my part, it is not just easy optimism to fill up one of my talks. It is a conviction based on much thinking of what is likely to happen after this war and what sort of world is likely to arise. Of course I am positively aware that the post-war world controlled by men like Mr Roosevelt and Mr Churchill will not be one in which there will be much hope for us. I am not among those who think we could gain what we want by negotiating with these people, but it is extremely unlikely that either Roosevelt or Churchill will survive into the post-war world.

I don't say, and have never suggested, that we are going to get all we want and all that is necessary to our future security and happiness just by asking for it. We cannot expect to sit back and have all that we have been robbed of handed back to us; but I need hardly say that to you, you know it well already. The men who are now in Belfast and Derry jail are a proof, if any proof is wanted, that Ulster nationalism is as living as it ever was, and not only the

42. In 1943 the occupying Japanese set up a native government in the Philippines, which had been a self-governing 'commonwealth' under US suzerainty before the war.

men in jail but those whom the combined efforts of the English and American forces have not been able to put in jail. Very little may be heard of these men just now in the war news of the world, where the Philippines, India and other nations in their struggle for freedom may appear to be having more success, and we delight in that success, but your time is coming too. How it will come [...] I am not going to try to prophesise, but I want to remind you of this from time to time; I know well how isolated you must feel, cut off as you are from the rest of Ireland and cut off from Europe. There you are in the very centre of the Anglo-Saxon armed camp, hearing nothing but tales of Anglo-American achievements and seeing the constant parade of Anglo-American armed force – you are the most isolated group in the world. While I do not for a moment think you are in need of any words of mine to tell you that all this apparent might is by no means invincible, your own national spirit, your own simple love of your own fields and hills, is stronger than it and in the end will outlast it. The English and Americans are there because they are paid to be there, but you are there because you could not live happily anywhere else.

Mr Roosevelt and Mr Churchill have sent their troops to our corner of Ireland, and while Chicago and Manchester corner boys, who I daresay did not know the difference between Ulster and Uruguay, are overrunning our country, many of those who love it and know every mountain, every little town and lough in it, are in prison. But this war is not only being decided on the battlefields of Europe; in a less sensational way it is also being decided in the prisons and on the hills of the Six Counties, for the determination and endurance of these Irishmen is also playing its part; and even you ordinary people of the Six Counties in your homes can have an important part in deciding what sort of world comes after this war. It is not necessary for you to do anything more at present than to keep yourselves from being for a moment influenced by all the apparent might of England and America. As long as you remain true in your minds and hearts, that is a great thing. You are our bridgehead, you are our forts behind enemy lines. It is only when peace comes that the importance of the part you are playing will be clearly realised.

12 October 1943

Tonight I will speak to you about the Irish prisoners in Dartmoor and other English jails. These men you may consider the first casualties of this war. They had declared war on England several months before the outbreak of this world war, and no country has had a better reason for fighting than they had.[43] It was well realised here in Germany [... which had acted] to protect her own people who had been maltreated by the Poles and to bring back the German city of Danzig to Germany.

That handful of Irishmen started their campaign in England to bring to an end the persecution of Irish nationalists in the Six Counties and to bring the Six Counties back to Ireland. Their aim was very similar. Their action was an amazingly brave one. They did not engage you in war. They carried on their campaign in the heart of England. [...] It may be that we as a nation had not been prepared to stand behind them and give them our sole support. It may also be that many of you believed, and may still believe, that they were mistaken. Well, I am certainly not going to argue about that or to try to convince you to the contrary. Since those days [...] so much has happened in the world that I do not think that many Irishmen, no matter what their personal opinions may be about the best way of regaining our lost territory, will feel anything but pride in these men. We have seen the Anglo-American air forces devastate some of the finest towns of Europe, killing thousands of civilians in the process, and we have heard Mr Roosevelt call this a part of his crusade. Well, I am certainly not going to use the

43. See n. 17.

word 'crusade' after Mr Roosevelt has used it, because he has made it dirty. [...] these Irishmen in their lonely campaign in England in the early days of 1939 were fighting for something far more worth fighting for than the English and American armies have any conception of. Now they have been for years in English convict prisons [...]

These men do not ask for our sympathies; they do not need sympathy. What they need is that we stand behind them and recognise them, even at this late hour, as having fought on behalf of Ireland, bravely and truly. The enemy soldiers who are captured or the enemy fliers shot down over England are sent to prisoner-of-war camps. The fellow-Irishmen of ours, soldiers of the republic, are shut up with thieves and cut-throats who set on them. It may be true to say that we in Ireland have one ground of quarrel with England – partition. If a gangster were to kidnap one of our children it might be strictly true to say that we have only one ground of quarrel with the gangster. [...] We shall not hide the real difference existing between us and England in this manner, and one of the most outstanding and vital of those differences is the fact that Irishmen and women are suffering in English prisons [...] with no contact with their homes in Ireland, [forced] to wear convict clothes and having to withstand all the ingenuity of a system designed to break their spirits. I would willingly forgo speaking to you at home if I could speak for a few minutes to these men and women – you have no very urgent need of my words, but I could certainly be of some help to them in their obscure and silent struggle. [I hope] that you remember them and, I think I may say, not only remember them but [make] up your minds to recognise that no peace is final until they once more were free.

16 October 1943

In speaking to you in Ireland I have always tried to avoid all politics. By that I mean I have only tried to see how we, as a people, might come out of this war with the possibility of a happier and securer life than before. I have no interest whatsoever in power politics and intrigues of statesmen, no matter to what nation they may belong. I have the greatest suspicion and dislike of all politicians, and so far as I come under their notice at all they have the same suspicion and dislike for me. [...]

I came here to Germany in 1940 because I saw it was essential that at least one or two Irishmen should be here in Germany while there were thousands in England and America, but I am certainly not sorry that I came. Here from Germany I can say what no Irishman would be allowed to say anywhere else, neither in England, America, nor in Ireland itself. I can speak to you here from Germany[44] and tell you the truth about this war, and I shall go on doing so as long as the hospitality of the German wireless is given me, even though there may be a group at home who would do whatever they can to stop me speaking to you and to impute to me motives of personal gain or ambition. If ever the position was so altered that you were no longer flooded with English newspapers, English and American broadcasts; if our own newspapers were to give up publishing the hours of the BBC programmes or were to publish as well as these the hours of Continental broadcasts in English; then I would gladly give up speaking to you. For I have no special love of broadcasting. I am neither a professional propagandist nor a professional politician, but as long as I feel subjected to all that the Anglo-American propagandists can do to

44. David O'Donoghue has noted that Stuart here asserts four time in three sentences that he is in Germany, whereas we know that the Irland-Redaktion had been broadcasting from Luxembourg since August due to bomb damage suffered by the Rundfunkhaus in Berlin. See O'Donoghue, *Hitler's Irish Voices*, p. 132.

make you believe that Anglo-American imperialism will create a
world in which you will be happy and secure, then I feel that I
must avail myself of the opportunity I have of putting another
point of view before you. Not that, as I have often said, I believe
for a moment that most of you are at all likely to be taken in by
this Anglo-Saxon propaganda. I know very well that you are not,
but all the same it may sometimes be an encouragement, even to
the most staunch of you, to be able to turn on the wireless and
hear someone of your own, speaking the language which you
understand and saying the very things that you in your hearts have
been thinking or even saying the evening before.

Sometimes in the evenings here I think of so many little Irish
villages which I know and I wish so much to be in any one of
them. To be sitting there in a cottage and listening to what some
of you had to say about this whole business. What a relief that
would be, to hear you talk for a bit, and I myself not to have to
say anything. Well, that time will come, please God, and meanwhile I hope that some of you will sometimes of an evening say to
yourselves or each other, 'Well, he hasn't so very much to say but
at least he seems to believe what he says and he isn't just another
of these damned English and American politicians.'

19 October 1943

As I sat down to write this stuff to you this afternoon it was a
rainy, awful day here in Germany, and at times instead of writing
I began to think of what it was like at home. I was in the Wicklow mountains, in Meath and the Antrim hills, and for a few
moments I wished I was there and not here. I wished I was there
at home with only my own work to do and that I could forget the
war. But that was not for long.

[...] now is the time when it is impossible to keep silence.
There is a huge army of writers and public speakers, of journalists

and broadcasters, in England and America, to say nothing of Australia, Canada, New Zealand and other parts of the earth, who are using the English language to try to convince the world that this war is a British and American crusade for liberty, humanity and idealism against the forces of aggression and barbarism. I do not flatter myself that I can do very much against this, but the little I can do I will do. And now I am speaking not only as an Irishman but as a member of that human race which Messrs Churchill and Roosevelt are so keen on saving, and I say what thousands and millions of others would say too, all over the world, if they had the power of expressing themselves and the opportunity of doing so. They would say that they don't want this sham idealism and this pseudo-freedom which Churchill and Roosevelt's army of publicists are forever promising them. There are millions of people in the world today who want one thing from England and America, and that is to be left alone. That is what the people of India want, the people of Burma, of the Philippines, of Iceland, of the Azores, most of the peoples of South America, the Liberian Negroes, the Arabs of Palestine, the peoples of Iran and Iraq, not to speak of our own people in the Six Counties. All these people, with others that I have not mentioned, form a very considerable part of the population of the earth and none of them, curiously enough, are interested in being saved, liberated or protected by the English and American crusaders; and all that the army of writers, journalists, broadcasters in England and America can do will not convince them that an Anglo-American victory is their only chance of peace and happiness. I am no prophet and I do not pretend to know what would be a perfect solution for all the social and national problems and difficulties that exist in the world. One thing I do know, and that is that men like Churchill and Roosevelt and their advisers are the last men on earth capable of dealing with these problems and difficulties.

I dare say the same [thought] has crossed your mind as the one I am going to stress. If a committee of six average Irishmen, let us say a farmer or two, a National University student, a Civic Guard and an IRA man, were formed into a committee with sovereign powers to settle all the present problems of the world, they would make a far better job of it than Churchill, Roosevelt and company. The reason is, of course, that they would be sincere and disinterested, however badly informed they might be in certain cases, whereas Churchill and Roosevelt [...] have no interest whatever in anything but making as many millions of people as possible bow down before the pound or the dollar. [...] Irishmen have already shown that they will speak out, even if they have to hold up the programme in a Belfast cinema to do so.[45] I am proud to be speaking in such company.

23 October 1943

The sort of world that the English and Americans would like to make, if successful in this war, is becoming ever clearer. Sometimes it seems suddenly to come clear in some comparatively small incident and one looks back and wonders why one had not realised it before and why many far clearer signs have been ignored.

[*There follow several incomplete sentences commenting on 'the whole Anglo-American policy' in the war, which he describes as 'a policy of world domination such as has never before been planned' – a description that some listeners may be 'half inclined to [see] as an exaggeration, a piece of pro-German propaganda'.*]

But now, I think the [...] minded of you in Ireland will see that something very like world domination really is in view. I do not want to exaggerate, or go in for sensationalism; I am not suggest-

45. On Easter Saturday 1943, Hugh McAteer (see n. 14 and 25) appeared on the stage of a cinema on the Falls Road in Belfast 'to read a statement of IRA policy and to call for a minute's silence in memory of the 1916 dead' (Fisk, *In Time of War*, p. 379).

ing that either England or America want to hold the nations of the world under direct military dominance, but I think there is no doubt that they intend by the setting up of a chain of naval and air bases all over the world, and by an intensification of their control of the world's markets, to become virtually all-powerful. Let us face this question coolly and [...] let us even give certain English and Americans credit for believing that by such an arrangement they could ensure peace in the world and that such a war as the present could not break out again. Even this, of course, is an illusion, for even supposing everything turned out as the most optimistic of them believe, it is very doubtful how long England and America would see eye to eye. There would also be the presence of Russia in the world. But leaving all this aside, even if some sort of peace could be secured by world domination, it would nevertheless be a tragedy for the human race. [...]

[*There follow several fragmentary sentences in which Stuart argues that 'you cannot set up military bases in other countries without arousing the suspicion and hostility of the best elements in those countries' and criticizes the idea of 'an international police force largely made up of English and American warships and aircraft'.*]

[...] by some accident someone in England may hear it and simply put me and most of you down as unbalanced fanatics. If so, and if only one such person should begin to have a doubt about whether after all we are such fanatics, it will be a tiny step nearer a lasting peace that sooner or later has got to come.

26 October 1943

[*G2: 'Beginning missed'*] [...] tasks for us Irish in this war to try to keep a sane and balanced outlook, in the midst of all the feverish feelings, extreme bitterness, and desire for revenge. In the belligerent countries it is natural that there should be these things, especially among the civilian population, though I must in fairness say that here in Germany, in spite of all the terrible sufferings of a large part of the people through the destruction of their homes, there is, side by side with the grim determination, a surprising lack of anything in the nature of a distorted [...] outlook. The task of all true neutrals, and that of Ireland in particular, [is to] try to see beyond the smoke and noise of war. We have got, even while being spectators of some of the greatest battles in history, to always remember that sooner or later all the battles will be over, and then will begin a task in its own way as hard as the hardest battle, the re-fashioning of life, so that the maximum of security and freedom may be had by all. [...]

Indeed, I know that for many of you the struggle to live and to look after your families quite rules out the possibility of your having much idle or wasteful enjoyment, but in so far as you have a certain peace and security denied to so many people today, it is your task to try to grasp the truth about what is happening in the world and to see that your children as they grow up grasp it too. [*G2: 'Remainder of broadcast useless owing to intermittent failures in reception'*]

30 October 1943

[*G2: 'Beginning missed, apparently referring to Hallow Eve'*] [...] It is a day which more than any other brings back memories of home [...] of an evening specially celebrated in the country. These memories of the soft autumn night in the hills and the children with masks or blackened faces going from door to door make these Halloweens that we're spending cut off from home so full of the Irish atmosphere. I believe that what makes a nation great is this thing that I can only call atmosphere – some quality of landscape, climate, culture and tradition all blended into one and from which the people of that nation draw their strength. It doesn't matter whether a nation be large or small as long as it has this; its people will be ready to fight for it and die for it. But equally important, they will have something to give to the rest of the world. For a people must be first deeply affected by their own national spirit before they can be of any value at all to the world in general. There can be no such thing as internationalism until the hearts of people are internationalised, until people lose this half secret and holy love that they have for the way the evening falls over certain woods – and this, thank God, will never happen. All the internationalists and imperialists will not succeed in convincing people that evening falls in very much the same way all over the world, and that a mountain in Ireland is much the same thing as a mountain in England or Norway. If you or I had been born of Burmese parents and spent our childhood amongst the hills of Burma we should feel in our hearts that Burma was the most beautiful place on earth, and [...] we should never rest until we got the English or any other foreigners that tried to dominate us out of it.

No doubt that is very much what the Burmese felt, and still feel; their history shows how much they must have loved what I call the atmosphere of their own country. They have fought and suffered for it for generations, and now at last they are being let alone to live their own lives, and soon, if all goes well, Burma will have something unique to give the rest of the world. I have simply taken Burma as an example because it has been lately in the news. What I say of Burma is true of all those nations which really are nations and not yet political puppets set up by large nations for their own purposes or financial parasites on great powers. You and I, though we are not Burmese, can rejoice with the Burmese people, not by some motive of propaganda but sincerely, because we are glad that in another small part of the earth people are going to have a chance to live [...]

[We] must see to it that at least as far as one small island is concerned there is only one belief, belief in ourselves to create a peace-

ful and fruitful life on our own soil and according to our own traditions.

2 November 1943

There have been many references in the English press lately to the
post-war world. Papers like the Manchester *Guardian* and the
Observer have been busy warning small nations that they can't
expect to have the same margin of freedom as they had before the
war. [...]

Neither the opinions of the English press around 1939, nor
their opinions now, nor their opinions in another five years, are of
any real importance to us. What is important is that as many sincere voices as possible should be raised at this decisive moment,
and especially voices coming from the small nations themselves, to
state plainly and clearly that no system of aggression [...] will ever
lead to peace.

Unfortunately, there are many small nations at the present
moment over whom England and America can exert enough pressure one way or another to keep them either silent, or enforce
agreement. But there are others whose press is still free to express
their views on the Anglo-American plans as they slowly are being
revealed. Both in the Far East and in Europe, both in the press and
over the wireless, there has already been enough said to convince
any sincere English or American statesman that there are many
small nations who will never co-operate in any plan which means
renouncing a vital part of their freedom. It is a pity that you in Ireland are so isolated from the news of what is happening in the
world. While you hear more or less reliable war reports of the
actual fighting, you are largely dependent on English and American news services for the news of what is going on behind the battlefield and so, of course, you are cut off from just those more or
less powerful nations whose outlook would be of such value and

interest to you. Anglo-American publicity would like to make you, and everyone else, believe that the only real opposition to them, and their plans, comes from Germany and Japan because Germany and Japan have other aggressive plans of their own. But this, as you know, is very far from being true.

What you cannot know, however, is how determined [...] many of the peoples of the smaller countries are feeling towards the Anglo-American conception of a post-war world. It is the duty of everyone who belongs to a small nation, and who has the opportunity, to add his voice to the others. I am glad to be able to do so on behalf of Ireland. I say that as far as we are concerned we have not the slightest intention of co-operating in any English or American scheme for Europe, even if their schemes could ever be put into practice. Europe owes her place in the history of world civilisation and world culture neither to England nor America; indeed it was Ireland that helped Europe through her darkest period and kept the little flame of civilisation alive at a time when it was in danger of being blown out. The time, I believe, is coming when we can help Europe again. By keeping the flame of nationalism alive we can spring from the revolution of all those small peoples who survive within their own spirit and freedom as a guarantee of the greatness of Europe. She still is full of the great creative spirit and this spirit owes much of its strength to the spirit of the small nations of Europe among which Ireland, free and undivided, will take her place.

6 November 1943

As far as England is concerned there is a very great difference between this war and the last. I spent the latter half of the last war at an English public school, and though I know something about what the feeling was there, especially on a section of the young generation [...]

[*There follow several fragmentary sentences in which Stuart contrasts the present war with the First World War, stressing the difference between a war in which English troops fought 'with their backs to England' and one in which they were fighting 'far away in Italy' and bombing German cities.*]

What must be the result of all this? What, in the end, can be the result of accustoming a whole generation to the worst form of violence and terrorism without any compensating spirit of heroism or real comradeship? What can be the effect on the civilian population of seeing photographs in the papers of the devastation of Hamburg and other cities? These are questions the answers to which are not pleasant to contemplate. What will happen to people who have learned nothing but how to destroy the largest number of other people's homes in a single night when that activity is taken away from them? [...]

You need not ask me what all this has to do with us; it has a lot to do with us. After the last war, we in Ireland did not escape from the terrorism and violence which some of the English troops brought back from the war. The Black and Tans were [responsible] for much of this terrorism. What is going to happen in England after this war? There is every prospect of worse violence and terrorism. You cannot one day proudly exhibit photographs of rows and rows of houses blasted to ruins [...] and the next day expect [children who see the photographs] to look on life as sacred. You cannot one day greet the crews of aeroplanes that rain bombs on men and women and children in this criminal phase[?] as heroes and the next day expect them to settle down quietly in an office or on a farm. Many of them no doubt will only be too glad to do so, but [there are] others in whose nature violence and terrorism has been roused and developed which cannot be so quickly overcome again. I do not pretend to know what is going to happen; it is quite possible that the passions roused in these people by every means possible will afterwards be turned against their own politicians. It is possible, and there would be a certain justice if it were so [...]

[If we] cannot stop English papers from coming into our country altogether, we should at least keep the worst of them, with their gloating over murder and devastation, away from the youth of Ireland, and we ourselves should use our neutrality to keep a true and balanced outlook.

13 November 1943

The recent resolution of the Labour Party of Northern Ireland bringing up the whole question of conditions in the jails there in which Irish nationals are imprisoned, is an event [...] which can give [...] a great measure of hope for the future.[46] It is another indication of the essential unity of outlook between all true Irishmen. Round all local politics or parties, I believe that we've come to a question of what sort of Ireland you want to build up in the future, [on] which we all pretty much agree. That is our task when this war ends, to create in our own little corner of the earth a community in which all have a chance to live in peace and to do some constructive work. Our best answer to the [...] world police forces, strategic bases and the outside control of small nations, being planned by the enemies of Germany, is for us to start even now preparing our own comparatively humble schemes to bring unity, peace and security to one small island. As the battles become more widespread and rage with an ever-increasing intensity, this must be our aim. I see the great chance we are going to have of at the same time achieving that goal for which all Irish nationalists have fought and also died, and of giving the lead to other small nations after this war, in rebuilding their community on a foundation of peace and goodwill. That is a great task. [...]

46. Unidentified.

I cannot ever forget the responsibility that I have in speaking to you. My own future and that of my children are dependent on it, just as yours is. I have as much reason as any of you in trying to make Ireland a place where after this war I can live and do my own work, with those that are dear to me, in security and peace. I do not make these talks, as I cannot but suspect that most of the English and American publicists make theirs, that is to say, just [as] part of the great propaganda machine, in which they are paid to work as workers are paid to work in a factory. I tell you only what I passionately believe [...] [T]here are none of you who need have the slightest fear that you will ever hear from me words that I am paid to speak or that I speak in order to in some way improve my own immediate position.[47] This may be the case with only too many of the writers who have given their services to the British and American broadcasting programmes, but that is no concern of ours. Those of you who have read my books can see that my belief has not changed. [*G2: 'Passage completely blotted out by noise'*] [...] I admired Hitler from the first days of power in Germany. In another [book] of mine [...] written in 1932 and published in New York and London in 1933, I described a clash between brownshirts and government forces in Munich, in which I did not hide my sympathies for the revolutionaries, as they then were.[48] Some of these books were primarily political, and I only mention them now because I want those of you who listen to me to be sure that what I say now is, in different words, what I said then. Of this, at least, you can rest assured. You may sometimes disagree with me or think me mistaken or even wonder whether I am speaking from my own convictions or for the purposes of propaganda. But if it

47. In a diary entry of 1 August 1942, Stuart wrote, apropos his wife and children: 'I had been a bit careless perhaps over knowing whether what I was sending home was enough. Now they seem to have less money and [I] must send more. Anyhow for these talks alone, if I only do one weekly, I get about 250 RM a month.' See 'Selections from a Berlin Diary, 1942', *The Journal of Irish Literature* V, 1, January 1976, pp. 84–5; this selection follows Stuart's original diaries faithfully.

48. The novel referred to here is *Try the Sky*.

was not possible to speak to you with the deepest sincerity, I would not speak to you at all.

16 November 1943

[*The transcript begins with fragmentary sentences referring to 'the Anglo-American war fever and hysteria'.*]

[…] what is worse than the wireless is the English popular press. I have neither the time nor the inclination to read these papers, but when I do happen to see some, I am sickened by what I find in them. Before I began writing this talk I was looking through a few at random. In the *News Chronicle* of October 19th, there was published a report through a paper correspondent under a headline – the things the military were doing as they retreat in Italy. This report was a fairly long and detailed description of the finding of corpses, mostly those of children, murdered and mutilated in an Italian town evacuated by the German troops. Examining this report as a writer, from a technical point of view so to speak, it was quite obvious that […]

[*Here follows a fragmentary passage in which Stuart notes that the report 'mentioned the Christian names of some of the murdered children, so obviously invented to increase the emotional effect of this story on readers'.*]

To anyone, such as myself, who has lived among Germans and has met and got to know many German soldiers, such a story is not even worth contradicting.

[*The transcript concludes with several fragmentary sentences in which Stuart appears to express his concern that 'such stories appearing week after week' might have some influence on Irish people, and states that*

'I am not going to waste the few minutes in trying to prove that this and other similar stories are not true'. The G2 transcriber then notes: 'Remainder of broadcast hopelessly interrupted. From a word picked up here and there, Stuart is quoting a further story.']

20 November 1943

As the war goes on it becomes more and more obvious that the problems that are going to arise after it, and the difficulties to be overcome before lasting peace can be hoped for, will be enormous. English and American politicians have shown over and over that they have not the slightest conception of how to solve these difficulties. The post-war world, of which they had control, would, I believe, simply be North America magnified a thousand times. It would be a world full of hatred, suspicion, intrigue, assassination and minor wars.

What, it may be asked, do we in Ireland, who are neutral, hope to do to prevent such a calamity? In one way we cannot do very much, it is true; we are a small nation without financial or military strength. All the same, I believe there is something we can do towards insuring that the post-war world is not the sort of place that Messrs Roosevelt and Churchill dream of. We have our own problems and difficulties, we have above all partition, and it is our task to solve these national problems of ours in a manner that will lead to the peace and unity of our island. We have seen the sort of hell on earth that a country can be turned into by the methods of the great financial powers. We have had an example in North Africa, to go no further, of the horrors that result when great powers, who do not even agree together, try to administer a piece of territory for their own ends.[49]

49. This seems to be a reference to the confusion that arose in the French colonies of

It is our task to see if we cannot solve the Irish problem in the very opposite manner to that believed in by England and America. I believe this can be done – it depends largely on you, the Irish nationalists in the Six Counties – but the first thing we must remember, a thing that no English or American politician can grasp, is that all the great and important changes in history have come from inside the community [itself] and not because of pressure exerted from outside. First of all, you in the Six Counties must believe so strongly in your complete solidarity with the rest of Ireland that you are ready to endure all the hardships that such a belief involves. You are Irish and you have a long and heroic tradition behind you. It is true that you are only a comparative handful of people judged [against] the vast numbers of which modern armies are composed. If we were to be obsessed by figures, as Mr Roosevelt is, then we might indeed despair – what are some thousands of Irish nationalists compared with the millions of troops, the hundreds of thousands of aeroplanes and tanks which Mr Roosevelt is always boasting about? – but the truth is the figures are not so important to these people as it seems. Not the size of communities but the intensity with which they feel and the strength of their faith, that is what matters and that is what is going to matter more and more.

You Irish nationalists in the North may seem to the English and American politicians of no very great consequence. Their minds are only concerned with calculations in which vast numbers are involved, they are only interested in the old game of power politics. Either this war will end with a victory for power politics and money politics, and humanity will be plunged into another dark age, or there will be the beginning of a new conception of social and national life. These are the ultimate issues at stake, and

---

North Africa, which had fallen under German–Vichy control, after they were captured by the Allies. The High Commissioner for the territories was Gen. Henri Giraud, an American creation, who (among other missteps) illegally deposed the Bey of Tunisia following the ousting of the Germans.

they are not only at stake on the battlefields of Europe and Asia; in our own Six Counties we have the same forces opposed to each other. You Irishmen and women in the North have nothing with which to oppose the great money powers whose troops occupy the Six Counties but faith, endurance and an intense love of your own homeland and way of life [...] It is not the millions who hardly know what they are fighting for or why they are in the Six Counties or North Africa or Italy who will be victorious; those who know why they are enduring, those whose faith is intensest – and I believe we are among them – they are the ones who in the end will see their longing realised and the peace they suffered for finally achieved.

30 November 1943

The real value of nationalism has never more clearly been shown than in the case of Ireland during this war. If we had not had the living national spirit deeply rooted in the past we would not have been able to maintain our resistance to the propaganda and other forms of pressure which our position between England and America made it inevitable that we were subjected to. The fact that we have not only refused England and America military [and] strategic help but that the vast majority of our people have withheld their sympathy from them and their cause is something that we may be proud of. We have shown that one small country, although in an unfavourable position, can retain our independence of spirit and cling to the truth [...] Do not be afraid that our example is being lost on the rest of the world. Of this I can speak from firsthand knowledge, and I tell you that many people have been heartened and inspired by seeing Ireland remain resolute.

[...] whereas at the outbreak of this war most continental Europeans knew little or nothing about our history, our status, or even our geographical position, today we are one of the small nations in which most interest is being taken. So far we have had no military task in this war but we have an immense spiritual one. Our three or four million people have to keep a hold on truth and sanity while around us on both sides of us a hundred and fifty million or more are being swept away by a nightmare [...]

[*There follows a fragmentary passage in which Stuart refers to the 'spectacle of those Latin American countries' – presumably those who aligned themselves with the Allies – and says 'I believe it could not have happened had there been a living spirit of nationalism' in those countries.*]

We have been hearing many attacks upon Irish nationalism from English and American publicists. The main reason [...] is that it is one of the forces which the power of money cannot overcome. The failure of all attempts to involve us, either strategically or emotionally, on the Anglo-American side in this conflict is due to the fact that we have learned to think and feel for ourselves. For generations we have thought and felt for ourselves and not as circumstances or expediency dictated. That, I believe, is the secret of our powers of resistance. Through all these centuries of our struggle [...] nothing mattered except to be able to think and feel for ourselves. I do not want to boast on your behalf but I think we should feel proud that stubbornly and courageously and [...] against all the propaganda [...] we have not for a moment forsaken our own souls. With England on one side of us and America on the other, with English and American troops overrunning a corner of our island [...] [*G2: 'Remainder of talk inaudible owing to noisy reception'*]

7 December 1943

Twenty-one years ago tomorrow four Irishmen were executed in Dublin. It is not out of any idle sentiment that I wish to recall the past tragedy, that we recall the memories of Rory O'Connor, Liam Mellowes, Dick Barrett and Joe McKelvey.[50] 'Tis because today, perhaps more than at any other time in the years between, we see how completely right they were in what they stood for. There were, unfortunately, many Irishmen at that time who looked on the attitude taken by these men and their comrades as too extremist and dangerous. Now, I think, we as a nation are beginning to understand that if we have been saved from the worst present dangers and horrors, it is only because these men and their predecessors had the vision and courage to be extremists in the past. Those small nations who for generations had exchanged extremism for comfort and, as they believed, security, were amongst the first to totter in this conflict. Today it is only the fearless that will survive; and if we can boast of a certain fearlessness, from whom have we learnt it? From men like Cathal Brugha, Liam Lynch, Michael Collins, the men of 1916 and so back through the centuries. Today all is clearer than it ever was before. It is because of the dynamiters of last century and not because of the men who condemned them, that we survive. It is because of Rory O'Connor, Mellowes, Barrett and McKelvey that today we are outside this conflict, and not because of the men who looked upon them as enemies [...]

Today is celebrated another anniversary which has very much to do with the one about which I have been speaking. That is the twenty-sixth anniversary of Finland's declaration of independence. Mr Ryti, the Finnish president,[51] in a speech has spoken of the spirit which makes nations great and which has nothing to do with the

50. See n. 15.
51. Rysto Ryti, president of Finland 1940–4.

[181]

amount of their armaments and even less with their gold reserves or the extent of their trade. Finland is a great nation in the sense that Ireland is a great nation, and her president points out [that] the future of his people, as of ours, depends first on this inner spirit [...] People who looked upon the 1916 men as heroes were slow to accept [that] the men who fought against the Black and Tans had equally furthered the spirit of nationalism, and when these men in their peril were accepted there was another hesitation before the whole nation lauded O'Connor, Mellowes and their comrades for carrying on the unbroken tradition. And so it is today. And that is why I want to stress that there is no good in honouring the memory of these men whose anniversary occurs tomorrow without recognising the fact that their spirit is still alive in Ireland today. It is not the task of most of you to take part in the actual physical struggle against English and American troops. What these troops stand for, it is the task of all of you to oppose. Above all it is your duty to Ireland never to accept the present social conditions in our country as inevitable. They are not inevitable. They are due largely to past centuries of English occupation.

No greater loss could have been suffered by Ireland than was suffered by the execution of Liam Mellowes. He saw very clearly that freedom for us was not only a political but also a social question. He understood that in fighting England we were fighting much more than a foreign power who dominated us politically and geographically. He saw that equally disastrous was the fact that the dominant ideal in Anglo-Saxon communities, the ideal of money as supreme, had also found its way into our own life.

On Sunday night I happened [to hear a talk] on behalf of St Bridget's Orphanage. In the course of this talk the speaker described conditions among the poor families in Dublin. All I could say was, what was revealed in that five minutes would not make one proud of being Irish. I do not believe that the speaker was exaggerating in the slightest. He was telling of what he himself had seen while engaged on his work among the Dublin poor.

It was a shocking picture but it is one that, after all, I myself and I think most of you were already quite aware of. It is a question that concerns all Irish nationalists [...] It is not my business to suggest what form the attack on the present social structure, if it can be called structure, of our lives, should take. That is a matter for you all to resolve. While a handful of brave men are carrying on the fight against the forces of the enemy in the North it is essential that you should remember it is only half the fight; the other half is your task in the future.

11 December 1943

In the last weeks there have been conferences, speeches, special reports, and communiqués, but in none of them [have] been the things that people all over the world were wanting to hear.[52] In none of these greatly publicised and widely broadcast utterances was there the slightest indication of the necessary vision and understanding for the rebuilding of society. It was the same old tale all over again, the same sort of talk that we had at all the League [of Nations] meetings and conferences from 1919 until the present war, only with this difference, that now America is playing the part that France did before; and of course there is no need for the statesmen concerned to hide their aim as they had formerly to do. They can now show quite openly that they care nothing for the tradition of Europe, the culture of Europe or the lives of the people of Europe. The whole thing is for them so much territory with so much population to be split up and divided in ways dictated by economics and political expediency. Not one word in all these weeks of reports and speeches about the things that make peace valuable and without which peace is no better than war; on

---

52. Churchill, Roosevelt and Stalin held their first tripartite meeting at Teheran in November 1943.

the contrary, one got the impression that everything uttered by these elderly and weary materialists were words that one had heard long ago and which had been stale and hopeless even then.

But in the midst of all this there was one voice which must have given many people some comfort and strengthened their faith: that was the speech made by President Ryti of Finland. Most of you probably did not hear this speech and it was certainly not reported by the English or American news agencies, nor is it necessary for me to go into it now. All I want to do is to recall that the Finnish president showed an outlook in complete contradiction to that of Churchill, Roosevelt, Smuts and their colleagues. He asserted that it was the inner spirit of a nation that made that nation great and became a basis for a peaceful and useful life for the people of that nation. He rejected the ideas which have formed the policy of the great materialistic countries, a policy which has created huge empires and caused great wars. We in Ireland have been fighting for generations against this policy and this outlook. We have been fighting against the way of life which is disastrous to our own. We have for generations refused to accept the argument that we would be better off quietly to take our place in a great and prosperous empire and give [up] our impracticable claims to living our own lives in our own ways.

General Smuts is an example of someone who also once believed that the human spirit was something superior to all great semi-military, semi-financial combines calling themselves empires, commonwealths or anything else, but he has travelled far since those days. He speaks now of small nations and wealthy nations, of great nations and weak nations, as if wealth and poverty, greatness and insignificance, could be measured completely in terms of trade figures, gold reserves and armaments. He dismisses France and Italy as of no more practical account, apparently unconcerned by the fact that in doing so, he's dismissing two of the greatest sources of culture that the world has seen. General Smuts would have once welcomed and understood the words of the Finnish president; now the only language that he understands is that of the political financiers.

It is not men like Roosevelt and Churchill, men grown old in materialism, brought up in the tradition of political intrigue, men to whom banking is one of the most important human activities – it is not such men who can now save the world. That has been growing ever clearer but never can it have been so clear as it has now become after the utterances of the last week or so, with their utter lack of anything that could have raised an answering spark in one single heart.

18 December 1943

After this war there are going to arise very many difficult problems to be solved before any real peace. We shall, however, be only called on to solve one of them – that is, of course, the Six County problem. I am not now speaking of the problem of getting rid of the English and American troops of occupation, but of the next stage in the solution, which is the reincorporation of the Six Counties in the rest of Ireland. There is no good getting rid of a hostile military base on our territory and leaving another kind of hostile base in the form of an anti-national spirit which would at any subsequent moment be ready to form the bridgehead for another occupation.

It may appear to some of you that I am exaggerating this difficulty and [that] once the English and American troops have left the north-east corner of Ireland those people who are most reactionary there would pretty soon become contented members of the Irish nation. Well that may be so, but much depends on circumstances which we cannot yet foresee and for this reason there is little use in going into the problem in detail. But I believe it is a good thing for us, even now, to face the fact that there is a problem. Of course these people are Irish, and they may be expected to accept, at least after a generation, the fact that the only government that has a real right to control them is an Irish government. But although they are Irish they have been steeped in the English tradition and the English outlook.

I believe that the first and likeliest common ground that Irish nationalists will have with the comparatively small group of Northern unionists will have a social basis. When the gulf between the two on other questions may seem unbreachable there still can be sincere agreement when it comes to a question of everybody being assured of the necessities of life. Once it becomes evident that the English social system and outlook is quite incompatible with the happiness and security of a large number of people in whatever community that system holds sway, that will be the beginning of Irish unity. We cannot hope to achieve that unity if we in the rest of Ireland do not show ourselves ready to reject the social and economic system left to us as a heritage of the English domination. For in this, and in all the other problems which will confront the world after the war, fine phrases will not be any good. If we in the rest of Ireland can arrange our social life in a way that the most defenceless of our people are protected from the economic disorders which we will probably be faced with after this war, then we would have one ground for unity which would be appreciated in the Six Counties, even by non-nationalists.

England and the Empire are probably not going to be very pleasant places to live in when this war is over; the war will have to be paid for one way or the other. But we in Ireland have a very great chance to create a community in which security is universal. We can do this best [...] in co-operation with our fellow-countrymen in the North, no matter what their previous political opinions. Therefore, as I see it, and I think as most of you see it too, our future independence and unity are bound up with our social life. The work of making Dublin and Belfast cities in which all the citizens have a chance of peace and happiness is not two problems but one. It can only be done by all Irishmen uniting to do it [...]
[*G2: 'last three or four words too indistinct to record'*]

21 December 1943

Tonight I want to say a few words about our present relationship with the United States. It is a subject which has, I believe, been much discussed at home. The whole question is an extraordinarily complex one. [...] [*G2: 'long noisy and distorted passage'*]

In the present struggle not only has the United States government supported England in her occupation of our territory, but I do not think it is an exaggeration to say that without this American support England could not have been in a position to have kept their army of occupation in the Six Counties. But even that is not the whole of the question [...] [*G2: 'further noisy and distorted passage'*]

For whatever our recent association with America, our past association with the continent of Europe is [...] an older one [...] We may be told that our neutrality is not getting us any friends; personally I very much doubt that. I don't know what qualifications the people who tell you that have to speak for America and the Irish in America, but I, for my part, can tell you this: our neutrality has gained us many friends in Europe, not only in Germany, but in the small nations too. It has, moreover, increased our number of friends in India [...] [*G2: 'remainder too indistinct for transcription'*]

25 December 1943

[*The following paraphrase of Stuart's talk appears in the BBC Monitoring Reports kept in the British Library and the Imperial War Museum.*]

Today is a day of looking back, not only on personal memories, but on the past of our nation. When I began these talks, because

I was cut off from Ireland, unable to hear what was happening there, I read and re-read as much of the writings of Padraig Pearse as were available in Berlin. Pearse had always seemed to me one of the greatest Irishmen. As soon as I had written a talk I asked myself if there was anything in it contrary to Pearse's outlook; if there was, I tore it up and wrote another. There is no time to tell you which of his writings I found most helpful, and I cannot refer to the book as it was destroyed in a recent raid on Berlin, but a few sentences I remember: 'A nation's fundamental idea of freedom is not affected by the accidents of time and circumstances; it does not vary with the centuries or the comings and goings of men or empires. The very substance of truth does not change, nor does the substance of freedom.' Those words made everything clearer than it was before. I saw there was no need to look for new policies; all we Irish had to do was to remain steadfast in our old faith.

28 December 1943

The fifth Christmas of war was marked by messages [...] from the national leaders and statesmen of many countries. There was one remark made in one of these about which I think it necessary to say something. That was a sentence of Roosevelt's to the effect that the United States troops were fighting for something that could be best symbolized by calling it the message of Bethlehem. Now I'm not going to take up time in saying all the obvious things that could be, and are being, said about such an utterance. I don't suppose any of you listening to me look on such a statement as anything but a bad symbol. But there is one aspect of [this] Roosevelt-as-a-new-St-Francis business which is depressing. Whatever Roosevelt is, I imagine he's a fairly clever politician, and he would not go on posing as the great and simple Christian if there were not many of his own people ready to take him seriously. That is the worst aspect of the matter, that there are people to be found today, in America at least, who do not know the difference between good and a degraded and perverted [religion] [...] That as I see it is the worst thing that could happen to humanity and not wars, though God knows they are bad enough. But it is even worse that for the masses of people the great truth that is the basis of our life and culture should be twisted and caricatured. I will even say that it is less sad when people reject these things altogether. It is less dangerous for people to deny themselves [religion] altogether than to pretend to serve it [...] It is less dangerous and also less sickening. Let me put it like this: what can be the mentality of people who really believe that Mr Roosevelt is in the great Christian tradition, the tradition of the Christian saint and mystic? Any attempt to answer that question would give an appalling picture. Such people in their outlook form an even more insurpassable barrier to that state of world peace and world enlightenment than do those who reject Christianity altogether.

That isn't my own personal view of the matter. The Roosevelt mentality is one that simply cannot be understood in Germany. People here are asking is he really serious and can any of his own people take him seriously? Here people are too close to the spirit, the unchanging Christian tradition, to be aware that in the great commercial communities such as the United States there is a tendency to make Christianity into something which gives successful businessmen a solid respectability. [...]

If America, the America of Mr Roosevelt, was to come out of this war victorious, it will mean the letting loose of a flood of sham spirituality over the whole world. Mr Roosevelt and his followers would then be in a position not only to preach their commercialised Christianity to the world but to do their best to enforce its acceptance. [...]

You in Ireland can do much to resist the spread of this heresy of commercial Christianity from the United States. I spoke to you on Christmas day about Padraig Pearse; it now appears to me that Pearse really did what Roosevelt pretends he is doing. Pearse was inspired by religious motives even as a national leader. I am not going to point out to you in further detail the gulf which separates these two men; I should perhaps even apologise to you for mentioning them together. You in Ireland have the task, as I've often said, of seeing to it that our corner of the world is not overrun with perversions of truth and sham idealism. It would be better to be overrun by a foreign army than for that to happen, but I believe we shall survive this war without either happening and that we shall even see once more free that part of our country already overrun.

1 January 1944

I wish those at home, and all those of you listening to me, a happy and peaceful new year. I think of a few of you here and there all over Ireland, on both sides of the border, who perhaps have been listening to me on and off now for quite a long time – a few of you who find what I say at least more personal and sincere than, let us say, most leading articles in the newspapers. Not that I want to belittle the journalists who have to write these articles. It is no easy task for them to avoid saying anything to offend any group of their readers and at the same time keep on the right side of the party the paper happens to support and the business interests which support it. My task in speaking to you is much easier. It is much easier for me to be sincere because I don't have to please anyone or keep on the right side of any party. I do not have to try to say what I think will make the largest number of people turn on their wireless and listen to me.

[...] When I began to write this talk I said to myself, Here I am within another year [...] an awful prospect. Then I saw there was one way of making it not so awful but in fact making it a task that I can look forward to quite gladly: that was by speaking to those few of you in different parts of Ireland who listen to me with trust and interest. It is these few of you that make the writing and

speaking of these talks not a monotonous task but mostly something which I am glad to be able to do. [...]

I think of you in whatever parts of our country you are tonight,
in parts I know and in parts I don't know; I think of you not always
agreeing with every word I say, by no means, but as on the whole
agreeing that my outlook about our country and about this war and
the coming peace in relation to our country is more or less yours. As
I say, I am thankful not to be a journalist [... and] not to be a politician and have to convince myself and others that my outlook represented the outlook of such and such a contingent of our
population, or worst of all [...] one of the English or American publicists who have to begin by showing people that in a world of darkness they alone are the bringers of reason and enlightenment [...]

In the year that is beginning, there will probably be events that
will vitally affect our future. As long as I have the opportunity of
speaking to you I will try to judge of these events from the point
of view of an Irish nationalist here on the continent of Europe, an
Irish nationalist who wants Ireland to be free and at peace, in a
world free and at peace. And in this connection my New Year wish
is that those of you who have listened to me during the past year
will go on listening and that I shall have the good luck to retain
your trust until there is no more news to speak to you any more.

8 January 1944

[*This broadcast was not transcribed by the G2 monitor, who logged
that the recording was 'unfit for accurate transcription' due to noise.
The BBC transcript that follows is patently not a verbatim transcription – its short sentences are noticeably inconsistent with Stuart's
familiar meandering cadences – but its language is clearly Stuart's.*]

It has become quite clear that England and the USA are really
fighting to preserve the old social and financial order. Does Ireland

want to remain in that old order or not? What do you want to become after this war? It is not enough to talk about freedom and nationalism. After the last war a group of comparatively small nations was created by the politicians and financiers of England and France. Poland, Czechoslovakia and Yugoslavia had governments based on the old capitalist system. The creation of these countries was hailed with a lot of shouting about freedom and nationalism. Yet their freedom was purely one of prestige and brought no blessing to the lives of their peoples. We in Ireland must never make that mistake.

Irish nationalists must see that Ireland does not become another of these little republics in which the old order reproduces itself. It is of no importance at all that the Tricolour should fly from the City Hall in Belfast instead of the Union Jack if Belfast workers are to find it as hard to live and support their families as before. Such freedom is merely illusion and such nationalism a farce and a danger. English politicians will be ready enough to let us have back the Six Counties if they are sure that the whole of Ireland will remain closely tied up to the old system.

We Irish have still very much to do to bring our social life on to a level with our national life. The first thing to do is to face the truth. Until Dublin becomes a much better place for the average working family to live in than Belfast, we lose more than half the force of our claim to Belfast. This may not be a very palatable statement, but I think that to most of you it is quite obvious. And Dublin cannot become a socially better and happier place than Belfast except by a more complete break with English financial and social traditions.

How to achieve the union of our national and social life into one great movement which will include the return of the Six Counties, is something that must be talked about and discussed by you at home. What Roosevelt and Churchill stand for, we repudiate, because it means not only partition, but also extreme social injustice.

11 January 1944

Tonight I want to speak especially to you Irishmen in the North who see in this war a means whereby your homes will once again become part of Ireland. You are in the great Ulster tradition. It does not matter whether your families came to Ireland in the times of James Stuart, at the beginning of the seventeenth century, or whether they were there before, or only came afterwards. All that matters is that you feel yourselves Ulstermen and Irishmen and that it is the Irish way of life rather than the English that suits you. Your leaders have seen in this war an opportunity for the Six Counties to become once more part of Ireland; they are undoubtedly right. At the end of this conflict, if not before it, I believe that Ireland will have a chance of becoming united and free such as she has never had before during the long centuries of occupation.

To some of you it may seem like over-optimism. You in the North, with the evidence of the power of the enemy constantly before your eyes, may naturally wonder how we are going to throw off such a formidable opponent. Never before have so many foreign troops been in Ireland, not even at the height of the Black and Tan war, but behind this appearance of might there is considerable weakness. I have never gone much into military matters in these talks because I do not pretend to be competent to speak about them, but because you in the Six Counties are so isolated and so exposed to English and American propaganda, I think there is no harm in mentioning a few facts obvious to any impartial observer here in Germany. To begin with there is plenty of evidence that people in the United States, best qualified to judge, do not believe in the possibility of defeating Japan. While Roosevelt and his publicists are talking about all the territories which they mean to take from Japan, the experts, the people who will still be in power long after Roosevelt is no longer president, are quietly discussing the possibility of coming to an understanding with Japan.

It is good for us to remember this, when we might be inclined to think despairingly of the mass of American troops in occupation of our territory. The position of the United States, despite all the Roosevelt propaganda, is not by any means so secure as it might seem. Indeed, if the present American administration remains in power long enough to attempt to carry out this ambitious plan to provide the greater part of the manpower for the attempted invasion of Europe and of later launching a great offensive in the Pacific, it is quite certain that America will not be able to stand the strain. The United States, both by its geographical isolation and its high degree of industrialisation, is well fitted to act as an arsenal and to supply her two principal allies with the great mass of armaments; whether, however, she can even do this for long without widespread strikes, without inflation and the other preliminaries to social and economic upheaval, is extremely doubtful, but if she were to try as well to bear the brunt of two major campaigns, it is pretty obvious that there would be a collapse. The United States cannot be turned into a great military power in the sense that Germany or Japan or Russia are great military powers, and all the ambition of President Roosevelt will never alter this fact.

It is no secret that we are now on the eve of the greatest and most decisive battles of the war. What happens in the next few months is going to have a vital bearing on the political future of the world. Ireland is certainly not going to remain unaffected by the outcome of these battles. The successful invasion of Europe by England and America would consolidate their occupation of the Six Counties, whereas a defeat in Europe would tend to make their position there far less secure. I am not, however, suggesting that our fate is dependent on anything in the end but our own living faith and our own energy. At the most we can only expect to be helped by circumstances indirectly; our own battles no one can fight for us but ourselves.

15 January 1944

[*The transcript begins with several fragmentary sentences in which Stuart notes that 'all nations have their own special failings and blindnesses and I am not trying to make out that the Anglo-Saxon race have a monopoly of evil'.*]

The gratuitous abuse of any people is no part of my task in speaking to you as I see it. [...] certain English publicists [...] have once again discovered that the German people are a nation of uncivilised, uncultivated and brutal savages. No, with such examples of insanity before one it is all the more necessary to be sober and fair. But I think it is obvious that the Anglo-Saxon people have one special and very dangerous weakness, and that is a tendency to self-righteousness, which manifests itself most of all in wartime. It is right, however, to remember that the reaction usually sets in after the particular war is over. It is also true that a small section of people in England have always stood out against each successive wave of self-righteous war hysteria. In the Napoleonic war the hysteria began to appear in England, perhaps for the first time, but there were many people who refused to share it. [...] By the time the Boer War was over, which by the way was one of the hardest of all to justify, this self-righteousness had become something of a habit. All the same, a quite considerable section of opinion in England was always against it. But then, in the last war, this self-righteousness rose to its highest peak. While it lasted, England was swept by this wave, which eclipsed all previous ones. At the same time a small section of the people remained untouched by it, and very soon after the war was over a violent reaction set in. Writers like Richard [...][53] described their own hatred as a mass hysteria, and many people

53. The ellipsis is in the G2 transcript; the writer in question may be Richard Aldington, to whose novel *Death of a Hero*, based on Aldington's experiences in the First World War, Stuart made a (slighting) reference in his diary on 19 December 1942.

asserted they hated it too even while being carried away by it. There was a flood of anti-war books and for a time the popular view in England seemed to be that almost all that had been written or said about the war, while it lasted, had been nothing but lies and propaganda intended to arouse the necessary emotionalism.

Why am I reminding you of all this? you may ask. What has it to do with us in Ireland? I think it has this much to do with us: we have the task, as I see it, of keeping a balanced judgement in the midst of the lies, exaggerations and emotional distortions around us. And this becomes far easier when we remember that in perhaps a few months – in a few years at most – the people in England and America who are now shouting about crusades and liberation will not dare to open their mouths, or if they do open their mouths, so short is public memory, it will be to ridicule and pour contempt on all their previous activity. So it was after the last war in England and so it is going to be after this one, not only in England but to an even greater degree perhaps in the United States. And just as in the last war, there is now a small group in England, and possibly a considerably larger group in America, who see through the whole sham. These people, some of them writers, have now no chance to be heard, but their time is coming. When the Roosevelts and Churchills have disappeared as completely as the Wilsons and Lloyd Georges did, then some very different voices will be raised in the Anglo-Saxon world. We, for our part, have only to hold on to the truth as we see it, and there is little doubt that, even now, there are many who are grateful to us and to whom our sanity is an inspiration.

22 January 1944

[*The transcript begins with two fragmentary sentences in which Stuart states that 'one of our greatest tasks at the present time is to think for ourselves'.*]

[...] And I think that this is a thing that most of you who are listening to me do not find at all difficult, for it is certainly a characteristic of us Irish to think for ourselves and to be sceptical rather than credulous. That is a very good thing in the present world crisis. It may make it difficult for us to unite and even difficult to find a satisfactory government universally accepted, but it ensures that we will not be easily influenced or carried away by foreign propaganda. We are not going to accept things simply because we are told to. And if there were more people in the world like that, this war could not have taken place.

Let me only take one example among very many. For instance, it seems to me, and I expect to you too, if the United States soldiers in Italy would ask themselves what they are really doing there it would begin to dawn on them that there was something really wrong with the whole policy of Roosevelt and those responsible for sending them. They are told that they are there to liberate the Italians and secondly as a means of attacking Germany, and presumably most of them accept these statements in a half-hearted sort of way and go on fighting in the same half-hearted sort of way. Of course the time will come when the truth will dawn on them – it always does – but possibly not until a few years after the war is already over. That is what happened after the last war. But if they were now to begin to think for themselves and examine the reasons for them being sent into battle they would come to some very interesting conclusions.

To begin with, the statement that they are there to liberate the Italian people is one that would fall to pieces under a little sober examination. Even the average not-very-well-educated American [...] today knows that the Italian people under Mussolini were not in such urgent need of liberation as all that. If it came to a question of whether a few million of their own people in the United States, small farmers in south-eastern[?] states, unemployed in the great American cities, or the Italians in Fascist Italy were in greatest need of liberation in the days before the war, the average American left to himself would have known the answer very well. An American would not have to read a book like John Steinbeck's *Grapes of Wrath* to get an idea as to what was happening in his own country. He couldn't help knowing it or hearing first-hand accounts of it. Maybe if he himself was lucky enough not to live in one of the afflicted states or amongst the forgotten men in the great cities in the days before the war it would have appeared ridiculous to have told him that he would go and fight to liberate the Italians. He would certainly have answered that liberation should begin at home.

Since those far-off days he has heard so much propaganda that he doesn't really think for himself any more at all. All the same, I daresay he has become a little sceptical about the whole liberation of Italy. He knows that the process involves hundreds of Italian people dying of typhus every week and a few more hundreds dying directly or indirectly of starvation. They have to go through all this in order that later on they can be given a government approved of by Roosevelt. Even this is doubtful because no one really knows whether, even if these American soldiers succeeded in occupying the whole of Italy, Roosevelt would be in a position to choose an Italian government or whether, as is happening in North Africa, marked differences of opinion would not arise among the occupying forces. In any case the whole outlook for the Italian people would be equally uncertain and [...] gloomy.

No, any American soldier who really began to think for himself would come to the conclusion that the best thing that he and his comrades could do would be to commandeer enough boats to take them straight back to the United States, and, if they still wanted to do any fighting, to start a fight there for the liberation of millions of their own fellow countrymen. But of course this would not happen; the same old propaganda would be kept up and millions would believe it, and so it goes on. Meanwhile, you at least should refuse to believe anything at all – yes, even what I say to you in these talks – until you have thought it all over for yourselves.

5 February 1944

[*G2: 'Start missed'*] [...] When one speaks of America it is very hard to say exactly what one means. Do we mean the America of Roosevelt, Morgenthau, Henry Kaiser[54] and their colleagues? An America which believes that civilisation consists in large gold reserves, the latest measures in mass production, in business methods [...] with a light varnish of cheap idealism thrown in? That is the America that is today all powerful, but beneath all this there is another America, a very different America, whose voice has not yet been heard except in one or two of her writers, an America that is trying to find her own culture and way of life. Which of these Americas is going to triumph will depend, at least to some extent, on the outcome of this war. Should America come out of this war victorious then there would set in a period in which the supercilious angles[?] of Roosevelt and men like him would probably sweep through the country. [...] whether America will at last find her own soul or whether she will be sidetracked into imperialist dreams is one of the things that the next few months or at most years will decide.

Meanwhile we in Ireland have nothing to worry about as far as our relationship with the United States is concerned. We are not one of the South American nations to be made crawl at the heel of corrupt American politicians and financiers. We know very well that there are many Americans who are ashamed of what their government is doing in South America, who are profoundly sorry that America sent troops to the Six Counties and who are disturbed at events in North Africa. I had several long talks with Mr Cudahy[55] in Berlin during the summer of 1941. Mr Cudahy, who

---

54. Henry Morgenthau: US Secretary of the Treasury. Henry Kaiser: shipbuilder largely responsible for the resurrection of the US Navy after the attack on Pearl Harbor.

55. John Cudahy, who served as US envoy in Dublin before the war, later became ambassador to Belgium, from which position he was sacked for entertaining German officers after the occupation; he then went to Berlin where he worked as a war correspondent.

had been American ambassador in Dublin and at the outbreak of war in Brussels, voiced a point of view shared, I believe, by not a few Americans: he saw America, had she remained out of this war, being with Ireland a great power for the preservation of truth and sanity in the world. Mr Cudahy is dead and I believe it is honouring his memory to recall his determined opposition to the whole outlook of Roosevelt and his colleagues. Cudahy was a great American and I believe that his point of view will be justified, if not today at least by a new generation of Americans. As long as there is a United States government in power that keeps troops on part of our soil there can be no question of anything but a feeling of hostility on our part towards that government. If and when there is a new spirit in America, then I think that no one will be quicker and more glad to recognise it than we Irish. But until then there is nothing for us to do but to wait and to refuse to be sidetracked by reminders of the close ties between the two countries in the past.

Appendix

The files of the Politisches Archiv des Auswärtigen Amts – archive of the German Foreign Ministry – on wartime propaganda broadcasting to Ireland contain several references to talks by Francis Stuart and, most intriguingly, a transcript of a talk dated 9 February 1942, some five weeks earlier than the earliest surviving talk in the Irish and British files. As I have not been able to ascertain the precise status of this transcript – a task complicated by the fact that the archive is moving from Bonn to Berlin and is closed to researchers – I reproduce it here separately from Stuart's other talks, to which it seems more a cousin than a sibling.

An item given as 'Francis Stuart – Talk' appears ninth and last on a list of items apparently for broadcast on 9 February 1942, starting at 10.45 p.m. Under a similar heading in the same file appears a corresponding transcript, with the initials 'F.S.' typed in the heading and the name 'Francis Stuart' handwritten nearby.

The main problem posed by the transcript is that its tone and level of detail are subtly but noticeably different from those of Stuart's other talks. These differences are perhaps explainable by the fact that this was Stuart's first talk; the appearance of uncharacteristic elements here may simply be evidence that Stuart decided, after an initial broadcast with which he might not have been satisfied, to change his style. Stuart was certainly capable of the rather harder, more engaged tone of this talk, as, for example, in his 1939 piece for *The Young Observer*. It must also be noted that while there are divergences between the tone of this talk and that of the later talks, the basic themes and, more tellingly, the cadences of the sentences do seem Stuartian. There are also more specific correspondences: the reference to 'patent-medicine manufacturers', for example, is echoed in Stuart's talk of 19 August 1942.

Even so, the differences in tone and content between this talk and the remaining talks are striking enough that we must consider the possibility that in this talk Stuart was reading from, or adapting, a script or notes prepared by someone else. Bruce Lockhart's *Retreat from Glory*, referred to in the talk, is not the sort of thing Stuart usually read, or at least not the sort of thing he usually talked about reading. The explicit anti-Semitism at the end of the 9 February 1942 talk was never repeated in the subsequent talks, nor was the specific praise of the Nazi daily *Völkischer Beobachter*. These divergences might conceivably reflect a change in style more than in substance – overt anti-Semitism and praise of a Nazi newspaper would have been at odds with Stuart's posture that he wasn't making propaganda – but they are notable nonetheless. Perhaps more tellingly, certain highly rhetorical words used here – 'pander', 'exploit', 'pawn' – never again appear in the transcripts; 'popular' and its variants occur four times here and only four times subsequently; 'cheap' occurs twice here and only twice more. Meanwhile, the second-person plural pronoun 'you', perhaps the most crucial single element in the intimate ambience that Stuart obviously wished to create between himself and his lis-teners, occurs some six hundred times, or about once every seventy-five words, in the surviving talks between March 1942 and February 1944; it occurs not once in the 780-word transcript of 9 February 1942.

The strongest piece of external evidence that the 9 February 1942 talk was of a fundamentally different status from the subsequent talks is a passing remark by Stuart in his diary for 24 March 1942: 'Wrote a second talk which I will give one day soon over radio for home.' The first talk, obviously, was the one that was broadcast to Ireland on 17 March 1942. Stuart's remark, assuming it is not simply a mistake (which seems unlikely), doesn't rule out the possibility that he gave a talk on 9 February 1942, but it does suggest that Stuart did not *write* any script before the St Patrick's Day one. On the balance of evidence, a plausible hypothesis would be that the 9 February 1942 talk was drafted in some form by someone other than Stuart, and adapted and recorded for broadcast by Stuart himself, not necessarily under his own name.

There are, of course, other possibilities. One is that the talk, whatever its origins, was never broadcast. There is no sign of this talk in the G2 or BBC files, although this in itself proves nothing: both sets of monitors missed talks by Stuart on several occasions. Neither the G2 nor the BBC files are compre-hensive enough in their transcription and logging to rule out the possibility that the talk was beamed to Ireland but went unrecorded due to either poor reception or inattention – the latter being a more plausible state of affairs in February 1942 than subsequently, when the G2 monitors in particular were listening keenly for Stuart's talks. It might also be that the talk was a test of Stuart's abilities as a broadcaster, never intended for the airwaves; it is cer-tainly probable that such a test took place, although the manner in which this talk is listed after a number of news items would seem to suggest that it was not a test. Another, quite straightforward, possibility is that the 9 February 1942 talk was written by Stuart and broadcast to Ireland, just as the subsequent talks were: this is the view taken by Andreas Roth, apparently the first researcher to have done extensive work in the relevant German file, in a paper on Stuart's broadcasts forthcoming in the journal *Irish Historical Studies.* Given the number of circumstantial indications to the contrary, however, as well as the impossibility of making a thorough study of files in an archive that is currently closed, I have opted to reproduce this talk as an appendix in order to indicate its uncertain status.

B.B.

9 February 1942

Democracy is a word being very much used by British and American publicists and it would be interesting to consider for a moment what sort of democracy really exists in England today.

To begin with, it is obvious that the word has lost almost all its original meaning. The mass of the people certainly do not rule in modern England – there is only one thing that rules there, dictates the policy of every government, and that is money. And the masses are simply used. They are exploited by big business – by newspaper-owners, patent-medicine manufacturers, by everyone, in fact, with something to sell. The English press, the streets, the countryside even, are full of advertisements all calculated to get the masses to buy this, that or the other commodity, and the popular newspapers themselves compete with each other in appealing to the popular taste. There is no attempt whatever to improve or educate that taste but in many cases only to pander to the lowest aspects of it. One has only to look at such dailies as the *Mirror,* the *Sketch,* the *Daily Express* or the *Daily Mail,* which unfortunately are exported in large numbers in to Ireland, to get an idea of one side of the working of English democracy.

As long as the masses are a means of profit they will be flattered and pandered to and supplied with cheap sensation in the forms of these newspapers, cheap cinemas, novels and such, all of which, alas, we have suffered from in Ireland too. But that section that ceases to be exploitable, the unemployed, being of no further use, are quietly, in peacetime, forgotten. As they are no longer pawns in the great money game they are let quietly alone.

In Germany, which does not boast of democracy, the case is very different. The people are not looked upon as fair game for clever and unscrupulous speculators. The press does not descend to the low levels of the English press in a frantic struggle for popularity. The *Völkischer Beobachter*, for example, which as a people's paper might be compared to one of the large popular English dailies such as the *Daily Express* or *Herald*, has a standard far above these. Try to imagine, for instance, an article on the front page of either of these two newspapers dealing in a serious manner with the different psychology of the present generation compared to the preceding one and tracing the influence of the war on the outlook of the youth of to-day. Yet such an article, based on a book by the writer Otto Gmelin (who incidentally visited Ireland in 1938), appeared on the front page of the last copy of the *Völkischer Beobachter* I happened to see, that of February 3rd. And moreover the ordinary German would be interested in such an article with the problems and arguments that would arise from it, whereas the ordinary reader of the *Daily Herald* or the *Daily Express* expects, apart from the news, which must also be given in easy and attractive form, something much lighter and more sensational. Germany, in short, is quite free of all those aspects of this so-called democracy which one might call mass-exploitation. For Germany is not ruled by money [...]

In the latter connection it is very interesting to read a book like *Retreat from Glory* by the ex-English diplomatist Bruce Lockhart. In this we are given a more clear insight than is usually allowed into what English methods were in Europe between the last war and this. We see how, while other countries were building up their armies, England was quietly consolidating her financial stranglehold.

Bruce Lockhart in the course of his interesting story quite casually refers to the Bank of England's representative in the national banks of several European countries. It seems scarcely to strike him as curious. He tells too of the large and efficient Intelligence department employed by the Bank of England for their international intrigues. He reveals something of the financial spider-web with which England entangled Czechoslovakia, the old Austria and several other countries, including Yugoslavia, in the weaving of which he played a prominent part. And, as might be expected, whether it is negotiations about an Anglo-Czech bank in Prague or the buying up of Serbian forests in Dalmatia, it is largely London Jews who figure in the dealings.

Yes, let us not forget it, the democracy that we hear so much about is simply the name for a complex and highly efficient system which sets money above everything else and which up till now has been operating with success in England and America. With success, that is, for the handful who control the machine.

Sources

ARCHIVAL SOURCES

Military Archives, Dublin
   G2/X/0127: transcripts and summaries of foreign wireless broadcasts
   G2/0214: personal file on Francis Stuart and Iseult Stuart

National Archives, Dublin
   DFA A72: file on Francis Stuart
   DFA 205/108: 'German Broadcasts to Ireland'

National Library of Ireland, Dublin
   MS 8184: Joseph O'Neill papers
   MS 29,515: typescript of *Men Crowd Me Round*, play by Francis Stuart
   MS 29,516: typescript of *Strange Guest*, play by Francis Stuart

Public Record Office of Northern Ireland, Belfast
   CAB 9CD/207: transcripts and summaries of foreign wireless broadcasts

University of Ulster, Coleraine
   Francis Stuart Collection

Imperial War Museum and British Library, London
   BBC Monitoring Reports, Daily Digests of World Broadcasts, 1942–44

Public Record Office, Kew
   HO 45/25839: Statement of William Joseph Murphy, 19 January 1945

Politisches Archiv des Auswärtigen Amts, Bonn/Berlin
   Sonderreferat Irland, Deutsche Propaganda nach Irland, Sendemitschriften Bd. 3

PRINTED SOURCES

Anon. 'Francis Stuart' [obituary]. *Guardian*, 4 February 2000.
—. 'Francis Stuart' [obituary]. *Irish Times*, 5 February 2000.

——. 'Francis Stuart' [obituary]. *The Times*, 3 February 2000.

——. '"Painful Insight" Writer Honoured.' *Irish Times*, 22 October 1996.

——. 'Pillars of Society: Kevin Myers.' *Phoenix*, 30 July 1999.

Arendt, Hannah. *Eichmann in Jerusalem: A Report on the Banality of Evil*. New York: Penguin, 1994.

Arnold, Bruce, et al. Letter to the Editor. *Hibernia*, 19 June 1980.

Barnwell, William C. 'Looking to the Future: The Universality of Francis Stuart.' *Éire-Ireland*, Summer 1977.

Bartlett, Thomas, and Keith Jeffery. *A Military History of Ireland*. Cambridge: Cambridge University Press, 1996.

Battersby, Eileen. 'Entering the Lists.' *Irish Times*, 3 June 1995.

——. 'Ever the Outsider, Still Unrepentant.' *Sunday Tribune*, 11 February 1990.

——. 'Nothing But Doubt.' *Irish Times*, 14 November 1996.

——. 'Prophet of Hindsight Who Outlived Both His World and His Century.' *Irish Times*, 3 February 2000.

Bell, J. Bowyer. *The Secret Army: A History of the IRA 1916–1970*. London: Anthony Blond, 1970.

Beller, Steven. *Vienna and the Jews 1867–1938: A Cultural History*. Cambridge: Cambridge University Press, 1989.

Benjamin, Walter. *Illuminations*. London: Fontana, 1992.

Bergmeier, Horst J.P., and Rainer E. Lotz. *Hitler's Airwaves: The Inside Story of Nazi Radio Broadcasting and Propaganda Swing*. New Haven and London: Yale University Press, 1997.

Berkley, George E. *Vienna and Its Jews: The Tragedy of Success, 1880s–1980s*. Cambridge, Mass., and Lanham, Md.: Abt Books and Madison Books, 1988.

Bewley, Charles. *Memoirs of a Wild Goose*. Dublin: Lilliput, 1989.

Bielenberg, Christabel, and Charlotte O'Connell. Letter to the Editor. *Irish Times*, 10 December 1997.

Boland, Eavan. 'The Ghetto Writer.' *This Week*, 10 August 1972.

Bowen, Elizabeth. 'New Novels' [review of *In Search of Love*, inter alia]. *New Statesman and Society*, 14 September 1935.

Brennock, Mark. 'Francis Stuart Elected to Highest Position in Aosdána.' *Irish Times*, 11 October 1996.

Burke, Raymond Patrick. 'The Representation of Jews and "Jewishness" in the Novels of Francis Stuart.' M.A. thesis, University College Galway, 1989.

Burns, James MacGregor. *Roosevelt: The Soldier of Freedom 1940–1945*. London: Weidenfeld and Nicolson, 1971.

Calvocoressi, Peter, Guy Wint and John Pritchard. *The Penguin History of the Second World War*. London: Penguin, 1999.

Carpenter, Humphrey. *A Serious Character: The Life of Ezra Pound*. London: Faber and Faber, 1988.

Carroll, Joseph T. *Ireland in the War Years*. Newton Abbot: David & Charles, 1975.

Carter, Carolle J. *The Shamrock and the Swastika: German Espionage in Ireland in World War II*. Palo Alto: Pacific Books, 1977.

Caterson, S.J. 'Joyce, the *Künstlerroman* and Minor Literature: Francis Stuart's *Black List, Section H*.' *Irish University Review*, Spring/Summer 1997.

——. 'Stuart, Yeats and the Artist's Self.' *Writing Ulster*, no. 4, 1996.

Coetzee, J.M. 'Going All the Way.' *New York Review of Books*, 2 December 1999.

Cole, J.A. *Lord Haw-Haw—and William Joyce: The Full Story*. London: Faber and Faber, 1964.

Cooney, Patrick. 'Unforgiven Soldier.' *Guardian*, 29 April 1999.

Corcoran, Neil. *After Yeats and Joyce: Reading Modern Irish Literature*. Oxford: Oxford University Press, 1997.

Cornell, Julien. *The Trial of Ezra Pound: A Documented Account of the Treason Case by the Defendant's Lawyer*. London: Faber and Faber, 1966.

Coulter, Carol. 'Stuart Rejects Charges of Anti-Semitism.' *Irish Times*, 12 January 1998.

Cowley, Jason. 'Supported by a Pillar of Cloud.' *Observer*, 28 May 1995.

Cronin, Anthony. *Heritage Now: Irish Literature in the English Language*. Dingle: Brandon, 1982.

—. 'Life, Art and the Novel.' *Irish Times*, 28 February 1975.

—. 'A Life of Revelation.' *Sunday Independent*, 6 February 2000.

—. 'A New Barrage in the War over Francis Stuart.' *Sunday Independent*, 10 October 1999.

—. 'Stuart an Innocent Abroad.' *Sunday Independent*, 30 November 1997.

Cronin, Sean. *Frank Ryan: The Search for the Republic*. Dublin: Repsol Publishing, 1980.

Cullingford, Elizabeth. *Yeats, Ireland and Fascism*. London: Macmillan, 1981.

Davidowicz, Lucy S. *The War against the Jews 1933–45*. London: Penguin, 1990.

Deane, Seamus. *Celtic Revivals: Essays in Modern Irish Literature 1880–1980*. London: Faber and Faber, 1985.

—. 'Francis Stuart: The Stimulus of Sin.' *In Dublin*, 17 December 1982.

—. *A Short History of Irish Literature*. London: Hutchinson, 1986.

Documents on German Foreign Policy 1918–1945, series D, vol. VIII–X. Washington, D.C.: Government Printing Office, 1954–7.

Doherty, M.A. *Nazi Wireless Propaganda: Lord Haw-Haw and British Public Opinion in the Second World War*. Edinburgh: Edinburgh University Press, 2000.

Donovan, Katie. 'In Honour of Francis Stuart.' *Irish Times*, 10 October 1996.

Duggan, John P. *Neutral Ireland and the Third Reich*. Dublin: Lilliput, 1989.

Durcan, Paul. *Ark of the North: For Francis Stuart on His Eightieth Birthday, 28th April 1982*. Dublin: Raven Arts, 1982.

—. *Greetings to Our Friends in Brazil: One Hundred Poems*. London: Harvill, 1999.

—. Letter to the Editor. *Irish Times*, 31 October 1997.

—. Letter to the Editor. *Irish Times*, 19 December 1997.

—. Note on Francis Stuart, *Waterstone's Guide to Irish Books*, ed. Cormac Kinsella. Brentford, Middlesex, 1998.

Eagleton, Terry. *Crazy John and the Bishop and Other Essays on Irish Culture*. Cork: Cork University Press, 1998.

Eatwell, Roger. *Fascism: A History*. London: Vintage, 1996.

Edmondson, C. Earl. *The Heimwehr and Austrian Politics 1918–1936*. Athens, Ga.: University of Georgia Press, 1978.

Edwards, Ruth Dudley. *Victor Gollancz: A Biography*. London: Victor Gollancz, 1987.

Elborn, Geoffrey. *Francis Stuart: A Life*. Dublin: Raven Arts Press, 1990.

English, Richard. *Radicals and the Republic*. Oxford: Clarendon Press, 1994.

Fenton, James. 'Auden's Enchantment.' *New York Review of Books*, 13 April 2000.

SOURCES

Fichtner, Paula Sutter. *Historical Dictionary of Austria*. London: Scarecrow Press, 1999.

Finneran, Richard, George Mills Harper and William M. Murphy, eds. *Letters to W.B. Yeats*, vol. 2. London: Macmillan, 1977.

Fisk, Robert. *In Time of War: Ireland, Ulster and the Price of Neutrality, 1939–45.* Dublin: Gill & Macmillan, n.d.

Foster, R.F. *Modern Ireland 1600–1972*. London: Penguin, 1989.

—. *Paddy & Mr Punch: Connections in Irish and English History*. London: Allen Lane, 1993.

—. 'Portrait of the Artist as a Young Nazi.' *Sunday Times*, 24 October 1982.

Fraenkel, Josef, ed. *The Jews of Austria: Essays on their Life, History and Destruction*. London: Valentine, Mitchell & Co., 1967.

Greene, David H. 'The Return of Francis Stuart.' *Envoy*, July 1951.

Hamilton, Alastair. *The Appeal of Fascism: A Study of Intellectuals and Fascism 1919–1945*. London: Anthony Blond, 1971.

Hamilton, Hugo. Letter to the Editor. *Irish Times*, 4 December 1997.

—. 'Understanding Francis Stuart.' *Writing Ulster*, no. 4, 1996.

Hanly, David. 'Francis Stuart, the Torc of the Town.' *Sunday Tribune*, 13 October 1996.

Harmon, Maurice. 'The Achievement of Francis Stuart.' *Writing Ulster*, no. 4, 1996.

—. 'Generations Apart: 1925–1975', in *The Irish Novel in Our Time*, ed. Patrick Rafroidi and Maurice Harmon. Lille: Publications de l'Université de Lille III, 1975–6.

Higgins, Aidan. Letter to the Editor. *Irish Times*, 17 December 1997.

Hogan, Eugene. 'A Man of Simple Pleasures Plays a Final Trick.' *Irish Independent*, 5 Feburary 2000.

Hone, Joseph. *W.B. Yeats, 1865–1939*, 2nd ed. London: Macmillan, 1962.

Joannon, Pierre. 'Francis Stuart or the Spy of Truth', translated by Grace Neville and Pól Ruiseal, in *The Irish Novel in Our Time*, ed. Patrick Rafroidi and Maurice Harmon. Lille: Publications de l'Université de Lille III, 1975–6.

Jordan, John. 'Name Calling.' *Hibernia*, 12 May 1972.

Kearney, Richard. *Transitions: Narratives in Modern Irish Culture*. Dublin: Wolfhound Press, 1988.

Kehoe, Emmanuel. 'The Life and Times of Francis Stuart.' *Sunday Press*, 23 July 1978.

Kennedy, Michael. *Ireland and the League of Nations, 1919–1946*. Blackrock: Irish Academic Press, 1996.

Kenner, Hugh. *The Pound Era*. Berkeley: University of California Press, 1974.

Keogh, Dermot. *Jews in Twentieth-Century Ireland*. Cork: Cork University Press, 1998.

Kermode, Frank. 'Estrangement.' *The Listener*, 23 March 1972.

Kerrigan, Gene. 'Aosdana Make a Show of Themselves.' *Sunday Independent*, 30 November 1997.

Kiberd, Declan. *Inventing Ireland*. London: Jonathan Cape, 1995.

Kilfeather, J.B. 'Blackened Reputation.' *Fortnight*, January 1983.

Kilroy, Thomas. 'The Autobiographical Novel', in *The Genius of Irish Prose*, ed. Augustine Martin. Dublin and Cork: Mercier Press, 1985.

—. 'The Irish Writer: Self and Society, 1950–80', in *Literature and the Changing Ireland*, ed. Peter Connolly. Gerrards Cross: Colin Smythe, 1982.

Klemperer, Victor. *I Will Bear Witness: A Diary of the Nazi Years, 1933–1941*. New York: Random House, 1998.

—. *To the Bitter End: The Diaries of Victor Klemperer 1942–45*. London: Weidenfeld & Nicolson, 1999.

Lane, Anthony. 'The Man in the Mirror.' *The New Yorker*, 9 August 1999.

Lazenbatt, Bill. 'A Conversation with Francis Stuart.' *Writing Ulster*, no. 4, 1996.

—. 'Selections from the Diaries of Francis Stuart.' *Writing Ulster*, no. 4, 1996.

Le Brocquy, Louis. Letter to the Editor. *Irish Times*, 2 January 1998.

Lee, J.J. *Ireland 1912–1985: Politics and Society*. Cambridge: Cambridge University Press, 1989.

Leland, Mary. 'Francis Stuart in Cork.' *The Cork Review*, Nov.–Dec. 1979.

Lentin, Ronit and Louis. Letter to the Editor. *Irish Times*, 15 December 1997.

Levenson, Samuel. *Maud Gonne*. London: Cassell, 1977.

Lynch, Brian. Letter to the Editor. *Irish Times*, 2 January 1998.

MacBride, Maud Gonne. 'Letter of the Month: Fascism, Communism and Ireland.' *Ireland To-Day*, March 1938.

McCartney, Anne. 'Francis Stuart and Religion: Sharing the Leper's Lair', in Robert Welch, ed., *Irish Writers and Religion*. Gerrards Cross: Colin Smythe, 1992.

—. 'The Significance of the Self in Francis Stuart's Work.' *Writing Ulster*, no. 4, 1996.

—. '"Transported into the Company of Women": A Feminist Critique of Francis Stuart.' *Irish University Review*, Spring/Summer 1997.

Mc Cormack, W.J. *The Battle of the Books*. Mullingar: Lilliput, 1986.

—. *Dissolute Characters: Irish Literary History through Balzac, Sheridan Le Fanu, Yeats and Bowen*. Manchester: Manchester University Press, 1993.

—, ed. *A Festschrift for Francis Stuart on His Seventieth Birthday*. Dublin: Dolmen, 1972.

—. 'Francis Stuart: The Recent Fiction', in *The Irish Novel in Our Time*, ed. Patrick Rafroidi and Maurice Harmon. Lille: Publications de l'Université de Lille III, 1975–6.

Macdonald, Mary. *The Republic of Austria 1918–1934: A Study in the Failure of Democratic Government*. London: Oxford University Press, 1946.

MacEoin, Uinseann. *The IRA in the Twilight Years*. Dublin: Argenta Publications, 1997.

McGarry, Fearghal. *Irish Politics and the Spanish Civil War*. Cork: Cork University Press, 1999.

McHugh, Roger, and Maurice Harmon. *Short History of Anglo-Irish Literature*. Dublin: Wolfhound, 1982.

Mac Intyre, Tom. 'Back to the Wall: A Personal Memoir', in W.J. Mc Cormack, ed., *A Festschrift for Francis Stuart on His Seventieth Birthday*. Dublin: Dolmen, 1972.

Mazière, Christian de la. *Ashes of Honour*. Translated from the French by Francis Stuart. London: Allan Wingate, 1975.

Miles, Hamish. 'New Novels' [review of *Glory*, inter alia]. *New Statesman and Nation*, 2 September 1933.

Montague, John. Letter to the Editor. *Irish Times*, 20 November 1996.

Moroney, Mic. 'Aosdána Rejects Call for Stuart Resignation.' *Irish Times*, 27 November 1997.

Mulkerns, Val. Letter to the Editor. *Irish Times*, 1 December 1997.

Mulqueen, Éibhir. 'Francis Stuart's "Journey" Ends at Clare Graveside.' *Irish Times*, 5 February 2000.

Murphy, Daniel. *Imagination and Religion in Anglo-Irish Literature 1930–1980*. Blackrock: Irish Academic Press, 1987.

Murphy, Hayden. 'Case for the Cause of Francis Stuart.' *New Edinburgh Review*, Spring 1984.

Myers, Kevin. 'An Irishman's Diary.' *Irish Times*, 19 March 1991.

—. 'An Irishman's Diary.' *Irish Times*, 24 October 1996.

—. 'An Irishman's Diary.' *Irish Times*, 22 October 1997.

—. 'An Irishman's Diary.' *Irish Times*, 17 December 1997.

Natterstad, J.H. *Francis Stuart*. Lewisburg, Penn.: Bucknell University Press, 1974.

—. 'Francis Stuart: The Artist as Outcast', in Heinz Kosok, ed., *Studies in Anglo-Irish Literature*. Bonn: Bouvier Verlag Herbert Grundmann, 1982.

—. 'Francis Stuart: At the Edge of Recognition.' *Éire-Ireland*, Autumn 1974.

—. 'Francis Stuart: A Voice from the Ghetto.' *Journal of Irish Literature* V, 1, Jan. 1976.

—. 'An Interview' [with Francis Stuart]. *Journal of Irish Literature* V, 1, Jan. 1976.

—. 'Locke's Swoon: Francis Stuart and the Politics of Despair.' *Éire-Ireland*, Winter 1991.

Noakes, Jeremy, and Geoffrey Pridham, eds. *Documents on Nazism, 1919–1945*. London: Jonathan Cape, 1974.

North, Michael. *The Political Aesthetic of Yeats, Eliot and Pound*. Cambridge: Cambridge University Press, 1991.

O'Brien, Conor Cruise. 'My Call for a Stuart's Inquiry.' *Irish Independent*, 29 November 1997.

—. 'A New Barrage in the War over Francis Stuart.' *Sunday Independent*, 10 October 1999.

—. *Passion and Cunning*. London: Paladin, 1990.

O'Brien, Máire Cruise. 'Why Francis Stuart's Stance Outrages Me.' *Sunday Independent*, 30 November 1997.

O'Brien, Stephen. 'Writer Stuart Joins Arts Elite in Day of Déjà Vu.' *Irish Independent*, 22 October 1996

O'Byrne, Robert. 'German Years Cast Long Shadow Over Stuart's Work.' *The Irish Times*, 3 February 2000.

—. 'Repeated Disputes Made Him Well Known'. *Irish Times*, 3 February 2000.

O'Connor, Ulick. 'Alienation of a Black Swan.' *Sunday Independent*, 13 November 1994.

—. 'A Stuart Recrowned.' *Sunday Independent*, 8 July 1990.

O'Donoghue, David. 'Francis Stuart – The Truth.' *Sunday Independent*, 14 December 1997.

—. *Hitler's Irish Voices*. Belfast: Beyond the Pale Publications, 1998.

—. 'Stuart Had Many Reasons for German Stay Including IRA Role.' *Irish Times*, 3 February 2000.

Ó Drisceoil, Donal. 'The Neutralization of Irish Public Opinion during the Second World War', in *Ireland and the Second World War*, ed. Brian Girvin and Geoffrey Roberts. Dublin: Four Courts, 2000.

O'Faolain, Nuala. 'Black and White Views that Leave Us Blinkered.' *Irish Times*, 15 December 1997.

O'Faoláin, Seán. 'New Novels' [review of *Try the Sky*, inter alia]. *New Statesman and Nation*, 21 January 1933.

—. 'A Wild Irishman' [review of *The Great Squire*]. *John O'London's Weekly*, 24 February 1939.

O'Halpin, Eunan. *Defending Ireland: The Irish State and Its Enemies since 1922*. Oxford: Oxford University Press, 1999.

Orwell, George. *Collected Essays*. London: Secker & Warburg, 1961.

—. *The Road to Wigan Pier*. London: Penguin, 1989.

O'Toole, Fintan. 'Forcing Art to Confront the Reality of Experience.' *Irish Times*, 5 November 1996.

—. 'Stuart Has Confronted Outcome of His Actions.' *Irish Times*, 5 December 1997.

—. 'The Survivor.' *Writing Ulster*, no. 4, 1996.

Oxaal, Ivar, Michael Pollak and Gerhard Botz, eds. *Jews, Antisemitism and Culture in Vienna*. London: Routledge & Kegan Paul, 1987.

Petit, Chris. 'Journey to the End of the Night.' *Guardian*, 23 June 1995.

Pound, Ezra. *Selected Prose 1909–1965*. New York: New Directions, 1973.

Pye, Patrick. Letter to the Editor. *Irish Times*, 14 November 1996.

Ricks, Christopher. *T.S. Eliot and Prejudice*. London: Faber & Faber, 1994.

Ross, Michael. 'H for Human.' *Sunday Times*, 6 February 2000.

Roth, Andreas. '"I'm glad to have this opportunity of saying a few words …": Francis Stuart's Broadcasts from Germany 1942–1944.' *Irish Historical Studies*, forthcoming.

—. Letter to the Editor. *Irish Times*, 1 December 1997.

—. Letter to the Editor. *Irish Times*, 31 October 1997

—. *Mr Bewley in Berlin*. Dublin: Four Courts, 2000.

Ruesch, Alfred R. 'Francis Stuart: The Language of Suffering.' PhD thesis, New York University, 1975.

Sheehan, Ronan. 'Novelists on the Novel: Ronan Sheehan talks to John Banville and Francis Stuart.' *The Crane Bag*, vol. 3, no. 1, 1979.

Shulman, Holly Cowan. *The Voice of America: Propaganda and Democracy, 1941–1945*. Madison: University of Wisconsin Press, 1990.

Sontag, Susan. 'The Artist as Exemplary Sufferer', in *Against Interpretation*. New York: Delta, 1966.

Sproat, Iain. 'In All Innocence: The Truth about P.G. Wodehouse and the Nazis.' *Times Literary Supplement*, 29 October 1999.

Stephan, Enno. *Spies in Ireland*. Translated from the German by Arthur Davidson. London: Macdonald, 1963.

Stern, Fritz. *The Politics of Cultural Despair*. Berkeley: University of California Press, 1974.

Stuart, Francis. *The Angel of Pity*. London: Grayson & Grayson, 1935.

—. *Angels of Providence*. London: Victor Gollancz, 1959.

—. *Black List, Section H*. Foreword by Colm Tóibín. Dublin: Lilliput, 1995; London: Penguin, 1996.

—. *The Bridge*. London: Collins, 1937.

—. 'The Catholic Dream.' *Irish Times*, 26 September 1972.

—. *The Coloured Dome*. London: Victor Gollancz, 1932.

—. *A Compendium of Lovers*. Dublin: Raven Arts, 1990.

—. 'Dublin Long Ago.' *Icarus*, Spring 1976.

—. 'An Extract from *Who Fears to Speak*.' *Journal of Irish Literature*, V, 1, Jan. 1976.

—. 'Extracts from a Berlin Diary.' *Irish Times*, 29 January 1976.

—. *Faillandia*. Dublin: Raven Arts Press, 1985.

—. *Der Fall Casement: Das Leben Sir Roger Casements und der Verleumdungsfeldzug des Secret Service*. Translated from the English by Ruth Weiland. Hamburg: Hanseatische Verlagsanstalt, 1940.

—. 'Fighting the World' [review of *Ezra Pound: The Last Rower*, by C. David Heymann]. *Hibernia*, 8 October 1976.

—. *The Flowering Cross*. London: Victor Gollancz, 1950.

—. *Glory*. London: Victor Gollancz, 1933.

—. *Good Friday's Daughter*. London: Victor Gollancz, 1952.

—. *The Great Squire*. London: Collins, 1939.

—. 'Hearts of Darkness' [review of *A German Love Story* by Rolf Hochhuth]. *Hibernia*, 10 April 1980.

—. *The High Consistory*. London: Martin Brian & O'Keeffe, 1981.

—. *A Hole in the Head*. London: Martin Brian & O'Keeffe, 1977.

—. *In Search of Love*. London: Collins, 1935.

—. 'Introduction' to *After the War is Over*, ed. Dermot Bolger. Dublin: Raven Arts Press, 1984.

—. 'Ireland a Democracy? The Real State of Affairs.' *The Young Observer*, 1 December 1939.

—. *Julie*. London: Collins, 1938.

—. *King David Dances*. Dublin: New Island, 1996.

—. *Lecture on Nationality and Culture*. Dublin: Sinn Féin Ard-comairle, 1924.

—. Letter to the Editor. *Irish Times*, 13 December 1938.

—. Letter to the Editor. *Irish Times*, 19 December 1938.

—. Letter to the Editor. *Irish Independent*, 5 October 1939.

—. Letter to the Editor. *Irish Times*, 12 June 1970.

—. Letter to the Editor. *Irish Times*, 22 October 1970.

—. Letter to the Editor. *Irish Times*, 9 August 1971.

—. 'Letters to J.H. Natterstad.' *The Journal of Irish Literature* V, 1, Jan. 1976.

—. 'Literature and Politics.' *The Crane Bag*, vol. 1, no. 1, Spring 1977.

—. *Memorial*. London: Martin Brian & O'Keeffe, 1973.

—. 'A Minority Report.' *Irish University Review*, Spring 1982.

—. *Mystics and Mysticism*. Dublin: Catholic Truth Society of Ireland, 1929.

—. 'New Yorker Chic' [review of *Janet Flanner's World: Uncollected Writings 1932–1975*]. *Hibernia*, 24 January 1980.

—. 'Nocturne at the Cable Shop.' *The Cork Review*, Jan.–Feb. 1980.

—. 'On Liam O'Flaherty: Recollections of a Great Spirit.' *Adrift*, no. 3, 1985.

—. 'Patrick Kavanagh: Earthy Visionary.' *Hibernia*, 25 July 1975.

—. *Pigeon Irish*. London: Victor Gollancz, 1932.

—. *The Pillar of Cloud*. Introduction by Hugo Hamilton. Dublin: New Island Books, 1994.

—. 'Politics and the Modern Irish Writer', in *Ireland at the Crossroads*, ed. Patrick Rafroidi and Pierre Joannon. Lille: Publications de l'Université de Lille III, 1979.

—. 'President de Valera', in *Great Contemporaries: Essays by Various Hands*. London: Cassell, 1935.

—. 'The Public Man' [review of Yeats's *Uncollected Prose*, vol. II, edited by John P. Frayne and Colton Johnson]. *Hibernia*, 31 October 1975.

—. 'Purgatory' [review of *Lenin in Zurich* by Alexander Solzhenitsyn]. *Hibernia*, 23 April 1976.

—. *Racing for Pleasure and Profit in Ireland and Elsewhere*. Dublin & Cork: Talbot Press, 1937.

—. *Redemption*. Introduction by Paul Durcan. Dublin: New Island Books, 1994.

—. 'Selections from a Berlin Diary, 1942.' *The Journal of Irish Literature* V, 1, Jan. 1976.

—. 'The Soft Centre of Irish Writing', in William Vorm, ed., *Paddy No More*. Portmarnock: Wolfhound, 1978.

—. *States of Mind: Selected Short Prose 1936–1983*. Dublin: Raven Arts Press, 1984.

—. 'Talking to Ourselves.' *Irish Times*, 23 November 1971.

—. *Things to Live For: Notes for an Autobiography*. London: Jonathan Cape, 1934.

—. *Try the Sky*. London: Victor Gollancz, 1933.

—. '2016.' *The Cork Review*, Nov.–Dec. 1979.

—. 'The Water Garden.' *The Cork Review*, Mar.–Apr. 1980.

—. *Victors and Vanquished*. London: Victor Gollancz, 1958.

—. *We Have Kept the Faith: New and Selected Poems*. Dublin: Raven Arts Press, 1982.

—. *The White Hare*. London: Collins, 1936.

—. *Women and God*. London: Jonathan Cape, 1931.

—. Untitled memoir of W.B. Yeats, in Francis MacManus, ed., *The Yeats We Knew*. Cork: Mercier Press, 1965.

Stuart, H. [Francis]. 'In the Hour before Dawn.' *To-morrow*, no. 2, September 1924.

—. 'A Note on Jacob Boehme.' *To-morrow*, no. 1, August 1924.

—, and Cecil Salkeld [*recte* W.B. Yeats]. 'To All Artists and Writers.' *To-morrow*, no. 1, August 1924.

Stuart, Iseult Gonne. 'Five Letters from Iseult Gonne Stuart.' *Journal of Irish Literature* V, 1, Jan. 1976.

Stuart, Madeleine. *Manna in the Morning: A Memoir 1940–1958*. Edited and introduced by Dermot Bolger. Dublin: Raven Arts Press, 1984.

Tóibín, Colm. 'Stuart's Raison d'etre is to be Outside the Pale.' *Sunday Independent*, 7 December 1997.

Travis, Alan. 'Payments that Forced Wodehouse into Exile.' *Guardian*, 17 September 1999.

Webb, W.L. 'Hunting Stuart.' *Guardian*, 16 April 1975.

Welch, David. *Nazi Propaganda: The Power and the Limitations*. London: Croom Helm, 1983.

Welch, Robert. *Changing States: Transformations in Modern Irish Writing*. London: Routledge, 1993.

Wheal, Elizabeth-Anne, Stephen Popa and James Taylor. *A Dictionary of the Second World War*. London: Grafton Books, 1989.

Winkler, Allan M. *The Politics of Propaganda: The Office of War Information 1942–1945*. New Haven and London: Yale University Press, 1978.

Yeats, W.B. *On the Boiler*. Dublin: Cuala Press, 1938.

—. *Uncollected Prose*, vol. II., ed. John P. Frayne and Colton Johnson. London: Macmillan, 1975.

Zeman, Z.A.B. *Nazi Propaganda*. London: Oxford University Press, 1964.

Index

Attempts to index Stuart's broadcasts by theme foundered for two reasons: the ubiquity of a handful of intertwined themes – Irish unity and neutrality; the lies of Allied propaganda; Anglo-American cultural, political and economic perfidy; the virtues of 'Europe' – and the vagueness of the language with which Stuart usually expressed himself. Certain minor themes in the broadcasts are indexed here, as are references to the major themes in the Introduction; in the text of the broadcasts, the major themes appear *passim*. The heading 'Stuart, Francis' provides only the basic signposts to his biography and references to his written works; for his views on, say, Burma, see under Burma. But it is probably best if, before consulting the index in search of particular references, the reader reads Stuart's talks straight through.

Abwehr 32–5, 37, 50
Aldington, Richard 195n
Algeria 105n
Allies *passim in Broadcasts*
  bombing 51, 142, 145–6, 150, 156–7, 162, 173
  desertion of troops 128
  propaganda 39, 50–1, *passim in Broadcasts*
America *see United States*
Andrews, J.M. 127n
anti-Semitism 2n, 4, 14–15, 17, 18–26, 29, 42–3, 56–7, 202, 204
Antrim, Co. 78, 85, 103, 131, 134, 145, 165
Aosdána 55, 58, 59
Arabs 143, 166
architecture 1–2
Argentina 156–7n
Atlantic Charter 104
Auslandorganisation (Dublin) 38
Australia 91, 135, 165–6
Austria 2, 6, 26, 204; anti-Semitism 2n, 14–15, 17
Azores 166

Badoglio, Gen. Pietro 141n
Bakar, Pandit 87
Barrett, Richard 96–7, 181
Battersby, Eileen 5n
BBC 4, 108, 112, 125, 147, 150, 164
Beckett, Samuel 57–8
Belfast 85–6, 167, 192
Benes, Eduard 47, 135, 151
Benjamin, Walter 18
Berlin University 3, 29, 30, 78, 113–14
Beveridge report 108
Bewley, Charles 26
Black and Tans 173, 182, 193
Blueshirts 17
Boer War 195
Böll, Heinrich 58n
Bose, Subhas Chandra 87, 138, 160
Bowen, Elizabeth 21n
Britain 7, 39, 40–1, 47, 48, *passim in Broadcasts*
  architecture 1–2
  radio 2, 3
Brooke, Sir Basil 127–8, 135

brownshirts 8–9, 17, 29, 175
Brugha, Cathal 114, 155, 181
Burke, Raymond Patrick 47n
Burma 155, 166, 170
Büro Concordia 36n

Canada 135, 165–6
Casement, Roger 36–7, 96
Céline, Louis-Ferdinand 18
Chamberlain, Neville 86
Chile 156–7n
Churchill, Winston 48, 51, 83–4, 90, 101,
    104, 105, 109, 127, 135n, 138, 143, 146–7,
    158, 160, 161, 166–7, 177, 183n, 192, 196
civil war (Ireland) 1, 5, 6, 17, 116
Clissmann, Helmut 28, 33n
Collins, Michael 181
communism 16, 17, 50–1
Connaught Rangers 107
Connolly, James 96
conscription (Northern Ireland) 128
Cronin, Anthony 24, 27n
Crumlin Road jail 110n
Cudahy, John 199–200
Curtin, John 135
Czechoslovakia 40, 46–8, 51, 151–2, 192,
    204

Dáil Éireann 30, 127
Daily Express 203, 204
Daily Herald 204
Daily Mail 203
Danzig 40, 85–6, 114, 162
Dartmoor prison 100, 162
democracy 15, 16–17, 26–8, 79–80, 82, 85,
    90, 94, 95, 100, 108, 110, 203–4
De Gaulle, Charles 58n
Deutsche Akademie 29
De Valera, Eamon 15–17, 31n, 36, 39, 52,
    72, 83n, 92
Die Woche 78n
Dillon, James 102
Douglas, Maj. C.H. 116n
Dublin 1–2, 15, 99, 106–7, 182, 192
Dunkirk 112, 149
Durcan, Paul 56

Eagleton, Terry 57n
Easter Rising (1916) 16–17, 73–4, 91, 92,
    181, 182
economics *see money, unemployment*
Edwards, Ruth Dudley 55n
Egypt 105n
Elborn, Geoffrey 29, 37
Eliot, T.S. 19
England *see Britain*
Esmonde, Deputy 30
'Europe' 1–2, 39–40, *passim in Broadcasts*
Evans, Larry 107

fascism 13n, 16, 17–19
Fianna Fáil 52, 135
Fine Gael 52, 127, 131
Finland 132, 154, 181–2, 184–5
First World War 91–2, 150, 172–3, 195–6
Fourteen Points 75
France 1–2, 50, 70, 82, 95, 102, 110, 119,
    130, 145, 154, 184, 192
Franco, Francisco 17, 30n, 58n
Frankfurter Zeitung 78
Frederick the Great 89
Free India 87
Fromme, Franz 33n

G2 4, 28, 63–4
Gallimard 54
Gandhi, Mohandâs K. 79–81, 89, 90, 104
German Academic Exchange Service 28
Germany 5, 8, 25, 29–38, *passim in Broad-*
    casts; see also Abwehr
  architecture 1–2
  collaboration with IRA 32–6, 37, 48, 50
  Foreign Ministry 33–5, 37, 38, 38n
  invasion of Poland 30, 85n
  people 44, *passim in Broadcasts*
  propaganda 33–4, 35–6n, 38n, 52
Giraud, Gen. Henri 178n
Glendalough 70, 133
Gmelin, Otto 204
Goebbels, Joseph 38n, 45n
gold standard 120
Gollancz, Victor 54–5
Gonne, Iseult (wife of FS) 1, 28, 29, 34,
    56–7n

Gonne, Maud (mother-in-law of FS) 1, 56–7n
Görtz, Hermann 34–5, 50
Grass, Günter 58n
Great Contemporaries 15
Great Depression 95n
Guardian 171

Haferkorn, Hermann 34n
Hales, Seán 97n
Haller, Kurt 35
Hamburg 146, 173
Hamilton, Hugo 24n, 57–8
Hartmann, Hans 38n
Hayes, Stephen 32
Hempel, Eduard 33, 48n, 93–4n
Hitler, Adolf 4, 8n, 9, 41–2, 51, 80–1, 89, 90, 98–9, 118, 146, 175
Hollywood 82
Holocaust 14, 25
Hoven, Jupp 33n

Iceland 166
India 79–81, 85, 87, 104, 138, 143, 155, 160, 161, 166, 187
international finance *see money*
IRA 6, 32–6, 37, 39, 50, 83, 87n, 96–7, 100n, 110, 111, 135, 162–3, 167, 167n, 181
Iran 166
Iraq 166
Ireland *passim in Broadcasts*
 censorship 31n
 general election (June 1943) 52, 123–5, 126–7, 131–2, 134
 language 83
 literature 76
 military intelligence *see G2*
 neutrality 31n, 38–9, 45, 50–1, *passim in Broadcasts*
 nationalism 1–3, 4–6, 7–8, 18, 19, 40–1, 45–6, *passim in Broadcasts*
 poverty 27–8, 106–7, 182–3, 192
 refugee policy 27–8
 republicanism *see Ireland, nationalism (see also civil war, War of Independence)*
Irish Guard 36, 50
Irish Independent 30

Irish Press 116
Irish Times 30n, 116
Irland-Redaktion 4, 35n, 38–9, 42
Italy 17, 107, 110, 136–8, 140–1, 148, 149–50, 152, 154, 179, 184, 197–8

Japan 87, 135n, 155n, 157, 160n, 172, 193, 194
Jews 3, 4, 29, 42, 204
 Austrian 2, 3, 6, 14
 in Stuart's books 19–25, 50, 56–7n
Johnson, Lyndon 58n
Joyce, William 3, 33–4, 50, 87n

Kaiser, Henry 199
Kharkov 118
Kiberd, Declan 57
Kilroy, Thomas 58–9
Kristallnacht 14, 26, 30n
Kruger, S.J.P. 122

Latin America *see South America*
League of Nations 72, 73, 75, 80, 82, 95, 183
Lee, J.J. 48n
Lentin, Ronit and Louis 56
Lewis, Sinclair 76
Lewis, Wyndham 18
Liberia 166
Lincoln, Abraham 89, 90
Lipsey, S.M. 55
Lloyd George, David 196
Lockhart, Bruce 204
'Lord Haw-Haw' *see Joyce, William*
Luxembourg 164n
Lynch, Liam 114, 155, 181

McAteer, Hugh 96–7, 110n, 167n
Mc Cormack, W.J. 1n
McKelvey, Joseph 96–7, 181
MacRory, Joseph, Cardinal 93–4
MacSwiney, Terence 155
Maffey, John 30n
Mahr, Adolf 38
Malaya 87n
Malraux, André 58n
Maryborough prison 106

Mauriac, François 58n
Meissner, Gertrud (Madeleine) 33n, 49–50
Mellowes, Liam 96–7, 155, 181, 182
Mhac an tSaoi, Máire 20, 57
Millevoye, Lucien 56–7n
Mirror, The 203
money 41–3, 51, *passim in Broadcasts*
Morgenthau, Henry 199
Morocco 105n
Munich 8, 86, 175
Murphy, Const. Patrick 83n
Murphy, Hayden 9n
Murphy, William Joseph 35–6n
Mussolini, Benito 17, 140–1, 197
Myers, Kevin 56, 59n

Napoleon Bonaparte 80, 89, 90
Napoleonic war 195
National Museum (Dublin) 38
National Socialism & Nazis 4, 8–9, 18, 38, 41, 42, 43, 81; *see also Germany*
Natterstad, J.H. 5n, 13n
New British Broadcasting Station 36n
New Zealand 165–6
News Chronicle 176
Nixon, Richard 58n
North Africa 95, 105, 177, 179, 198
Northern Ireland 40, 46, *passim in Broadcasts; see also Ireland, nationalism*

O'Brien, Conor Cruise 27n
Observer 171
O'Connor, Rory 96–7, 181, 182
O'Donnell, Peadar 41, 87
O'Donoghue, David 45n
O'Donovan, Jim 32
O'Faoláin, Seán 9n
O'Flaherty, Liam 78
O'Neill, Eugene 76
Orwell, George 55n
O'Toole, Fintan 42, 53–4, 59

Palestine 166
Paris, fall of 114
Parnell, Charles Stewart 89–90, 116
Pearse, Patrick 96, 114, 188, 188–90

Philippines 160, 161, 166
Poepping, Hilde 33
Poetry 1
Poland 40, 46–7, 85n, 119, 135, 151–2, 192
Pound, Ezra 18, 116n
Protocols of the Elders of Zion 42
Punch 121–3

Republican Congress 87n
Romania 154
Rommel, Erwin 105n
Roosevelt, Franklin Delano 49, 90, 101, 104, 108–9, 117, 123, 133, 136, 138, 139–40, 146–7, 158, 159, 160, 161, 162–3, 166–7, 177, 178, 183n, 184, 185, 188–9, 192, 193–4, 196, 197–8, 200
Rostov, occupation of 118
Roth, Andreas 33n
Royal Oak 111n
Rugby 125n
Russell, Seán 35–6
Russia 1, 43, 119, 157, 168, 194; *see also USSR*
Ryan, Frank 33n, 35–6
Ryti, Rysto 181–2, 184–5

SA *see brownshirts*
Saar 114
St Bridget's Orphanage 182
St Kevin 133
St Laurence O'Toole 133
Salazar, António de Oliviera 58n
Salo Republic 141n
Sayers, Dorothy 55n
Scapa Flow 111
Schwarze Korps 29
secret stations 36n
Shakespeare, William 126
Sicily, battle of 136–8
Sikorski, Gen. Wladislaw 135
Sinn Féin 1, 2, 5
Sketch 203
Smuts, Jan Christian 135, 184
social credit 116
South Africa 135
South America 156, 166, 180, 199
Southern Illinois University Press 54

Soviet Union see USSR
Spain 17, 102, 110, 130
S-plan 100n, 162–3
SS 29, 141n
Stalin, Joseph 53, 183n
Stalingrad, battle of 43–5, 111–12, 113, 114, 118
Steinbeck, John 198
STUART, FRANCIS
  and Aosdána controversy 55–60
  broadcasting career 4, 34n, 38–49, 50–3, 64
  and German/IRA collaboration 32–6
  in Germany 29–38; see also broadcasting career
  imprisonment by French 50
  in Irish civil war 5
  publishing history 54–5
WORKS
  Black List, Section H 5n, 5–7, 16n, 27, 50–1, 53, 54, 55, 56, 60
  The Coloured Dome 8, 78n
  diaries 34n, 43n, 175n
  Der Fall Casement 36–7
  The Flowering Cross 49, 53
  Glory 9–12, 49, 55n
  The Great Squire 21, 23–4, 25n, 55n
  The High Consistory 53n
  A Hole in the Head 53n
  In Search of Love 21, 25n, 55n
  'Ireland a Democracy?' 31
  Irische Freiheitskämpfer 36
  Lecture on Nationality and Culture 1–3, 4–6, 14, 39, 57n
  Julie 21–3, 24, 25n, 55n
  letters to newspapers 26–8, 30–1
  Memorial 53n
  Pigeon Irish 7–8, 27, 110
  The Pillar of Cloud 49, 53
  'President de Valera' 15–17
  Redemption 49, 53
  Things to Live For 12–15, 17, 55n
  'A Trip down the River' 54

Try the Sky 8–9, 12, 55n,
Victors and Vanquished 25, 50, 53
Women and God 19–20, 27
Stern, Fritz 19
Stuart, Ion 89
Stuart, Iseult see Gonne, Iseult
Stuart, Madeleine see Meissner, Gertrud
Sturmer, Der 29
Sudetenland 114
Swift, Jonathan 15n
Synge, J.M. 114

Teheran conference (1943) 183n
Tóibín, Colm 5n, 58
To-morrow 1n
Treaty, Anglo-Irish (1921) 2, 5, 16
Tunisia 178n

unconditional surrender 146–7
unemployment 28, 94, 95, 119, 125, 137, 203
United Kingdom see Britain
United States 7, 47, 48, passim in Broadcasts
  literature 74, 198
USSR 7, 43–5, 154n see also Russia

Versailles, Treaty of 85n, 114
Vienna 2, 14, 19
Vittoria Emanuele, King 141n
Völkischer Beobachter 204

Walshe, Joseph 48n
War News 116
War of Independence (Ireland) 16, 91, 116, 173, 182, 193
Weizsäcker, Ernst von 33
Williams, Thomas 52, 83n, 91–2, 105, 121
Wilson, Woodrow 75, 140, 196

Yeats, W.B. 1n, 15n, 17, 18–19, 114; On the Boiler 18
Yugoslavia 46, 192, 204